Nigel Frith teaches poetry at Oxford University.

THE LEGEND OF KRISHNA

THE
LEGEND
OF
KRISHNA

Nigel Frith

Schocken Books • New York

First published by SCHOCKEN BOOKS 1976

Copyright © Nigel Frith 1975

Library of Congress Cataloging in Publication Data

Frith, Nigel.
  The legend of Krishna.

  1. Krishna. I. Title.
BL1220.F74 1976   294.5′2′11   75-35449

Manufactured in the United States of America

To My Parents

Contents

Introduction

Do the gods exist? Some people seem to think so. Undoubtedly they exist as concepts. The idea of a glorious god of beauty, of the Muses and the sun, is an established concept in people's minds to which we give the name Apollo; just as the concept of a fierce war-god and hammer-wielder is known as Thor. In some countries also the concepts of various gods have a strong influence on people. Thus the gods might not only exist as things in the mind, but have power. But can they exist outside the mind? I myself do not think so.

But admitting that, one has admitted nothing: for what is the mind? It is the region where lives the whole spirit of an age, where all actions are given birth, where everything is controlled. A concept such as political freedom has shaken the world in recent times. Perhaps this concept is itself a kind of god, spurring man on to a better life, a more responsible individuality.

The concepts of war, or love, or justice rule our own lives within the greater pattern. Perhaps these concepts are best realised and defined as gods. The nearer we draw to them, the greater the power they give us. We may well derive great spiritual benefit from reading about them and thinking about them as gods. But religion has slowly dropped them, science done well without them, and art, feebly, now looks the other way.

I believe it is time we opened ourselves once more to the world of gods – not with superstition, but clearly recognising that we are dealing merely with fancies, and merely for the purpose of wisdom and delight. This book is an attempt to deal again with the world of gods, a world which until recently has been the traditional matter of the arts. It takes as its subject the mythology of the East, for many of the gods are alive and well and living in India.

The god Krishna, however, is extremely well and uniquely Indian. He embodies some of the most attractive things about that ancient civilisation. The heroic spirit of the old Sanskrit epics is found in Krishna's adventures as warrior and dragon-slayer. The wisdom of the yogis is embodied in the instruction Krishna gives to his friend Arjuna, which is set out in the *Bhagavad Gita*, that Indian bible of a mere eighteen chapters. Also in Krishna we find the exoticism of the East, as shown in his rich life as a Raja, and his harem of 16,000 concubines, and the warm-hearted earthiness, which as A. L. Basham notes is especially found in Indian culture, is met with in Krishna's hilarious youthful pranks, when he lived a life of irredeemable mischief among the cowherds of Braj. But perhaps most typical of all, and the most popular and striking quality of Krishna, as he is worshipped today in India, is the luscious eroticism of his life with the milkmaids in the forests of Vrindavan: here the very great talent of Classical Sanskrit poets in evoking a love-world of surpassing sensuousness reaches its climax in the accounts of the great Rasmandala, the dance with the cowgirls.

Krishna of all Indian gods is also the one of whom the West is becoming increasingly aware. No other Indian god has had a devotional hymn in the Top Ten. No other Indian god has his picture with his favourite Radha sold in thousands as a greetings card. The Krishna-Consciousness movement are often to be seen dancing in their orange robes, and clashing their cymbals, in Western cities. The *Bhagavad Gita* is selling in numerous editions, ranging from the briefest paperback to the most enormous scholarly edition, and forms the key work not just to the Krishna-Consciousness Movement, which has some sixty-four centres all over the world, but to the meditation movement of the Maharishi Mahesh Yogi, whose membership is over 400,000. Krishna has been on television in a ballet, on the radio in a work for soprano and orchestra. He appears as a dominant lover-god in the recent spate of glossy books on the secret doctrine of Tantra. He can be bought on packets of incense, and worn in little medallions bought from shops in the King's Road. If ever a god has managed to be with it, Krishna is with it. He will probably end up as the only pop idol who wasn't really there.

But perhaps he *is* really here. The good thing about being a god is that unlike the human species on which you are modelled, you don't suffer from senility or death. Krishna has been going in India for some two thousand years or more, and now he seems to be taking new life in the West. It is the object of this book, as I shall explain later, to create in the reader some tangible idea of Krishna as he exists in the world of gods, the celestial world which we can perceive dimly not through our senses but through our imagination. This world is necessarily made up of fables and situations which embody truths of the psychological world rather than the material world, and it is into this world that I wish forcibly to push the reader by the power of the narrative I have built up. It may be as well therefore in order to counter this fabulousness, to give in this introduction the blunt historical facts which surround and lie behind the cult of Krishna.

The popular Hindu idea of Krishna is that he actually existed as a prince of Mathura and later Dwarka thousands of years ago, at the time when there was a great war between the Pandavas and the Kurus. Although a man, he was nonetheless an incarnation of Vishnu the Preserver of the Universe, who takes bodily form whenever the race of men reach a crisis in their affairs, and evil begins to overpower the good. In this form he taught the warrior Arjuna, and his teaching has been preserved in the *Bhagavad Gita*. Before he became a warrior and a teacher, he lived the life of a cowherd in Vrindavan near Mathura, which is situated on the Jumna between Delhi and Agra.

This history like many Indian histories is hopeful rather than probable. As Basham points out in his *Wonder That Was India*, the Krishna legends and indeed Krishna as a person or god, seem to be made up of a number of layers. It could possibly be that there was a hero prototype for Krishna, who was connected with the wars which have their legendary record in the *Mahabharata* – the great war epic of India. As such he would have been recorded during the composition of the epic, which as W. G. Archer puts it in his excellent book on the literature and artistic representations of Krishna, 'crystallised' sometime between the fourth century BC and the fourth century AD. From this he could have developed as a popular hero, who was nonetheless somewhat detached from the fighting.

The *Bhagavad Gita*, which is essentially a section of the great epic, is nonetheless probably an addition, and was not part of the original story. It seems to me possible that the author of it was attracted by the detached part Krishna played in the war, and thus found it very suitable to his character, and slotted it in at a very dramatic point in the tale. Krishna's wisdom therefore, and his role as a teacher, is probably an accretion to his original role as warrior. It is rather as if King Arthur, who perhaps represents a much embellished memory of an actual person, had been given by a later writer a passage in the

11

Morte d'Arthur, in which he lectured Sir Bedivere on the merits of a holy life.

The most popular aspect of Krishna: his life as lover and cowherd, seems to be an even later addition to the legends. Basham believes that he may originally have been a fertility god in Southern India. The name Krishna means black, and in Tamil verse there are records of a black god who plays a flute and dallies with the milkmaids. This cult may have been brought to the North by a wandering tribe. As it blended with the already existing legends of Krishna the Prince, it must have given popularity to the idea that Krishna who was once a mere cowherd eventually overcame the grim tyrant Kamsa, and established himself as a Raja in his stead. This concept of a rags-to-riches story obviously went a long way towards making Krishna an ancient Indian pop idol.

A final element in the legend probably grew up spontaneously: the stories connected with Krishna's childhood. Most great heroes acquire a fairy-tale childhood somewhere along the line, and Krishna's is very satisfying on this score. Indeed there are very great similarities between the story of Krishna's nativity and that of Christ's. They were both born in pastoral surroundings: Christ among the cows of a stable, Krishna among the cowherds. They were both threatened, because of prophecies of their greatness, by the tyrant of the land in which they were born: one by Herod, one by Kamsa. They were both miraculously saved by flight urged by the vision of a god or angel. And indeed the similarity between the names of Krishna and Christ have prompted some to see more in this than the coincidences of popular taste.

While the conception of Krishna probably developed in this way, from a dim legendary warrior, to a teacher, to an exotic beguiler of hearts, the cult of Krishna must have followed the same progress. Thus at the time in which the epic *Mahabharata* was 'crystallising', Krishna was considered to be a merely human hero; but by about the second century BC, as we know from the account of the Seleucid ambassador Megasthenes, Krishna was looked on as an incarnation of Vishnu. This semi-divine quality of Krishna must have given rise to worship of him, and it was thus natural that when the additions were made to the *Mahabharata* around the second century AD, the distillation of the sacred teachings of the time would have been put into his mouth.

Krishna's role in the *Bhagavad Gita* added greatly to his prowess, for this short book is a beautiful summary of Indian philosophy and religion. In it Krishna gives the teaching that one should seek to grasp the self: the very source of our consciousness, and having grasped it remain in the self throughout all one's actions. This is the essence of the great religious works which make up the most ancient part of Indian literature. But Krishna also teaches that if one places all one's love and faith in him, one will similarly attain the aim of human life. This looks forward to the cult of Krishna as a god of love.

The idea fostered here of Krishna as a god to be loved, and the concept which may have come from a similar Southern god of Krishna as a great lover himself gave rise to the cult of bhakti. In the twelfth century Ramanuja, who was from Southern India, started a cult of devotion to Vishnu and his incarnation, Krishna. In the sixteenth century, Chaitanya led his disciples in devotional singing and dancing, from which the orange-clad Krishna-Consciousness devotees that parade in Oxford Street are directly descended. The cult of bhakti is thus a kind of superheated fan-club worship: the devotees become so drunk with love of their idol that their whole psychological make-up is purified and refined to a state of constant ecstacy. That is the aim at any rate.

Just as Krishna himself is made up of numerous layers which embody different ideals, so the standing of Krishna today in India is a blend of all these things. Almost every sect of Hinduism – and Hinduism out of all religions is the most free and comprehensive – gives Krishna some veneration. Even amongst the sternest and most unemotional Sankhya followers, or those who seek to find the self by rigorous intellectual inquiry, Krishna is venerated because of his teaching in the *Bhagavad Gita*. Simultaneously, among the most primitive tribes, and even among those who practise the orgies of Tantra, Krishna is still venerated because of his own erotic exploits, and his sumptuously erotic love-affair with Radha the cowgirl. Krishna for some reason or other is everybody's favourite, for a god who is simultaneously a naughty child, daring lover, mighty warrior, and great teacher, certainly has something to offer everyone. Wherever you may look he is incorrigibly there, and now even in the West he seems to be haunting the streets.

I have given a purely factual account of the rise of Krishna as a personality and as a cult, so that readers of this book may be without any illusions about who Krishna really was: like King Arthur, he is ninety-nine per cent legend. The purpose of this introduction is thus to give the facts. But the purpose of the book itself is just the opposite of this. There are hardly any facts about Krishna, as I have indicated. On the other hand there are plenty of fables and legends, and indeed these fables and legends are more what he truly *is* than the account of his possible historical origins and subsequent cults. Krishna *is* his story. In the imagination of it he lives, and by the imagination he can alone be perceived. What I have written therefore is a story which blends all the most famous legends about Krishna's life, and unites them into a single, huge fable, which gives, I hope, the most forcible impression of Krishna.

In order to do this, I drew on all his various literary and artistic manifestations which are not very available to the public. His first literary appearance is in the *Mahabharata*. It is difficult for anyone to consult this document as it is approximately a million words long, translations are rare, and when you find them they extend in massive volumes over whole shelves of libraries like the Indian Institute in Oxford. The *Bhagavad Gita*, which is an excerpt, is easy to get hold of. Krishna's most comprehensive literary appearance, however, and the one in which the legends of his cowherd origin feature, is in the *Bhagavata Purana*, which dates from the ninth or tenth century AD. Translations of this are difficult to find, and even when you have found them, they do not really give a complete picture of Krishna as he is worshipped today, for the immensely popular story of his love for Radha the cowgirl does not feature. This part of the legend is most truly recorded in lyrical love-poems by bhakti poets, especially in the delightfully sensuous *Gita Govinda* by Jayadeva, and also in the beautiful miniature paintings which W. G. Archer has so well documented in his book. The many layers which we noted of Krishna's nature are thus pretty much scattered in their source-material.

As the object of this book is to give a unified impression of Krishna as he is understood today, I have mingled the legends of these various sources. I include the story of his nativity, his childhood pranks, his battles with monsters, the tournament and his fight with Kamsa from the Puranas. I take from the love-lyrics many romantic episodes described by Radha, and from the *Gita Govinda* the dramatic structure for the great Rasmandala dance. But in order to give an impression of Krishna's life as a hero in the *Mahabharata,* and his role as a teacher in the *Bhagavad Gita,* I have invented a few incidents in the centre of the book, which show Krishna as a warrior, and indicate the nature of his incarnation, and the realisation of his teaching of the self. I have also gone further than this, and in the hope of giving a comprehensive idea of Hindu mythology, I have involved in the story all the major Indian gods, and given sketches of the three celestial worlds of Mount Meru, Varuna's ocean kingdom, and Yama's Hell, together with a reworking of the ancient Vedic myth of Indra's fight with the drought-demon Vritra, which culminates in the climax of the coming of the monsoon. The book may thus serve not just as a comprehensive account of the nature of Krishna, but as an allegorical guide to Indian mythology, and certain important aspects of Hindu religion.

What is more truly my aim, however, is not to give information so much as experience of Krishna. If the gods live at all, then they do not live in time, but have their meaning in the vast world of the mind – or to put it in modern terms the collective unconscious. This is a strange, dark world, which we only experience when unwittingly pushed into it, when a strange yearning or relish makes us seem to be in contact with something more than meets the eye. I want the reader of this book to get some such feeling of the spirit of Krishna, as it is embodied in the legends. I want him finally to be overpowered by the sheer lusciousness and impetus of Krishna as a god. And in order to do this I have written the book in a particular way, the background to which I should now like to explain.

There is no modern literary form which could express the excitement, the sensuousness and the emotional impact of the Krishna legends. The technique of the modern novel serves very well for the everyday: the minutiae of our day-to-day actions and thoughts. Modern poetry similarly has a very small range, and modern drama remains rooted to the superficial aspects of contemporary life. Krishna, however, and his story, are not part of the mundane world. He embodies deep spiritual truths, and powerful psychic experiences of the inner mind: the mind that houses our loves, our dreams, our longings, and also our most ghastly fears. Clearly therefore the modern literary fashions have to be rejected *en masse* as inadequate to the great task of giving the impression of Krishna.

I decided therefore to go back to the literary forms which, in the

15

way they have been used in the past, have by far the most powerful effects. No recent writer, not even Tolstoy or Pasternak, can compete with the really great writers, who have used that most powerful of forms: the epic. The epics of Homer and Vergil, the Titanic wars of the *Iliad*, the fabulous journeys and monsters of the *Odyssey*, the deep, moving pictures of the *Aeneid*, are undoubtedly some of the most perfect and potent things in all literature. The poets themselves were obviously two of the most skilful and imaginative writers who ever lived, but the form in which they worked was also great in itself. The epic is both the grandest, the most simple, and the most perfect literary form. It is also the most direct. In it there is the perfect union of expression for the character of its heroes, the poetic qualities of its scenes, and the drama of its story. Compared with the novel, the story in an epic goes with incredible impetus and speed. Krishna's first main appearance in the world of record was in an epic. It seemed suitable then that I should choose the epic form for his story.

This book therefore marks a clean break with our current intellectual literature, and goes back to a much more direct and primitive form, in which the narrative is given in the raw. In the first place it encompasses far more plot than could be squeezed into a novel of similar size. The action extends over the whole universe, and not only men but all the Indian gods are involved in it, together with all the devils in Hell. However, I have rigorously followed the example of the *Iliad* and the *Odyssey*, and condensed this universal crisis into what really amounts to a single fable: that of Krishna the cowherd's acceptance of the challenge to fight at Mathura; this is the matter with which the book opens, and it is the outcome of the tournament which closes the book. It seemed to me that only by this sort of epic structure, which is seldom met with in the novel, could the necessary power be given to the story.

The epic technique of involving the gods with human actions I have incorporated. The epic tradition of a journey through Hell I have also used, and, in including a journey for Krishna which takes him over Asia and eventually to Heaven, I have followed the technique of Dante in his *Divine Comedy* by providing him with a guide. In this journey I have expressed the philosophical core of the work, and shown how the concepts enunciated in the *Bhagavad Gita* apply to the story. I have departed from the epic tradition in making many episodes comic or even farcical.

16

These ancient techniques I have revived, paradoxically enough, to communicate the story of Krishna with the greatest possible freshness and novelty. In every direction today we see the ancient things gathering power and capturing people's minds: old legends, old cults, ancient wisdom and ancient mystical practices. The enduring power of the old is proving to be the newest thing of all. By using Homeric techniques of narration and construction, I hope I have added something new to English literature.

But the main appeal of the epic form for me, and what I hope I have exploited most in telling the legend of Krishna, is its inherent universality of appeal. Unlike the modern novel, or modern poetry or drama, it is not a sophisticated form which appeals only to intellectuals. The epic's nearest modern equivalent are the 'lowest' forms of literature in print: American comics like Superman, Batman, the Heap, or – most epic of all – those which narrate the adventures of the red-bearded, hammer-clanging Norse god Thor. The epic then forms the raw, essential, potent core of literature, and once it begins to rear its head, like Krishna, it cannot be resisted. To ensure this quality in the book, I have written in the most basic and simple of styles. At first I tell the story as a fairy tale or childen's book – the current refuge of the epic – but as the meaning deepens I resurrect the style of Malory. If I can achieve half the magic, the pathos and the romance of his tales of King Arthur, I will be more than gratified.

There is one final technique which I have tried to incorporate: a strange one, an Indian one, with a rather mystical flavour. This is to do not with the form but with the purpose or the effect of the narrative. The ancient critics of Classical Sanskrit literature held that their plays and poems were designed to have a spiritual effect. According to whatever the subject was, and the skill of the writer, their works excited Rasa. Rasa means a mood or emotion or flavour which the reader experiences, and this could vary between eight or nine types: the heroic Rasa, the pathetic, the disgusting, the wonderful, the horrific, the comic, the furious, the peaceful, and the erotic. These states felt by the reader were considered to be akin to mystical experiences, and it was thought that the reader's soul was purified and enlivened by the experience. Indeed should the Rasa become powerful enough the reader could be plunged into a definite mystic trance.

17

The whole aim of this book is to work on the reader's mind so that he will gain through the experience of many different Rasas, a culminating Krishna-experience by the time he reaches the end. Although the narrative gives a full account of the Krishna legends, and manages to incorporate into his story nearly all the main Hindu gods, it is not primarily intended to be a guide-book to Hindu mythology. Although the book is also an example of a new form of literature, a much more concise, structured, and expressive form than has been used in this century, it is not primarily intended to demonstrate the new epic style. It is primarily intended to make the reader experience Rasa in all its forms. By a gripping, fast-moving story the reader should be led through a carefully arranged succession of different Rasas. This in turn should have a cumulative effect, so that for instance after the horror, pathos and disgust of the battle with the fiends, the luscious eroticism of the Rasmandala should swamp the reader in the famous Sringara Rasa. This cumulative emotional effect should be at its strongest at the very end of the book, and here a final realisation is intended to provide a sudden understanding of Krishna as a god.

PART I

Krishna and the Mountain

Book One

Kamsa Sends a Demon

Old tales are mellowest, and old ways of telling. I turn my back on the everyday world to bring you a story in ancient style. I take you into a legendary land, such as in the past men would celebrate in stories, where the deeper things of life may be pictured and brought alive. Read here of love and dragons, of gods and devils, heaven and hell. Read here of the world that lies closest to the heart, in which even now your deepest thoughts are born.

Read here of Krishna, wildest and idlest of heroes, who brought up as a cowherd became prince of richest India. Read of his love, Radha, the deep-hearted, she who stayed true to him throughout the torments of earth and hell, who was craved for by Kamsa the tyrant of Mathura, imprisoned and tortured by him to be his wife.

Read here of a drought, and of an army of demons that threatened to burn up India entire, and how Krishna, the hero who alone could defeat them, was cursed by the gods to be furthest from all assistance. Tangled and tight is the knot of error, to which our lives lead us through a thousand desires. Endless our trouble, unsolvable our anguish, till one touch of the ancient truth releases all from their servitude.

Follow this tale to the final answer, and you will read there the solution of all. You will be taken on a journey of meaning, from laughter and playfulness to bitterness and tears, from terror and revulsion to wonder and peace, from war and from battles to moonlight and love, from feasting and rejoicing to a state which has no name. Follow this sequence as the tale unravels, layer upon layer, and meaning upon meaning, and you will be brought to a state beyond all telling.

There was a tyrant ruled the town of Mathura in India. King Kamsa was his name, and he held all the people in a vice of fear and suspicion. Because of this one man, all the citizens were downtrodden, and they knew nothing of happiness or freedom.

But Kamsa, ruling with fear, himself feared, and like many tyrants a prey to superstition, put his trust in astrologers and sorcerers. And once he called a wise man to his palace, a wise man that lived nearby the gateway of the city, on its Eastern side. He came to Kamsa, wearing the long yellow robes of his faith, and carried a trident, symbol of his ascetic life.

And Kama said to the man 'Tell, wise man, tell. Shall I, King Kamsa, Raj of Mathura, indeed be a ruler, and never be beaten in battle or fight?'

And the wise man said in a loud voice, as if he despised the King, 'The King of Mathura shall be famous enough, and his throne shall be known to ages a thousand years from now. The King of Mathura shall be an unlucky King, for he shall be slain by a mere cowherd, a boy, coloured blue, brought up among the fields.' And the wise man, having said this, suddenly turned away with contempt and walked out of the court.

And Kamsa felt his heart grow cold. He knew well enough what boy this was the wise man mentioned, for there was such a one in a village near by, in the land of Braj, where the cowfolk lived. And this boy was known to have power over demons, and he had slain many devils in the past, and eaten their bodies before he sent them back to Hell. And Kamsa feared the boy, whose name was Krishna.

But Kamsa did not show his fear to his courtiers. Instead, as fearful people do, he scowled at them, as though they had done wrong, and glowering walked out of the palace. He came to a dark house in a gloomy part of the city, where there were rats and rubbish piled in heaps, and knocked on the door and waited. And a man came to the door, of horrible aspect, with a white moustache that faded to yellow at the ends. He had a bald head and eyes small and close together, and the eyes were never still.

'Call me up a powerful devil,' said Kamsa to him. 'Call me a demon, a snake of living fire, one that will burn all it touches, one that will dance in the lusts of a man's heart.'

And the horrible man took Kamsa into his dark house, and stood him by. And he drew a circle on the floor of the room with chalk and threw some corn in the air, and some water. And then he closed his eyes and chanted a chant.

'Demon of earth's burning, demon from the earth's very centre, come to the dark city now, now come to the word of the master.'

22

Suddenly there was a great flash and a roar of thunder, and into the circle drawn on the floor of the dark room came a devil, laughing and screaming, all made of fire and twisting with flaming scales.

'Command the devil what you wish,' said the horrible man.

Kamsa then said in a loud voice to the demon 'I command you fire-demon to fly to the country of Braj, and to seek out a boy called Krishna, coloured blue, and to eat him so that there is nothing left of him but dust and ashes.'

Then the horrible man rubbed away with his foot a part of the circle on the floor and the devil leapt out with a scream and flew off through the roof of the house. King Kamsa paid the man in gold, and then went back, dark and thoughtful, to his palace.

Book Two

Krishna and the Bathing Girls

Now Krishna knew nothing of all this, but was walking idly along by the side of the river Jumna, driving his cows. And he wore a garland of lotus-blooms about his neck, yellow against the deep, mauvy blue of his own skin, and as he walked he played on his flute a haunting melody, such as in the spring ravishes the heart of maidens, treading at the waterside their silken saris, and washing them until they are deep with colour and their gold thread gleams in the sun.

And Krishna, as usual, was in an idle mischievous mood. He heard the sounds of girls' laughter coming up from the river, and tiptoeing through the thickets and bushes of basil that grew along the riverside he saw a group of girls from his village, bathing in the water. And they were all naked, and splashed the waves over their soft sides, and wet their black hair. And all their clothes lay on the bank in little heaps.

Krishna let his cows go and walk in the woods and crept up to the river bank and picked up all the clothes and ran and climbed a tree. When the girls saw what had happened they shouted at him, and tried to splash him with the water, and told him to give them back their clothes at once.

Krishna called down to them 'If you want your clothes back, you must all come and get them from me, one by one.'

The girls were so annoyed at this that they screamed and shouted for help, for they were always being teased by Krishna. Just as they were screaming, the fire-demon which King Kamsa had called up in the dark house in Mathura flew past and heard the noise and sank down onto the ground. As soon as he had landed all the grass caught fire and began crackling and flaming, and smoke went up in black clouds to the sky. The fire-demon rolled on through the wood, and all the trees began to burn, and squeaked and hissed with pain. And the cows that were grazing in the wood found they were surrounded by the flames, and began to moo with fright.

Now Krishna, who was still up the tree by the riverside, heard the cows mooing, and saw the smoke. He jumped down from the bouncy branches and ran off to see what was the matter. And the fire-demon came closer, and burnt all the banks of the river.

The girls screamed and ducked under the water to stop being burnt, but Krishna jumped towards the demon and put his lips forward as if he was going to sip a drink, and sucked in a deep breath. And all the fire was sucked into his mouth and swallowed.

Then all was quiet again. The trees stopped burning and grew green again, and the grass stopped smoking and became juicy once more, and the cows were no longer afraid and began to eat the juicy grass. Krishna went to the river, and put his lips under the water, and blew out the fire-demon from his mouth. With great bubbles and steam and ash the fire-demon was drowned, and his body went floating down the river towards the city of Mathura.

When Krishna came back, all the girls were pleased to see him, and thanked him for saving them from the devil, and they all believed he had hidden their clothes so that they would have to stay in the water and not get burnt. But Krishna would still not let them have their clothes back. One by one they had to come out and give him a kiss before he would let them get dressed and go home. And as each of them came out he whispered to her that he would dance with her in the woods when the autumn moon was shining.

Now of all the girls that lived in the country of Braj, Krishna's favourite was Radha, a beautiful girl who lived with her brother in the biggest and best house in the village. And when all the girls had left the water and got their clothes, Radha alone remained.

Krishna said 'Won't you come out and give me a kiss?'

And Radha said 'If you want a kiss, then you must come in.'

So Krishna took off all his clothes and jumped into the water. But as soon as he came up to Radha for a kiss she pushed him under the water and then ran to the bank, and, as her clothes were still up the tree, she got dressed in his and ran off to the village. There was comment from the houses when they saw her in his clothes. There was laughter from the windows when they saw him in hers.

Book Three

Kamsa Plans a Tournament

When King Kamsa found the dead body of the fire-demon and realised that Krishna had killed it, he was so afraid he did not know what to do. He shut himself away in his room and would not speak to anybody.

However, a courtier called Akrura, who was a very crafty, clever man, went to the King, and told him that it was no good just to sit and sulk.

'If you want to solve this problem,' he said, 'call all your council together, and ask them what to do.'

So the King called his council. All round the gloomy streets went the King's messengers. Soon the palace was echoing with the sounds of important people talking and discussing things. King Kamsa entered, and they all fell silent.

'Now, my council,' said Kamsa, 'you all know my plans. I believe that I have the power to rule all India, and to make one great nation of what is now only a lot of little separate kingdoms. Soon all the world will know the greatness of the race of Aryans, and I will be known as the master of the earth.'

All the people of the council cheered as he said this, and shouted 'Hail Kamsa!' for they believed that he would become master of the earth and that they also would become great and famous men.

King Kamsa spoke on. 'But in the country of Braj, which as you know is a sacred country, and belongs to the god Indra, there is a little blue cowherd, and it is said that he will one day kill me. I have sent demons to eat him, but he has killed them. Tell me what I can do to destroy this boy, for he stands in the way of all our plans.'

One man said 'Wake the snake-demon Kaliya, that lives on the bottom of the Jumna, and tell him to swallow Krishna.'

But Akrura said 'Kaliya is old and meek, and Krishna would easily slay him. He has power over all demons, because he wears a magic bracelet.'

One man said 'Send soldiers into Braj to arrest him, and then have him executed.'

But Akrura said 'Braj is the country of the god Indra, and we do not dare to send our soldiers there. In any case, Krishna is protected by magic spells.'

Everybody fell silent, and did not know what to suggest.

And one man said 'Akrura, you are a crafty man, do you have a plan?'

'Yes,' said Akrura, 'My plan is this. Soon it is a big feast day with us, and I suggest that we should hold a tournament, a big meeting where everybody tries to win in races and trials of strength, and that in this tournament we should have a wrestling contest, and that everyone in the country around should be asked to come and wrestle, so that a champion of all India may be found. We must see to it that Krishna comes on that day to wrestle, and we can put against him the King's wrestler, who is a giant, and may easily beat Krishna and kill him, and even if he does not we may prepare a trap that will kill him unexpectedly. This is my plan.'

King Kamsa was pleased by this plan, and straightway he ordered that his builders and architects should be brought to him and he told them to build a great arena with ten thousand seats, and a great flat place of sand and grass in the middle where people could race and throw spears.

And the builders went out and knocked down a great space in a certain part of the city, and made all the houses flat that were there, so that people in that part of the city became homeless, and they cleared the ground and made it smooth.

And then the architects drew up plans to build a great circle of seats all on top of each other around the flat place, and they told the builders to bring stone, and they knocked down more houses and brought the stone from them to the arena. Soon vast seats were towering up all round the circle, with gangways in between for the people to walk up and down, and a great pavilion for the King to sit in and watch the contests. And when it was ready they set flags on the top, which fluttered in the sunny breeze.

And King Kamsa was very pleased, and sent out his messengers into the country all around to tell the people about the tournament. To the land of Braj he sent Akrura on horseback to tell the cowfolk and to see that they chose Krishna to be their champion.

27

Book Four

Blindman's-Buff

In Braj, meanwhile, where Krishna lived, all the villagers who looked after the cows were having a meeting. Radha's brother was there. As he had the biggest and best house in the village people thought of him as their leader. Just now they were discussing a difficult problem.

Radha's brother spoke to them. 'Dear friends, you all know that cows are for us very important things. We drink the cows' milk, and with it we make butter and cheese, we use cow hide for our shoes, and cow dung to make fires with, and all of us love our cows and calves and bulls. But now, alas, our cows are dying, because the summer is so hot that the grass is wilted, and the cows have nothing to eat. And the rains which are now due have not come.'

Radha's brother pointed to the sky, and all the cowfolk looked up, but there was not a cloud to be seen. In India it gets very hot in summer, so that if the rain does not come they have a drought, and everything begins to die.

Radha's brother then said 'But now things are even worse. To-morrow we have to send a whole herd of cows to King Kamsa of Mathura. Tomorrow also we have to sacrifice twelve cows to the god Indra, burning them in the fire, so that he will send us rain. But if we do this we shall have no cows left for ourselves. What can we do, my friends? All of you think, and see if you can find an answer.'

All the cowfolk were then silent, but nobody could think of a way out of their trouble.

Krishna meanwhile had gone to sing his favourite Radha a song. Outside her house he put a big swing, all gaily patterned in coloured silks, and big enough for two people to sit and swing on. And Krishna sat on it, and swinging to and fro he sang for Radha to come out and play.

As he sang, all the other girls came round him, and soon there were many listening to Krishna's song.

Radha came out at last, and said 'What do you want?'

And Krishna said 'You to sit on the swing.'

And Radha sat on the swing and said 'What do you want?'

And Krishna said 'You to give me the kiss you did not give me this morning in the water.'

And Radha said 'Why?'

And Krishna said 'Because your kisses are the best.'

Now Radha was feeling angry with him for teasing her that morning, and so she argued with him and said 'How do you know that mine are the best? You kiss so many girls that you don't know who is who.'

'O no I don't,' said Krishna.

'O yes you do,' said Radha.

And they would have argued like that all day, and all night too, if Krishna had not had a clever idea, and thought of another game they could play, for he loved playing games and fooling around.

Krishna jumped off the swing and undid his silk sash that was round his waist like a belt and said 'Tie up my eyes with this sash, and let's play blind-man's buff. I shall be blindfolded and chase you around, and when I catch any one of you you must give me a kiss, but as soon as I catch Radha and she kisses me I shall say "This one is Radha!" In that way I shall show you that I can tell Radha's kisses from anyone else's.'

Although the girls did not like the idea of being kissed by Krishna twice in one day, he started playing at once, and they had to agree. He blindfolded himself with his silk sash and then chased them round the village square.

First he chased this girl, and then he chased that girl, for although he could not see he listened to their footsteps and the rustle of their skirts. But the girls were too quick for him, and soon he was chasing them all over the village. The hens ran clucking out of the way and the geese honked. The dogs all started barking and all the village children joined in, shouting and screaming with laughter.

In the village meeting meanwhile, still no one had come up with an answer.

One man said 'I think we ought to send the cows to King Kamsa and forget about the god Indra, for unless we obey the King we shall all be put in jail.'

Another man said 'I believe we should sacrifice the cows to the god Indra, for unless we make Indra happy he will never make the clouds come and pour down the rain, and so we shall all die in the drought.'

29

After they had argued for a long time, Radha's brother said 'Let us sacrifice the cows tomorrow to the god Indra, and as for King Kamsa I shall go to him myself, and ask him to forget about the cows for this year.'

All the cowfolk thought this was a good idea, and one of them said 'Take your sister Radha with you too, for she will plead well with the King. All Kings like to please the ladies.'

All the cowfolk thought this was a good idea too.

And just as they had decided to finish the meeting and go and look for Radha to tell her that tomorrow she and her brother were to go to Mathura, a horseman came riding up.

It was the crafty Akrura, and he said to them 'Are you the cowfolk of Braj?' When they had answered him he said 'King Kamsa summons you all to a great tournament to be held in Mathura. There will be contests of running and chariot-racing and feats of strength, and wrestling. You are to choose a champion who will wrestle for you before the King.'

The cowfolk were excited by the news, for they loved festivals and tournaments, and they all began thinking what clothes they would wear.

And Akrura said 'Who will your champion be?'

And there was a big, fat man there, who loved boasting and pretending that he was strong, and he said 'I will be the champion of the cowherds, and I will beat the King's wrestler into a pulp.'

But Akrura looked serious, and said 'Have you not a blue man here, who is supposed to be a hero? Should he not wrestle for you before the King?'

And the big, fat man said 'No, Krishna is too silly. I am the man for a serious job like this.'

And Akrura said 'Take me to this blue man you call Krishna, and let us see what sort of a man he is.'

And so the cowfolk took Akrura towards the village square to look for Krishna.

Krishna meanwhile was still playing his game of blindman's-buff, and still he had not caught any of the girls that ran and laughed around him. And the reason he had not yet caught anyone was that Radha, with a frown and a wagging finger, was keeping them all away, for she did not want Krishna to kiss anybody but her.

But when he was tired Radha walked near to him in a lazy way,

30

and he heard her and caught her as she stumbled running away. All the girls laughed, and when he kissed her they waited to see if he would know it was Radha, and as Radha expected him to tell at once, she was very angry when he began the chase again, and she let him run a long time without allowing anyone to go near.

At last, however, she went near to him again and gave a little cough so that he would hear her, and this time she let him catch her easily, and she gave him a tender, loving kiss, just to let him know it was her, and all the girls knew that this time Krishna would be able to tell, for only Radha ever kissed him so sweetly.

But Krishna did not tell and began to run around again. And this time Radha was even more angry, and she pushed all the girls out of the way, and just as Krishna was running very fast she stood in his path so that he bumped into her so hard they both nearly fell to the floor.

But just as Krishna was about to kiss Radha for the third time, all the cowherds arrived with Akrura to look for Krishna, and were astonished to see Radha in Krishna's arms. And Radha's brother called out 'Radha!' so that Radha jumped with surprise and turned round and saw them, and Krishna, who did not know what was happening because of his blindfold, kissed the back of her head.

And Krishna took off his blindfold, and saw them all looking at him. But he pretended it was nothing, and whistled and looked at his nails, and wandered off round the corner. And just as he was passing where all the girls were standing, he turned round and pinched them so that they screamed. And all the cowfolk shook their heads, and thought that Krishna was being silly again.

Then the big fat man said to Akrura 'Krishna is a fool, as you see. You may tell the King I shall fight his wrestler for him, and beat him too.'

But Akrura, who wanted Krishna to be the champion so that he might be killed, said 'Cowfolk, you must choose carefully, for it will not be good for you if your champion loses, and he himself will certainly be killed. I shall come back in some days to hear whom you have chosen.'

And with that he rode away. The big, fat man felt a little frightened now at what Akrura said about being killed, but the cowfolk thought of him as a better man from that day forth.

But Radha's brother said 'Radha, you and I must go tomorrow to

31

King Kamsa of Mathura, for we must plead with him to forget about the herd of cows that at this time of year we have to send him, for the days are hot and our cattle are dying, and we cannot afford to send any away.'

Radha said 'I shall be glad to go with you,' and they went together into the house.

Then the cowfolk shooed their sisters away, who had been playing silly games with Krishna, and they all thought Krishna was stupid, and not fit to be their champion.

And now was time for the cowfolk to prepare for the night. All the cows were brought in from the woods and put into pens, where they would be safe from the wolves and tigers of the jungle, and the cowfolk got ready their suppers in their little thatched houses. Soon, after a good meal, they were asleep, while the Jumna flowed by, making a peaceful sound.

Book Five

Gods Get to Work

That night over the sleeping land of Braj, Agni, the god of fire, was riding by. He was huge, coloured red all over, and his hair was flames of fire. He rode on a fleecy ram with curly horns, and as he rode by in the dark night sky the flames of his hair and the red of his body made sparks fly like stars and the air smoke as if it had been burnt.

Agni was very angry, for he had seen that a fire-demon had been killed, and the fire-demons were Agni's friends. They helped him to eat up dead bodies, and sacrifices, when they had been thrown on the fire. And when dawn came Agni flew down to the land of Braj and landed on a mountain whose peak touched the sky.

In this mountain lived the god Indra, whom the cowfolk prayed to, and whom they sent cows as a sacrifice. Indra was supposed to live in heaven, far away in the Himalayan mountains, but now he was lazy, and preferred to live in the country and play with his friends in the mountain of Braj. And Agni came to the cave where Indra lived, and he stopped outside and called.

And out of the cave came a great loud voice, like the roaring of a lion, echoing in the rocks, and the voice said 'Put down the beef, and leave.' And Agni did not know what to do.

And there was a pause, and then the voice said 'Put down the beef. You will soon have rain.'

And then Agni got angry and shouted into the cave 'I have no beef for you, whoever you are. Now tell the god Indra I wish to speak to him.'

After a while there was a sound of footsteps, and the cave got brighter with a flickering light, and then Indra appeared at its mouth. He was a huge god, coloured gold, with big green eyes and a moustache as black as a thunder-cloud. And he had four arms, and one carried a thunderbolt, and one a rainbow bow, and one a leg of beef, and one carried nothing, but stroked his whiskers.

Indra recognised Agni and said 'Come into the cave. I thought you

33

were a cowman who had brought me his sacrifice, but you are the god
Agni, and gods are always welcome.'

Indra did not seem very pleased to see Agni, for they had quarrelled some time ago, and never had become good friends. He took
him deeper and deeper into the mountain, down dark corridors, and
soon they came into a great hall whose black walls were lit with
torches, flaming on the walls, and the floors reflected them in jet
black. And on the floors were big tables, and great warriors feasted
at the tables, drinking beer and eating beef, and dancing girls danced
at the other end of the hall.

Agni was jealous of all the feasting and said 'So, Indra, this is how
you live your days away from heaven. While we gods quarrel and
argue about men on the earth, you are feasting with the warriors who
bring the thunder.'

Indra did not answer, but saw that Agni was given meat and drink.
And when he had feasted, Indra said 'Why have you come to see me?'

And Agni replied 'This last day a fire-demon was drowned in the
river Jumna, and before this many devils and goblins have been
killed in this land. If it is you, O Indra, that do these things, then I
have come to ask you to pay back all.'

'I have better things to do than to kill devils,' said Indra. 'It is a
little blue cowherd that does these things. His name is Krishna. You
must ask him to pay you back, not me.'

'Krishna,' said Agni. 'Then I shall settle with him.'

And Agni left the feasting hall without a word more. He did not
want to stay long with Indra, for he feared his strength, remembering
past deeds.

So Agni flew down and dived into the river Jumna, and he came
across the snake-demon Kaliya stretched out on the bottom of the
river. Agni said to him 'Awake, Kaliya, and poison your waters. This
day you are to kill the little cowherd Krishna and drag down his body
to your grey-green depths.'

'O Agni,' said Kaliya, 'I have slept too long in these peaceful waters
to stir to do evil. My family are happy here, and we eat only the reeds.
We are too content to harm the men of the bankside.'

'Drown Krishna today,' said Agni, 'or I myself shall eat your wife
and little ones, and boil the Jumna dry with my fierce fires.' And Agni
shot up, and burst like a fountain of steam from the grey-green
waters. And Kaliya sadly told his wife what he must do, and told her

to look after her babies, that writhed and played on the weedy river-bed.

Radha and her brother meanwhile had made ready to go to Mathura to plead with King Kamsa. They put on their best clothes, so that they would look nice and King Kamsa would be glad to see them, and Radha looked beautiful in a lovely scarlet sari embroidered with gold thread so that it sparkled in the sun. And they both climbed onto a little bullock-cart, and waving goodbye to the cowfolk set off over the plain towards the great city.

It was now the day for the sacrifice of the cows to the god Indra, and all the cowfolk were very busy preparing things for the great ceremony, which was to be held at an altar at the bottom of the huge mountain in which Indra was living. The cows were made ready, and were decorated with garlands of white flowers, and offerings for the altar were brought and put into bowls and plates. There was a Brahmin in charge, who is a priest that looks after such things.

Now Krishna just happened to be passing, and when he saw the Brahmin getting things ready he thought it was all stupid and said 'Why do you prepare to kill those cows when we do not even have enough to give us milk and butter? Let Lord Indra look after himself and get his own beef. It is stupid to think that if you kill those cows and burn them Indra will be able to eat the smoke that goes up to heaven. If you want the grass to grow you should worship the little gods as well as the big ones: they will make sure the flowers bloom and the grass is juicy.'

But the Brahmin said 'Do not desecrate this sacred ceremony with your contaminated presence,' and threw a stone at him to make him go away.

And Krishna went for a walk down by the river.

It happened that some cowfolk children were playing by the banks of the river that day, and when Kaliya poisoned the water as Agni had told him to do the children drank it and became ill. And Krishna, who was passing, saw this and asked them what they had done.

'We tasted a little of this froth that floats so prettily on the grey-green water, and now we feel sick and don't know what to do.'

And Krishna ran to the water's edge and looked down. And from the depths of the river the great snake Kaliya came up, twirling and winding his body round. And the water grew dark as he came to the surface, and suddenly his snake's head reared up out of the water, dripping with yellow poison. Kaliya had seven heads, and all of them hissed and spat at Krishna, and his neck and head towered out of the water as huge as a great palm-tree that bends and streams in a hurricane wind. And Kaliya's heads rocked to and fro, waiting to dive and snatch Krishna from the bank.

But Krishna leapt up and swung himself onto Kaliya's heads, and danced on them, banging them each one with his feet, thumping a dance. And Kaliya grew weak and dizzy, and his eyes went misty with pain.

Out of the water then came Kaliya's wife, and bowing to Krishna she cried out 'O Krishna, spare my husband's life. It was not through his will that he came to fight with you, but the god Agni made him, or else he would burn us all. Let my husband live, and we will run away and trouble you no more.'

And Krishna felt sorry for the snake, and jumped onto the shore, and said 'Go, Kaliya, you and your wife and your little ones I shall not harm. But Agni will be angry with me and you for this. Go then, and swim down this river until you come to the sea, and swim in the sea Westward, and you will come to the realm of Varuna, the god of Ocean. Ask his mercy, and live with him there in his watery kingdom, where all is silent and calm.'

And Kaliya went with his wife and children and did as Krishna said.

The children of the cowfolk meanwhile ran and told their parents what had happened, but the parents, as they sometimes do, did not believe the children's stories, and still thought Krishna was only a lazy and stupid fellow.

Book Six

Indra's Ceremony

Soon the time came for the sacrifice, and loud horns were blown to summon everybody to the altar at the bottom of the mountain. The cowherds and the milkmaids came up, all dressed in their very best clothes, and formed a great ring around the altar. The Brahmin was in the middle and he got ready the rice, the fruit, the flowers, all to offer the god. They also brought up a huge bowl of soma, which was a special drink that Indra loved.

Krishna walked round the back of the people and came to where the cows were tied up ready to be sacrificed, and there was one cow tied to a little bullock-cart. Krishna saw two girls by the cart, and thought he would have some fun.

He said to himself 'O how I wish I were invisible,' and as soon as he said that he really did disappear. When he looked at his hand he could not see it, for some mischievous god had granted his request and Krishna was invisible for as long as he liked.

Krishna then went up to the cart and saw that the girls were sitting in it. 'That's very naughty,' he said, and the girls looked round and wondered where the voice came from.

Then Krishna pinched one of them, and she thought that the other girl had pinched her, and then he pinched the other and she thought that the other girl had pinched her, and just as they were starting to quarrel, he jumped into the cart and drove them off in it. Round and round they went, all over the countryside, and all the pigeons who were eating the corn flew up in terror to the treetops, and so did the crows to the rooftops.

The ceremony meanwhile had started. The Brahmin made a long, long speech, all in strange words that were taken from magic books called the Vedas, and in this speech he prayed the god Indra to ride out with his warriors and bring in the clouds with the rain.

And when the Brahmin had said this speech, he cried 'Bring in the cows!' and there was a great scream, and the bullock-cart came dashing in, and everybody scattered with fright.

37

When the Brahmin saw the two girls in the cart he grew very angry, and when they told him it had just run away with them he did not believe them and scolded them even more. And all the time Krishna, who was still invisible, sat in the cart and laughed his head off.

Because they had been interrupted, the ceremony started again from the beginning, and the Brahmin made his long speech again all about Indra and the rain. And Indra meanwhile up in the mountain was getting impatient, because he wanted his beef.

And the Brahmin cried out 'Indra, magic herdsman, send down your rains to refresh them.' And when he had finished his speech he came to the bit where rice and milk and flowers and soma are offered on the altar, and as he called out the name a cowman walked forward carrying the offering.

A man carried a large dish of rice, and another walked up with a big jug of milk, and another carried up a huge heap of little marigold flowers, all freshly picked, and finally the big fat man who had said he would be the champion wrestler went up, carrying a huge great big bowl, brimful of thick white sticky soma-juice. The bowl was so heavy he groaned, and his knees bent outwards as though he was going to fall down.

And when Krishna saw all this he shouted out in a funny voice 'Indra, magic herdsman, with a face like a juicy tomato.' And everybody gasped and looked about to see where the voice came from. The Brahmin was so angry he walked about staring at everyone to find who it was.

Then Krishna who was still invisible went along the row of cowfolk who held the offerings, and upset them all. He threw the rice on the floor and the milk in the air and the flowers at the girls, and the big huge bowl of soma he picked slowly up, held it high in the air, and then emptied it over the fat man's head.

Krishna roared with laughter, but the cowfolk were all frightened and everyone of them ran away. The offerings were trodden on, turbans and scarves were forgotten, the cows broke loose, and everything disappeared in uproar.

Indra, however, had been watching this, and grew so angry that he jumped down from the top of the mountain and landed just by the altar. He towered above the trees, and could see all the cowfolk running back to the village as though devils were after them. Immediately he strode after them, and arriving at the village he turned and blew them all back again with an enormous wind. The cowfolk all came tumbling back to the altar.

Next he took one great step and landed in front of the runaway cows, and these with his big hands he grabbed by the tails and dragged back to the altar. Finally he picked up all the scattered offerings and put them back in their dishes and plates, and he went himself and fetched an even bigger bowl of soma from the brewery in the village.

The god Indra was so big the cowfolk could not see him very well, but the Brahmin, sensing he was there, spoke to them all and said 'My friends, some devil must have stopped our ceremony, but now I feel Lord Indra is waiting for us to start again. Let us therefore continue with our rites.'

And once again the Brahmin made his long, long speech about Indra and the rain, so that even Indra himself was bored. At last it came to the offerings, and Indra smiled as the cowmen came forward carrying their gifts for his altar.

First came the man with the dish of rice, and Indra licked his lips, then came the man with the big jug of milk, and Indra sniffed and rubbed his hands together, then came the man with the heap of marigolds, and Indra laughed and his eyes gleamed at the sight, and finally came the big fat man carrying the great huge big bowl of soma, and Indra was very anxious and wondered if he should help, for the bowl was even bigger than the other and the man was staggering as if he were drunk.

Then Krishna who was still invisible went along the row of cowfolk who held the offerings, and upset them all again. He threw the rice on the floor, and the milk in the air and the flowers at the girls and the great huge big bowl of soma he picked slowly up again, held it up high in the air, and then emptied it over the fat man's head.

Indra was horrified. He staggered back from the altar, and took a deep breath, and then, so angry had he become, he leapt into the air, burning a path like a shooting star, and made the sky black above the whole land. He meant to punish the land of the cowfolk for what he had seen, and he roared in a loud voice for all his warriors to come and help him punish the cowfolk. And his warriors streamed out of the caves in the mountain, and flew to his side.

And Indra said 'Go, and bring clouds of hail, and throw down great hailstones on these people, that they may be stung and slapped

39

by a million balls of ice.' And the warriors flew off to obey his command.

All the cowfolk meanwhile, who had been made frightened by the mysterious happenings, were running here and there, not knowing what to do. It seemed to them that devils had jumped on them, and they were all afraid. Some of them hid in the trees, some behind the altar, and some amongst the cows who were mooing with fright.

Just then they heard a marvellous tinkling sound that seemed to come out of the sky, and a scent of jasmine was blown about on the breeze. Then all of a sudden the top of the mountain glowed with a flickering blue light, and Krishna appeared at the top, much larger than he really was, and around his neck was a garland of green leaves and woodland flowers. But the cowfolk thought he was some god, and did not see that it was Krishna all the time.

And Krishna spoke to them and said 'Little cowfolk, don't be afraid. I am the spirit of the mountain, and will never hurt you or do you harm. Why, though, do you spend so much time and waste your goods and cows by offering these things to Indra? Lord Indra is a powerful god, and can do without these things. Do not be afraid that he will not bring the rains. When it is time for the rains to come, then they will come. Why have you forgotten the elves of the wood? Give them a few flowers and they will look after you. And now farewell, little cowfolk, the mountain god bids you adieu. Remember my words and the grass and flowers will come back in time.'

With these words Krishna vanished, and the cowfolk stood looking up at where he was, silent with wonder. But then Indra's warriors came back, carrying and pushing the great clouds of hail, and Indra grabbed them and shook them out over the land, so that the cowfolk were pelted with enormous hailstones. And the cowfolk were stung and bruised by the hailstones, and cried for help, and did not know what to do.

Just then Krishna came up, sheltering under an umbrella, which he twizzled round on his shoulder, and which kept all the hail off him. And Krishna shouted to the cowfolk 'Come under my umbrella. I will shelter you, and save you from being hurt.'

And a few cowfolk who liked Krishna ran to him and tried to get under his umbrella, but there was not enough room. And the other folk who saw this shouted 'You are fools to trust a fool. Krishna cannot help you.'

But Krishna, when he saw that all his friends could not shelter under his umbrella, said 'Wait a little while, and I will get an umbrella big enough to shelter us all.'

And Krishna bent down and put his hand in a hole in the ground, just at the bottom of the mountain, and he heaved and shook and there was a tremendous crack, so that the sky seemed to split with the noise. Krishna put his hand in the rift that he had made in the earth, and pushed and squeezed, and the whole mountain began to shift, and as it shifted Krishna ran his hand underneath and with a mighty thrust lifted up the mountain and held it up over his head, and all the cowfolk were sheltered under it, and the hail did not fall on them any more.

Indra was even more annoyed at this. With his thunderbolt he smashed the clouds, and all his warriors in terror ran away, scattered over the whole earth. And Indra himself flew off in high rage towards heaven.

But the cowfolk were happy, and seeing how strong Krishna had shown himself to be, they all chose him to be their champion in the wrestling contest, and felt he would save them all. And so the ceremony of Indra's cows came to an end, and Krishna was the hero of the day.

Book Seven

Kamsa Sends the Soldiers

Agni the fire god was even more angry when he discovered that
Kaliya had failed to kill Krishna, and instead had run away to the
ocean. Straightway Agni plunged into the earth to visit the King of
all the demons, and try to get him to help. Down Agni went into the
black earth, and into the rocks under it, and into the caverns and the
hot boiling fire of Hell, and Yama the god of death and Hell sat there
on his throne, and his skin was green, his eyes the colour of copper,
and he carried in three of his four hands a trident, a mace and a
noose.

'Yama, great King of Hell,' said Agni, 'your demons have been
suffering on earth, and yet you have not stirred to help. Do you wish
all the devils to be killed by the little blue boy Krishna, or will you
not send all your devils out of Hell, and kill him so?'

And Yama replied 'Krishna is more than a boy, though I cannot
say what he is, and on his wrist he wears the ring of discernment, and
with this he has power over all my realm. Go, Agni, I cannot help you.
Indra rules in the land of Krishna, and not I.'

And the King of Hell looked with his gloomy eyes at the vast dark
regions under the earth, where there were black lakes and fiery
rivers, and he sighed. And Agni left him, scorning his laziness.

And Agni flew out of the earth with a shower of soil and fire, and
he leapt into the air and visited the realm of Surya the sun god. He
found the god racing across the sky in a chariot of gold drawn by
seven horses. Agni's eyes were dazzled by the sight, and he had to fly
hard to keep up with Surya's galloping horses.

And Agni shouted to him as the wind whistled past them 'Lord
Surya, Ruler of the Sky, I know that King Kamsa is dear to your
heart, for he rules the people of earth just as you rule the heights of
the blue sky, but have you not seen that he sits lazily in his city, and
does nothing? And why? All because he is afraid of a little cowherd
called Krishna. I think it is time you looked down on him, my lord,
and inspired him to do great deeds. Tell him now to send out his

armies into the land of Braj, for it is time for him to begin his conquest of India, and to become ruler of the world.'

With these words Agni dropped down to earth, and rested after his tiring flight, hoping that Surya would do as he said. And Surya thought about Agni's words, and his heart leaped with joy at the thought of great power and conquest, and immediately he looked down on Kamsa in his palace in Mathura.

Kamsa was sitting in his red sandstone palace, gloomily thinking about Krishna, and how he might trick him at the tournament, and Surya sent a beam of sunlight through the window which struck him on the shoulder so that Kamsa looked round to see who had touched him.

And Surya said 'Enough of this idling. Arise, O lazy King, leave your brooding thoughts, for it is time to begin your conquest of the world. Send out your legions now, and go North through the land of Braj.'

And Kamsa sprang up, on fire with this thought, and summoned his generals and told them to prepare for war. And he also summoned his architects and builders and told them he would use the great arena as a parade-ground for his troops and as a place to hold the mighty tournament which would mean the end of Krishna, and the King sat back well pleased, thinking that at last he was to become Lord of the World.

And the generals went out, and went round their troops and told them to pick up their arms and to clean their swords and spears and to make ready to march. And the builders went round and put banners on the arena for the great parade.

Radha and her brother meanwhile had arrived at Mathura in their bullock-cart and were brought before the King. Radha's brother spoke to him and said 'Great King Kamsa, we are from the village in the land of Braj, and it is now time for us to send you our herd of cows, as we do every year to pay our homage. But this year, O great King, there is such a drought that our cattle are dying, and we do not have enough cows to bring you and to live on ourselves. I plead with you, King, to forget about the cows for this year, and to let us live on what we have.'

But it seemed that the King was not listening, for he stared into space, as if thinking. And at last he said 'What? Forget your homage? Never. Send me twice as many cows this year to pay for your daring.'

43

And Radha went and kneeled before the King, and said 'O great King, do not punish us so, for we are faithful to you, and we have always sent you cows until this year. But now, look, King, there is such a drought that not half the cows are alive. Please forgive us and forget our homage, or we shall die.'

When Radha spoke the King said nothing but looked at her deeply, and when she had finished he waved them away and his courtiers took them out of the hall.

Now there was a certain wicked priest in the hall, and Kamsa called him and said 'That woman is very beautiful. Tell her and her brother they are to leave the land of Braj and come and live here in Mathura. I shall make him a chamberlain in my court. But as for the woman, she is so lovely you must find a way to take her away from her brother and bring her to my court. I want her to live with my wives in their harem. You understand?'

And the wicked priest nodded and said 'I shall obey, my lord.' The priest went after them and caught up with them just as they were coming to the walls of the city and he said to Radha and her brother 'The King has ordered that you are to leave your house in the land of Braj and to come to the palace. He has employment for you both. After three days you will bring your servants and all you own to the city, and I shall give you a house to live in, and work to do for the King.' And he turned and left them.

Radha and her brother were horrified at this news, for they did not want to leave their own home and all their friends in the land of their birth, and they feared being near to the wicked King Kamsa, for they did not know what he would do to them. And Radha was very sorry that she would have to leave her dear friend Krishna and never see him again. Sorrowfully they went back to their country in the bullock-cart, wishing they had never tried to persuade King Kamsa to forget about the cows.

In Mathura meanwhile the builders were soon finished with the arena. and the generals had soon summoned all their soldiers, who went in a great mass and marched into the arena to parade. With shining shields and flashing swords they marched up and down, and drums were banged and trumpets blown, so that all the town echoed with the noise. And all the shopkeepers and spinners and cooks and schoolboys came out to watch the soldiers marching up and down. And then King Kamsa came out of his palace on a high balcony,

44

and looked out over the arena, and all the soldiers shouted to him and said 'Hail Kamsa,' and all the people shouted 'Hail Kamsa.' And there was a cheering and a beating of drums.

And as Kamsa stood at the balcony, the crafy Akrura came up and stood by his side and said 'Worthy King Kamsa, it is time for me to go to the land of Braj and see if the cowfolk have chosen their champion to wrestle before the King. May I go in one of the chariots, so that I may seem an important messenger, and guide them into choosing the blue Krishna?'

And Kamsa said 'Take it and be gone, for soon the whole land of Braj will be full of my soldiers, and Krishna will be compelled to fight.'

So Akrura went off, and made ready a chariot, and drove off the horses towards the land of Braj.

And the soldiers in the arena before the King now stopped and drew up in their proper ranks, so that they looked like a great field of corn, rustling in the breeze.

And Kamsa shouted to them and said 'My trusty soldiers, who would gladly die for me every one, I have had a kind of dream, and in this dream a god told me that it is time to begin our conquest. Go forth then over the whole of India, and conquer all the people in my name. Some go South to the Deccan and some go West to Gujarat, and some go East to Bengal, and some go North to the mountains, and go through the land of Braj and make it mine. When you go into a town or village, if the people want to fight, then fight and kill them all, but if the people do not want to fight, then make them say "Hail Kamsa!" and make them swear to have me as their King, and take over their greatest houses, and rule them with power and sternness. Go forth then, soldiers, and in my name make all India one nation, so that I may be the Lord of the World.'

And the people all cheered and the soldiers all shouted 'Hail Kamsa, Lord of the World!' and then the soldiers marched round the arena, and as they went past Kamsa they saluted him, and then they went out of the city in great ranks to defeat all the people of India. In the sand they trod, they threw up dust that blackened the whole sky, and it was like a storm that darkened the whole land. And the soldiers marched on until it was night, but even then they did not stop but lit torches and went on in huge lines of flickering fire that were like monster snakes sliding over the peaceful land.

Book Eight

Radha Says Farewell

When Radha and her brother got back to the village, there was a group of cowfolk waiting for them to hear what King Kamsa had said. With sad heart they saw the sorrowful expression on the face of Radha, and at once she cried out 'O my friends, I and my brother have got to leave you, and to go and live with King Kamsa in Mathura, and we shall never see you again.'

And all the cowfolk were horrified at this news, and said to Radha's brother 'Is this true?' And Radha went into the house to weep.

And he said 'Alas my friends, it is true. We were not able to make King Kamsa forget about the cows at all, but he said that he wanted them and more, to make up for our daring in going there. We are in a worse position than ever before. The drought has not lifted, the King is angry with us, and I and Radha are to leave you for ever.'

Just as they were weeping and wailing at this, a great chariot was seen approaching over the plain, and soon it drew near, and in it was a charioteer, and the crafty Akrura.

And Akrura said 'Are these the cowfolk of the land of Braj?'

And the cowfolk said 'Yes, what misery have you brought for us?'

'I am come as an embassy from King Kamsa of Mathura,' said Akrura, 'and I am here to know if you have chosen your champion to wrestle at the tournament.'

'Yes,' they said, 'we have chosen Krishna the blue cowherd, for he is so strong he can lift up mountains.'

And just then Krishna appeared, and wandered up to see what was happening, and Akrura spoke to him and said 'Are you the blue Krishna, and do you accept to fight the wrestler before the King?'

And Krishna answered and said 'I am Krishna, but I will not wrestle with anyone before the King.'

The cowfolk were horrified at this, and said 'But Krishna, you must, for you will save us all.'

And Krishna looked at Akrura and said 'What is it like in your faraway city? Are the walls high, and are the streets gloomy? Are the people unhappy and servants of the King? Or is there laughing and dancing in the streets of the city, and is this King blessed as a servant of the poor?'

And Akrura said 'Indeed it is not such a weakling's city. Our walls are huge, and our streets are dark. Our people are afraid, and are slaves of the King. There is no laughter and dancing, for the King rules with an iron hand. Of such are the race of warriors made that will bring all India in conquest to our King.'

'In that case,' said Krishna, 'I will wrestle before the King, and I will tie the wrestler in knots so that he cannot be untied, and I will wrestle with the King too and overthrow him. Take this message back to your gloomy King Kamsa, that Krishna the hero will finish with him soon.'

And all the cowfolk cheered as he said this, and the crafty Akrura looked scornfully at him and went away.

Then the cowfolk told Krishna about Radha and her brother having to leave, and how King Kamsa had said he wanted even more cows than usual, and Krishna listened to all that they said and did not speak but looked grim, and at last he turned away and went walking in the forest.

Then Radha's brother joined her in the house and told her what had happened, and they wept because they knew that they had to leave their dear friends in three days' time. And all their friends came in, and wept too. It seemed to them that things were getting worse and worse, and they were afraid of worse still. 'What shall we do without you?' they said. 'For you always knew what was right and wrong, and knew what to do when anything happened.' And the little house was filled with the sound of weeping.

Now Radha wanted to tell Krishna that she would have to leave him and go to Mathura, but Krishna was nowhere to be found, and the night came and the darkness before she had seen him.

But it used to happen that when Radha and Krishna wanted to meet and talk where nobody could see or hear them they would go out into the jungle in the night and stroll through the trees. And Krishna, when he wanted her to come out and play, would blow a flute in the trees. And it so happened this night that as Radha was lying on her bed, unable to sleep because she was so sad, she heard

47

Krishna's flute in the forest and knew that he wanted to see her. And when she heard it she wept because she knew she had to tell him that they would not be able to meet any more.

Down the creaking stairs she went, and quietly out of the door, and Radha ran down the village street, which was quiet and still in the moonlight, except for a few dogs that looked up at her as she went past. And she came to the shimmering wood, that was all filled with the beams of the moon, and ran along the woodland paths and found Krishna leaning against a banyan tree playing his flute.

And Radha burst into tears and said 'O Krishna, have you heard that we are to go to Mathura and live there, and that we shall never be able to meet and play in the forest again, and that we are to be parted for ever?'

And Krishna did not speak, but smiled and took her hand and led her away into the forest. And he took her a way they had never been before, and it led them up the mountain, through thick bushes and over craggy rocks and up beside little streams and dense glades of bamboo, until Radha was quite tired with all the walking. But the walking made her stop crying, and soon she began to feel peaceful and happy again to be with Krishna.

After they had travelled for a long time, until the stars above them looked down curiously to see where they were going, they came over a ridge with a few tall trees, and then looked down to a valley, and the valley was round and in the middle of the valley, surrounded by beautiful flowering trees, was a lake, full of rosy and white lotuses. And Krishna led Radha down to the side of the lake and pointed across the still moonlit water and showed her an island that seemed to float on the lake.

Krishna said 'Do you see that island in the middle of this peaceful lake? That is the island of Everywhere, and is the centre of the whole world. Now Radha let us swim out in that lake, and live together on that green island, and forget all about the troubles that surround us, for once you have reached that lake you can never more be frightened by doubts or touched by sorrow. Will you come with me to the island?'

And Radha said 'No, Krishna, I cannot do that, for my brother would be so alone without me, and you yourself have promised to be the champion of the cowfolk. They can well do without me, for they have always been jealous that I am your favourite, but if you were to leave them they would have no protection against the tyrant Kamsa, and might very well be destroyed. We must both go back again to the land of Braj. But even so, this is such a beautiful place, let us walk around the lake and enjoy it for a while, for this is the last time you and I shall be together.'

So they walked round the lake together, and talked sadly of the times that lay ahead.

Meanwhile the soldiers were spread out over all the land, and they came to the village in Braj, while all the cowfolk were still asleep. With burning torches they arrived in the deep blackness and banged a loud drum and blew trumpets for everybody to awake, and when the people rushed out of their houses they seized them and made them prisoners, and accused them all of trying to escape.

And the soldiers seized all the houses in the village. And when Radha's brother came out they seized him and ordered him to tell all the villagers to swear that they would obey King Kamsa and be his servants. And the villagers all swore, and were made to shout 'Hail Kamsa!'

Radha and Krishna were still walking round the lake, and knew none of this that had happened. And Krishna said to Radha again 'See how beautiful that island is, and look also, there is a pavilion of white marble on it, built by some prince as a pleasure-house. Will you not swim with me to that place, and live with me there for always?'

And Radha wept and said 'Though all I ever want is that island and you beside me, and that we might be together as though we had always been so, and that there had never been a land of Braj and a house where I belong, yet I cannot come with you there, for you have sworn to help the cowfolk and be their champion, and I must be with my brother, who has looked after me for so long. Let us go back now to the village, and take this kiss to be my final farewell.'

So they kissed by the lakeside, and then went back up the valley that circled the lake. But as they reached the crest of the hill and looked down towards the plain, the dawn began to break, and in the grey light they saw the torches and the shields of the soldiers. Radha said 'Wait, Krishna, do not let us go back, for the soldiers have seized the village, and you will be captured. Look, how they run about, and see their spears and swords. O Krishna, I am afraid you will be hurt if we go down into the plain.'

But Krishna smiled and took her hand, and led her down the

49

mountain-side, into whatever fate was awaiting them. And the day came as they descended, and lit their steps with shining light, and all the plain stretched out before them, smoking with fires and darkened by the soldiers everywhere.

PART II

Vayu's Mission

Book Nine

Indra Summons the Gods

All this while in the highest heaven, the great god Vishnu, preserver of the universe, was listening to his wife Lakshmi telling him a story – and to listen with pleasurable detachment to a well-told story is a delight much like the delight of gods. And Vishnu was a huge god, with four arms, and he lay on a mighty serpent, coiled round like a rope, and they all floated on a sea of milk, which was indeed the ocean of eternity. And the story Lakshmi told was this very story of Krishna the kineherd.

And Vishnu listened, since in many shapes he had often come to earth to help mankind, and he had a natural interest in the fate of men. And each time Lakshmi came to the end of a part of her story she leant down towards the sea of milk and picked a golden lotus from the ocean surface and threaded it onto a silken band. And now eight lotuses were on the thread, and she had threaded on it also a bracelet that Vishnu had, for a joke to signal a certain part of her story. And having reached the eighth lotus, she stopped, and saw that Vishnu seemed to be asleep.

Lakshmi said 'Is the day so sultry that you fall asleep, or is my tale not gripping enough to keep you awake?'

And Vishnu said 'I do not sleep my darling, I do but dream. For many have been your stories that I have heard tell of earth, and in each I seem to be slowly enwrapt, until I take part in the story myself, and through them I have come down to man, to help them when the earth becomes bowed with sorrow.

'This story is pleasant enough, but yet soon I feel sad things will start to happen. For Kamsa and all his demons are evil characters, and they have plotted a lot of mischief. But who is this Krishna that is but a little cowherd, and yet can lift mountains sacred to the King of earth's heaven?'

And Lakshmi said 'To answer you that I shall have to go on with the rest of the story.' And she picked up another lotus from the lake,

53

and as she began to thread it on the silken band she told the tale, as you shall hear.

Now Indra, when Krishna had lifted up the mountain, zoomed to heaven like a volcano in his anger, all set to persuade the gods to punish the blue cowherd. Into the burning sky he shot, and soon he was flying over the foothills of the Himalayas, and down below were the winding valleys and crinkled ridges, all brown in the hot sun. And soon he was flying over peaks of snow and pinetrees, and soon there was nothing but blue snow, he was so high. And then where the clouds began to gather round the summits he came to the land of heaven, and above the clouds, seen here and there through breaks in the grey, were the golden walls of heaven, set high on craggy cliffs and amongst tumbling waterfalls, and behind the walls were terraces and rooftops and blossoming trees of gold that smelt of all delicious spices, and the sky above was purple they were so high.

And when the guards on the walls of heaven saw Indra they blew their trumpets and shouted that their lord was come back. But Indra was angry, and he summoned at once all the gods in council, and sent heralds to fetch them over the whole of heaven. And the gods came, and Indra's wife came also to hear what he would say.

And when they were assembled, Indra said to them 'Gods of heaven, an outrage! We have all been shamed. A little cowherd, a small blue boy called Krishna, has dared to stop my ceremonies in the land of Braj, and when I tried to punish them with a storm of hail, he lifted up the mountain, my mountain where I lived, and used it as an umbrella. Go therefore, my gods, and revenge your lord. Take Krishna away from the land of Braj, and throw him into the desert to starve.'

But the gods were a little shocked at what he said, and Indra's wife said 'That is a harsh punishment for a little cowherd. I do not think you should be so cruel.'

But Agni the fire god was there, who hated Krishna, and he said 'I think it is a good idea. He is a horrible little man, and deserves to be punished.'

And it looked as though Indra was going to have his way, and the gods would be sent to lead away Krishna into the desert, but then another god stood up, and this was Vayu, who was the god of wind, and Vayu said 'I do not think we should punish anyone without a fair trial. If someone is accused of something bad, then people should find out all they can about him to see if it is true or not, and so I suggest some god goes to earth to find out more about Krishna, and to see if he deserves such punishment.'

And the gods thought this was a good idea, and asked Vayu himself if he would do it. And Vayu said he would, and flew off to earth at once.

And Vayu flew all the way down to earth, coming into the thicker and hotter air of the plain, and when he reached the land of Braj he turned himself into the likeness of a wandering holy man, a yogi, a man who wears yellow robes and carries a wooden staff and walks here and there begging his food. And dressed like this, he came to the village.

Book Ten

Nanda's Tale

Now Vayu did not know anyone in the village in Braj, nor did he know who to ask about Krishna, and whether he was a good boy or not, so he decided he would ask the first person he met to take him to Krishna's father, and he would ask him about his son.

And he met by the roadside a red-faced man with a bottle, who was drinking and singing to himself, and this was Balarama, who was Krishna's brother, and in answer to Vayu's question he said 'Of course I can take you to the father of Krishna the cowherd, for his name is Nanda and he lives not far from here, and I should know anyway, because my name is Balarama, and I am Krishna's brother.'

And Vayu in a roundabout way asked Balarama what sort of a boy was Krishna, and Balarama said 'O, he is a devil. He loves fighting and killing poor innocent demons from Hell.' But Vayu decided he would wait and hear what Nanda said, and not believe bad things of Krishna too soon.

And he came to Nanda's house and went in, and Nanda was sitting eating some betel nut, which he had wrapped round in green leaves, and as he chewed away, Vayu greeted him and said 'I am a wandering yogi, and I have come to ask if you have a tale to tell of your son Krishna the cowherd, for I have heard much about him, as I travel by the way.'

And Nanda said 'He is but a little cowherd, who helps me look after the cows. Some people say he is a great hero, but I know that he is a simple boy, and but my son.'

And Vayu said 'Is he at all mischievous, and does he behave badly at times?'

And Nanda laughed and said 'Indeed he does, for he is always playing tricks on people, and when he was a little child, he loved to steal the butter. There is a story about this, if you would like to hear.'

And Vayu said 'Please tell it me, for I long to hear of Krishna.'

And Nanda said 'Once upon a time Krishna was playing in the forest with the other boys and girls, and as they ran around they made so much noise that a great wolf came out of the trees and watched them. And the wolf was hungry, and wanted to eat Krishna, and the wolf said to Krishna "May I play with you too?" Krishna said to him "What game do you play?" and the wolf said "Wolves and lambs." So they all ran round playing wolves and lambs, but the wolf was just waiting for a chance to bite Krishna, and he only pretended to play with the others. Now just as the wolf was going to jump on Krishna, Krishna said "We've played your game. Now you play ours." and the wolf said "What is your game?" and Krishna said "Human pyramids." And neither the wolf not the children knew what Krishna meant.

'Now Krishna had a plan, and he planned to get rid of the wolf and to get himself some butter all at the same time, for Krishna always loved butter, and would often try to steal it, and his mother grew so angry with him stealing the butter that she hung it up in the ceiling from a great big bowl, and Krishna could not reach it, as he was only little. But now he had a plan. So he drove the children and the wolf as well, like a lot of sheep, into his own home, and he said "Now we will all play human pyramids." And he put the children together and made them stand on each other's shoulders, so that they reached up to the ceiling in a great big pile, and Krishna climbed on top and reached and got the butter. And just as he did this, his mother came in, and she screamed at the sight of all the children, and threw up her hands. And all the children were so surprised they all fell down, and the wolf who was at the bottom of the pyramid was squashed quite flat. And we've used him as a doormat to this very day.'

And when he had finished his story Nanda laughed, but Vayu looked sad, because it seemed that Krishna really was a bad boy after all, who stole butter from his mother and used the other children to help him in his plan. So sadly Vayu said goodbye, thanked Nanda for the story and flew back to heaven.

But as he was flying back to heaven, Vayu thought he would call on Kubera, the dwarf god, for Kubera was always happy, and could cheer him up and as he came near Kubera's mountain he could hear from inside the clink of anvils and hammers, for Kubera kept a lot of dwarfs who worked in the mountain making gold bracelets and earrings and all lovely things.

And Vayu came into Kubera's palace, and he saw Kubera, and

said 'Can you tell me anything of Krishna. Is he a good boy or a bad boy?'

And Kubera laughed and said 'O, Krishna is a naughty boy, for he is always teasing the girls. He pinches them and steals their clothes when they are swimming and plays silly games on them all the time.' And Kubera leant forward and said 'You must be careful only to whisper his name in my palace, for all my maids are in love with Krishna, and sigh when they hear of him and start to cry.'

Then Vayu left Kubera and went back to the gods, and he spoke to them all and said 'I have found that Krishna is often a mischievous boy, and has played tricks on everyone in the land of Braj. It seems that Lord Indra was right to be angry with him, for what he says about Krishna, everyone else said too.'

Then Indra leapt up, and rubbed his hands with delight and said 'I shall punish him therefore so that he will never be the same.' And he called three gods forward, and he told one of them to take away Krishna's memory, and one of them to shoot Krishna with an arrow of love, and one of them to lead him into the desert and throw him down to starve. And the three gods flew off to do what they were told. But Indra's wife wept to hear what would happen to Krishna, for she felt sorry for him, and believed that really he was a good boy.

Book Eleven

Radha Brought to Trial

Now when the soldiers came into the village of Braj, all the cowherds were very frightened, and from that moment on everything started going wrong. Because they were frightened, and thought that the soldiers were going to kill them or make them prisoner and take them away, people started worrying and quarrelling with one another, and everybody was gloomy and afraid, just as the people were in the city of Mathura.

And other things started happening too, for Agni the fire god had a wife, and Agni's wife lived in a volcano, burning with fire. She hated Krishna, and she hated Radha for being Krishna's favourite, and she sat in her burning volcano thinking of plans to hurt them. And when she had thought of a plan she flew to the city of Mathura and came to the wicked priest of King Kamsa, and this was the priest who had told Radha and her brother they were to come and live in the city, the same priest that Kamsa had told to bring him Radha to be one of his wives.

And Agni's wife appeared to him in a dream and said 'Wicked priest, the great King Kamsa has put his trust in you, and he has told you that he desires Radha to be one of his wives. Go then quickly to the land of Braj, for Radha and Krishna are alone together in the forest. Catch them together and you can bring her away. Make her a prisoner and bring her to King Kamsa.'

And the priest jumped up, on fire with this plan, for he thought King Kamsa would reward him if he did this, and he hurried away in the morning streets of the town.

Now the gods who had been told to lead Krishna away to the desert, they also had been busy, and two of them came to where the horrible man who calls up demons lay, and they stood on either side of his bed and said 'Awake, O man that calls up demons, and go to the land of Braj, and get rid of Krishna for ever from the land. Make a magic potion that will take away his memory and get him to drink it, and then when he has drunk it and does not know who he is, lead

59

him away into the desert, and leave him there to starve.'

And the man jumped up, on fire with this plan, for he thought King Kamsa would reward him if he did this, and he hurried away, and as he came to the morning streets of the town he met the wicked priest, who was getting ready a great golden chariot with two horses to pull it, and the man said 'Take me, priest, to the land of Braj, for I have a plan given me by two gods to get rid of Krishna.'

And the priest said 'And I have a plan given me by one goddess to take prisoner Radha the favourite of Krishna. Jump in beside me, and let us be about our evil plots.' And he jumped in, and they raced off towards Braj, kicking up the dust in the low sunlight of the plain.

Now when Radha and Krishna came out of the woods, down from the mountain where they walked in the moonlight, they saw all the soldiers afar off in the village. And Krishna said 'There are too many soldiers for me to fight, and it is not good to kill men idly. Let us go amongst them, and do what they wish, for soldiers cannot rule long in a peaceful land.' And they went hand in hand towards the village.

And the wicked priest and the horrible man arrived in the village and shouted at once to the soldiers 'Where is Krishna and his favourite Radha?' And Krishna arrived with Radha and said 'Here.'

And the priest cried out 'Soldiers, seize those two you see there. They are enemies of our King and must be held prisoner.'

And the soldiers dashed at Krishna, and he let himself be taken. They took Radha and Krishna to a cowshed and threw them in the cowshed and locked the door. And the priest and the man gloated that they had them in their power.

And now even worse things began to happen, and all because the people were afraid, for Radha and Krishna, whom everyone in the village used to love, in a few hours became everyone's most hated enemy, and were cast out of the village and shouted at by all the people. And the way it all happened was this.

When Radha and Krishna were put as prisoners in the cowshed, all the girls in the village saw what had happened, and it so chanced that Agni's wife who had just been to see the wicked priest in Mathura was there also, high up in the air, burning with flame, and watching what was going on. And she thought of another plan which would hurt Radha and bring her into disgrace, and she flew down to earth and disguised herself as a milkmaid and went amongst the girls who had been watching all the time.

And Agni's wife said in a voice like a milkmaid's 'Sisters, do you see now that all this time Radha has been deceiving us? We thought she was a good girl who stayed in at nights in her house with her brother, and look, she has been wandering in the woods with Krishna, trying to keep him all to herself. She is a traitor to us all, and a traitor to her brother. Let us go and tell her brother what has happened.'

And in this way she made the milkmaids angry against Radha, and they began talking among themselves jealously, and they became furious, and all ran to Radha's house and called out her brother.

And the cowgirls shouted to him 'Your sister has been unfaithful, and instead of being in the house with you at night, has been out in the forests with Krishna the cowherd. She loves Krishna and she is his favourite.' And they were all so jealous, they said evil things against her, and called her bad names.

But the brother said to them 'Radha is not unfaithful, and she would not do the things you say. She is my sister, and would never do anything without telling me.'

And the soldiers came up and tried to make the milkmaids go back to their houses, but they would not be quieted. And the priest came to them and agreed with them and said it was all true that they said, and he cried out 'Radha is guilty. Bring her to the village square, and let us accuse her before all the people, and let us see what she can say.'

And the brother tried to stop them, but everyone was so excited they would not listen to him, and because they were together in an angry crowd, hatred and madness flew about among them, and they shouted and screamed that Radha was the cause of all their troubles and that it was because of her that the soldiers had come, and that Krishna too had betrayed them. And among all the shouting Agni's wife laughed and screamed with delight, for all the people were burning with rage just as if they were on fire, and she soared up into heaven beating her flaming wings, and went rejoicing back to her land and her raging mountain.

And the priest came to where Radha and Krishna were together in the cowshed, and he said 'Radha, you are to come and be tried before the people for unfaithfulness, for you have been shown to be the favourite of Krishna, and to have left your house to go with him at night in the forest. The people are enraged against you, and they must be satisfied.'

And Radha looked angry and said 'Then they are cowards and villains. Are these my friends of days ago? Do they so quickly turn against me when there are soldiers in the village, and do they fight against me instead of against that tyrant Kamsa who is oppressing them? O fickle people I scorn your weathercock natures.'

And the priest said 'Save your fiery speeches for your friends. Come to be tried.'

And Krishna said to her softly 'The days are mad, and the wars are come. This darkness has been sent to see by, and to sort out the false and the true. But do not fear, my little Radha, I shall always be with you. Me they cannot harm, and you have only to call me in the smallest voice, and I shall come to you from the ends of the earth.'

And they kissed, and she was taken away.

And when Radha had been taken away, Krishna sat in the cowshed for some time thinking what he should do. And while he was thinking, the man who could call up spirits came in with the potion of forgetfulness in a bowl, and without speaking he put it beside Krishna and went out.

And Krishna sat for a long while in thought, and the shouting outside in the square stopped and was silent, and without looking Krishna put his hand down to the bowl and picked it up and drank from it. And when he put the bowl down again he had forgotten everything he knew, so that he did not even know his name or who he was. And he sat very puzzled, silent, for a long time.

And when Radha was brought before the people, they howled and shouted against her, and poured on her all the hatred in their hearts, for the coming of the soldiers had made them all afraid. And Radha was put into the middle of the square so that the people were all around her. And Nanda, who had been talking to Balarama, heard these shouts and came out of his house, and they were astonished when they saw the great crowd and Radha in the midst, and Radha's brother held by the soldiers near by.

Nanda said 'What is this outrage? Why is this girl and her brother, the leader of the village, treated as though they were criminals, and held captive before their own friends?'

And the people shouted 'We are not her friends. She is an outcast.'

And the priest said 'Nanda, you were best to be silent. This is a lawful trial you see here, and it is done by the order of our ruler, King Kamsa, Raj of Mathura, and Lord of the World.'

62

And the people all shouted 'Hail Kamsa!'

And the priest said 'Be silent then, and watch the course of justice.'

Balarama said to Nanda 'Father, that man has a stupid face, and thinks himself a great one. Shall I call Krishna with my horn, and we can have fun with him and throw him in the pond?'

But Nanda said 'No, Balarama, for all our one-time friends have set their faces against us, and it is no longer the time for playing and games.'

The priest said 'On with the trial, and the charge is this. Radha, you are asked to tell this court whether or no you love the cowherd Krishna, and have become his favourite, and left your brother's house to be with him.'

And Radha's brother cried to her 'Radha, say nothing to these wicked men. They have no right to try you, nor need you tell your tale.'

And Radha said 'I have been asked to give the truth of what my heart holds best, and now you are all seated, and look as though you are waiting for a tale. I shall begin then, and tell the tale of Krishna, and how through the path of many years he came to me often and stole my heart away.'

Book Twelve

Radha's Tale

And Radha said 'You have asked me to say whether or no I love Krishna, and that is easily answered, for I do with all my heart. But how I came to love him, and to go with him in secret against my brother, this is a harder task and a longer story.

'When I was only a girl, and my heart knew nothing more than games in the orchard with the cowherd children, Krishna and I were always friends. He would pull down the branches of the mango trees, so that I could pick the best mangoes and we could eat them. But once when we grew a little older, Nanda sent us home together through the forest in spring, and before we had come back to the village in the land of Braj our hearts were stirred by a dawning love, and Krishna kissed me among the flowering trees.

'And later once, we had been sent to fetch curds from another village, the milkmaid girls to the other side the river, and we were late coming back, and reached the river at evening. There in the dusk Krishna and the other boys waylaid us, and they had taken the ferry so that we could not cross. And Krishna said we should all pay a toll, and the toll was in kisses, as you may guess. Long we all argued by the banks in the twilight, but we gave them our kisses because we were frightened of the darkness. But the boat was hidden, and still they would not let us pass, and the night came down and the stars went round, and all night I spent with Krishna in childish hugs and fondling.

'And Krishna became a menace to us little milkmaids, and he would tease us always and steal our curds, and once when he did so I grew so enraged I dressed as a constable and came through the trees, and I arrested Krishna and hit him with my truncheon. He was so perplexed, and stood there so still not knowing what to do, that all the cowfolk laughed and agreed that I had won that little game.

'But the years went by, and as I became older, it was no longer time for me to play games with Krishna, and I kept to the house and was faithful to my brother. And I became a woman, and had to behave in another fashion. But still my heart was gone to Krishna,

64

although now I stayed inside the house and saw him no more. The days passed drearily and I felt alone.

'One day, as I sat on the balcony of our house, looking down into the village street outside, Krishna happened to go by, driving the cows, and he looked up at me with those deep dark eyes and smiled at me with such a sweet smile that I felt my heart go to him as it had never done before, and I turned away and went back into the house. How my spirit swelled at that hour! I longed to go with Krishna, and yet I knew I could not. I was confused and overcome by the love that was inside me, and I felt hot and dizzy as though I had been drinking strong wine.

'From that day forward I kept away from the street, but Krishna would pester me with secret messages. Whoever I met would come bearing words from him, until I seemed to see Krishna in everything that happened.

'One day a flower-seller came to the house. She was an old lady, and I felt sorry for her, she was so poor and old, and I asked her in the house to look at the blossoms she had in her basket. I talked with her and smelt the flowers, sprigs of jasmine and ashoka blooms, lotuses from the lake and magnolias with rich perfume, and soon they all lay scattered on the silken carpet. I paid her for them all and asked which would suit me now to wear, and she took up a garland of golden azaleas and cast them round my neck and kissed me hard, and I saw then that it was Krishna in an old woman's disguise.

'I rushed him from my house and banged the door, and I ran to my room and fell on the bed weeping. How that kiss was to haunt me in the days and nights to come! O Krishna, such sweetness nearly tore the heart from my body.

'I grew sick at last with this trouble in my soul, and lay for many days lifeless on my couch. The moon burned hotly, and the fanning air was flame, my silk sheets were spikes and knives, and the soothing sandal sulphur. At last my brother seemed to despair of my life, and sent word everywhere to find a doctor that could cure me.

'Now it so happened that a strange yogi came into our village, and the people said he had done many great cures, for he was a wild-looking man, with matted hair caked in mud, and eyes fierce as tigers, and knew all the old spells, and my brother believed in this yogi and brought him to the house. I remember well when the yogi came in: he was like a man from my dreams, a demon-man who had chased me through the night, a savage magician always nearing as I struggled in my nightmare with unmoving limbs. The yogi sent them all away and saw to me alone.

'Without speaking to me or doing more than look into my eyes, he told me I was suffering from the disease of love. I was surprised at what he said, and amazed at his wisdom. So glad I was to find someone who knew my secret that I wept and cried that it was true what he had said, and I told him of my love for Krishna the cowherd, dwelling on all the sweet things that I knew about him. And when I had finished the yogi nodded and said "It is a common disease."

'And I looked at him and asked, not knowing whether I wanted it or not "And could you cure me?"

'And the yogi pulled off his ragged clothes and said "I am the very man to do it!" and it was Krishna.

'O, how I was overcome by shame and horror when I saw the blue limbs of Krishna beneath the yogi's tattered clothes, and when I knew that the doctor to whom I had praised Krishna and spoken so freely of my helpless love was none other than Krishna himself, nodding and smiling as I told him all. O, I was helpless then to put off his desire, and scarcely drew back when he took me in his arms, and the sighs and moans which his love wrung from me were hardly enough to call the others in to see us, for they thought they were all part of the doctor's cure. O Krishna, this was your wildest prank with me, and here was it you won your game.

'Now when Krishna left me, he told me that in four days time he would wait for me in the forest at the full moon, and I was to meet him there, and he would signal for me to come by playing his flute among the trees. And my brother and all he told I would be well again in four days time, and with that he went and left us alone.

'In four days time the rains came, and at night among the sounds of the rain and thunder I heard Krishna's flute warbling among the wind-blown trees, and I went to him that night and on all other nights when he has called me with the sounds of his flute in the deep forest.

'And this is how I came to love Krishna and to leave my brother to be with him late at night in the gloomy woods. The days I have loved are now over and gone, and I am a prisoner to the might of my enemies. Do with me as you wish, for it is no longer of any care with me. I have known Krishna and gone to the call of his flute, and I scorn you all with your threats and spears.'

Book Thirteen

Radha Condemned

And when the wicked priest had heard this, he turned to the people of Braj and said 'She has admitted her guilt herself, there is no need to call any forward to speak against her. I ask the people then, what is to be her fate?'

And the cowfolk cried 'Death,' for they were all jealous of what they had heard, and the envy of happiness is hard to bear.

And the priest said 'To death she shall be given, and as our leader and lord King Kamsa, Raj of Mathura, has ordered that if any woman in the realm be found guilty of unfaithfulness to any man she shall be put to death by burning, I shall take this woman to the city of Mathura and give her over to the King, to do as he will with her.'

But the people, who would rather she were burnt before them, did not cheer at this and fell silent, and Nanda, the old man, who was astonished at what he had heard, came forward and said 'By whose authority is this woman to be taken away from us? We are cowherds of the land of Braj and are in our own governing. You shall not take this woman away for she has neither had trial nor sentence nor is she in any way subject to King Kamsa of Mathura, be he raj or lord or leader or whatever you will call him.'

And the priest said 'Silence, old man, or we will take you with her to be burnt.'

And then Balarama came up and said 'You take her and I will take your head, you sour-faced priest. By this bottle I will, and with this bottle I will knock it off, and that I'll do this minute as well.'

But Nanda told his son 'Stay your hand, son. These are men, not fiends, and we must talk with them, for he who slays a man slays his own kind and turns his own against him.'

And the priest who was a clever man said 'Let there be no force one way or another in this matter. This woman has been brought to trial before the people, and the people must be judge, for King Kamsa wants everything that is right and fair. Do the people wish that I set this woman free?'

And the cowfolk shouted 'No!'

Now the fire god Agni had been hovering in the air above the land, and when he heard this he was delighted, and he flew off to greet his wife and said to her 'Well have you done, wife. The people hate Radha, and have called for her death. Soon her heart will be closed against Krishna, and we shall be free of him. Let us rest now. We have done a good day's work.'

And in Braj when the soldiers came to take Radha away her brother leapt forward to fight against them, and they took him too, and led them both to the cowshed to be prisoners. And as Radha returned she thought of Krishna there waiting for her, and had good hope that he would plot a way out for them all three.

But Krishna meanwhile had drunk the potion of forgetfulness, and when he had downed it the man that called spirits came to him, and seeing that Krishna did not know who he was he spoke to him in a soft voice and said 'Come, young man, you remember me. I am the kind man that loves you. Give me your hand then, for it is time you began your journeys.'

And Krishna, who was washed of all memories of where he was or what he had been doing, went with the man as meekly as a lamb, and the man took him away from the village and out into the plain. And he took him far away from the land of Braj, and brought him to the desert where the evil spirits live, and sat him down among the stones and sand and left him.

And so Radha and her brother came to the cowshed and went in. And she saw a blank space where Krishna had been, and her heart grew cold with fear. And Radha did not see him again from that day until the day she left her body and went down to the land of the dead.

And when the trial was over, the cowfolk began to walk away, but Nanda upbraided them and said 'O you fickle hearts, or rather you that have no hearts at all, how are you all so changed! How is friendship forgot when there are soldiers in the village, how is truth fled when there is a tyrant on the throne! And do you now turn against your oldest friends? Aye, such are men, that when they come in packs they come as wolves. Out of my way, you wolves and dogs!'

And the villagers marvelled that Nanda was so angry, who in the days of peace was the mildest of men, but they forgot him soon and went home to their houses, thankful that it was not they who had been accused.

And before very long the ox-cart was ready, and Radha and her brother were put in the cart, and the soldiers formed up on either side as guard. And Nanda and Balarama came in the growing darkness to bid farewell, and Nanda said 'Farewell, Radha, who are accused of the deepest heart. Now have the evil days come down upon us, and there is war and hatred over all the land. Have good courage therefore, and abide the settling in, for the great gods shall shake us to sift the good from the bad, but let them shake us never so hard, they shall never shake Krishna from our hearts. Farewell my friend, farewell Radha, let come what comes, all shall be well.'

And the priest told the guards to set off, and the ox-cart went in the evening air over the dusty plain, and brought Radha and her brother to the dismal city of Mathura.

Book Fourteen

Vasudeva's Tale

When the rosy dawn had touched the snowy peaks of heaven, Indra's wife got up after a night of little sleep. She was worried about Krishna, and though Vayu had told the gods he was indeed a mischievous boy who deserved to be punished she still could not believe it. So she called Vayu to her and asked him to fly down to earth and find out more about Krishna.

'Go, Vayu,' she said, 'faithful messenger of the gods, and dive into the earth, and greet Yama the god of the dead. Say to him I have sent you to see if there is anything he can tell you about Krishna, for that god knows the end of all men.'

So Vayu flew down to earth and dived into the black soil and came to the gloomy tunnels and fiery lakes of Yama, god of the dead, and Vayu said 'Hail, great King, Indra's wife has sent me to ask you if you know anything of Krishna, the blue cowherd. Can you tell me what he is really like, or what in days to come he will become?'

And Yama sighed and said 'What does it matter what anyone is or is not? You gods are so eager to be meddling in men's affairs. Leave them to time, my friend, and they will all come to me.'

But Vayu asked again about Krishna and said 'But have you heard of this herdsman? It seems he can do great marvels, and yet he behaves in a very mischievous way and causes everybody trouble.'

And Yama said 'I have heard of Krishna, but what he is I know not. He has power and power over my demons, and so I think he is no ordinary man. But if you are so keen to find out more about him, there is a man living in Mathurar, whom the King has thrown into prison. His name is Vasudeva. Go to him, for he has a tale to tell of Krishna the kineherd.'

Vayu thanked Yama and at once flew out of Hell and up into the clear air of the earth, and once more he disguised himself as a wandering yogi with orange robes and a wooden staff, and he came like that to the dismal city of Mathura, to look for this Vasudeva, who was in prison.

And once inside the tall city gates, Vayu began to ask the people there the way to the prison, but everyone he turned to pretended not to hear him and hurried by, and everyone he asked would not answer, for they were afraid and kept their faces turned to the ground.

But Vayu came at last to a huge building of red sandstone, and it had bars on the windows, and from inside came the sounds of clanking chains, and the groans of men, and Vayu thought this must be the prison and inside must be Vasudeva, so quick as lightning with his god's power he wished himself inside the walls.

And when he was inside he saw that he was in a great room, all dark and hot, with straw on the floor, and full of people in rags, who had long beards and looked sad and weary. But the people here were glad to answer Vayu, and quickly brought him where Vasudeva sat, and Vasudeva was a tall man who looked like a King.

And Vayu said 'Greetings Vasudeva, I wish you well, though you are in a dark place here and suffering misfortune, I have been sent to you because I wish to find out more about Krishna the cowherd. May I ask if you have heard of this person?'

And when Vayu said the name of Krishna, all the people in the cell looked round and were silent, and for a long time Vasudeva was silent. But at last Vasudeva said 'I have indeed heard of this person you mention, for I am Krishna's father, and suffer for it as you see.'

And Vayu was astonished when he heard what Vasudeva said, for Yama had not told him anything of this, and for a long time he could say nothing, but gazed at Vasudeva in surprise.

And Vasudeva said 'I see you are astonished, O holy man, and indeed you must believe what the world believes: that Nanda is Krishna's father, Nanda the cowherd in the land of Braj.'

And Vayu found his voice and said that this was so.

And Vasudeva nodded and said 'So does everyone think, for so things happened many years ago that brought my son, who was born a rich man's son in the city of Mathura, to be the son of a poor herdsman in the land of Braj. Aye, strange things happen when the gods come down to earth.'

But Vayu was still astonished, and said 'But how did this happen, and why have you let Krishna live so long with the cowherds, and have you not told him that he is your son?'

And Vasudeva said 'Perhaps you would like me to tell you the

71

whole story? We have time enough in prison, and it is only a little tale.'

And Vayu said 'Please tell me, for of Krishna I long to hear.'

And Vasudeva said 'Long, long ago, when Devaki became my wife, it was said by a priest who knew of future days that Devaki's eighth son would kill Kamsa the tyrant and rule as Raj in the city of Mathura. Now Kamsa even then was a jealous King, and he heard of this saying and threw my wife and me in jail. There did we live waiting for our eighth son to be born. Now it was winter when this happened, and the coldest that ever we knew, and outside of the prison we saw the snow come down, a thing that has not happened again to this day, and our son was born among the straw and candles of the prison.

'But I knew if my son were to live, he must be got away that night before the tyrant could lay hold of him. But the prison walls were high, and the bars were stout, and what could I do against the guards and soldiers? In the middle of the night, as the moon came down, I heard a voice in the stillness say "Take up your baby, and go into the land of Braj. Leave the babe there, and he will be safe from the tyrant. Up now, quick now, away!" And the voice faded as strangely as it came.

'I was fired by this message, and decided to obey it, for it seemed like a voice come from the gods themselves. I took up the baby, my little son Krishna, I wrapped up his little blue limbs in a blanket and cradled him in my arms against the cold, and I went towards the door of the prison. In the hushed darkness it slid open, and another door beyond it, and the barred gates that end the long corridors of that place, all slid open silently as I approached, and the guards and warders I feared would see me, them I passed, one by one with their bunches of keys, and all were locked in the soundest sleep. Soon I was out of the dark streets of the city, voyaging on over the snowy plain.

'But I came then to the river Jumna, and swollen with the melted snow it roared between its banks. I could not see how I could get over it, for the fording place was deep under the water and the ferry was nowhere to be seen. I dallied on the banks, walking here and there, not knowing what I should try to do. Just as I was about to turn back in despair my baby son Krishna stuck out his little blue foot towards the river, and at once the roaring waves went down and the river sank, and running quickly on the wet sand of the bottom I was able to get across and come to safety. I blessed the gods who were helping me on this night.

'And so I came to the village in Braj. I found the house of Nanda the faithful herdsman, and I found the baby girl, a child just born that night to his wife Jasuda, and I swapped my little Krishna for the girl and laid him instead of her in the wooden cradle. Back to Mathura I went, and all went well until I was safe again in prison. All that remained was to show Kamsa the girl and make him believe that it was the baby of my wife, and he would think that what the priest said could not be true.

'Well, the morning came and things did not quite happen in that way. Kamsa was enraged to see the little girl, and fearing even the strength of a little girl child, he picked her up to dash her to the ground and kill her. But as soon as he lifted her into the air, the baby turned into the goddess Devi, and roaring to heaven in a sheet of blue flame she spoke to us in a voice of thunder and said "Your son is safe, your little blue child, for he is no ordinary baby: he is the highest god come to earth again to save mankind, he is the keeper of the universe, Vishnu." And so she flew off to the realms of heaven.

'No one but my wife and I heard the goddess speak, but all were amazed nonetheless at what happened. Kamsa ordered that we live in prison for ever after, and went away angry to his palace again. My wife and I were sad at losing our little son, but we were happy enough to know that he would live, and with the knowledge that he is indeed Vishnu, the almighty, how can we lament at what has passed? Well, my friend, that is the story of the birth of Krishna, and how in the moonlight I took him from the prison, and ran with him silently across the frozen plain.'

And Vayu said 'It is a tale for always telling' and having spoken he felt suddenly so joyful, hearing that Krishna was none other than the mighty god Vishnu, that he shot off to heaven without pausing to throw off his disguise, and all the prisoners knew that a god had been with them as Vayu soared to the lofty mountains.

Book Fifteen

The Gods Rejoice

In heaven meanwhile Indra's wife had invited all the gods to her house, since she wished to tell them about Vayu's second mission. Although her husband was still angry with Krishna, she did all she could to make things happy. She sent to Kubera for some divine musicians, and got them to play their flutes and sitars on the terraces of her lovely mansion, and there were girls bringing sherbet, and golden goblets of soma, and the nectar of amrita. And all the gods came flocking to the house.

And when they were all assembled Indra's wife said 'Gods of heaven I wish to tell you that I have sent Vayu to earth once more to find out about Krishna the kineherd, for I could not really believe what he found before, that Krishna was a wicked and mischievous boy. It seems to me he is not wicked but just high-spirited, and that is I am sure what Vayu will find out.'

But Indra said gloomily with a snarl 'Let him be what he will, he is sent to the desert, and I shan't help him out of it.'

And a little red god that looked like an elephant, who was called Ganesha, said 'O Lord Indra, couldn't one of us fetch him back again? There is no need for you to go.'

And Indra said 'Fetch him back if you please, but he won't know who he is, for a god has taken away his memory, and that's that.'

But Indra's wife said 'Let us hope that what Vayu finds is good news, and then we can all become friends again, for once all the gods are friends, then everything on earth has a way of coming out all right.'

And Indra said 'I shall not be friends with any one. I have been shamed by a little blue cowherd in front of a lot of normal-coloured cowherds, and I am not ever going to forget the fact.'

And Agni, said 'And my fire demons have been killed by this ridiculous little boy, and I shall not forget that either.'

But before anyone could speak further, there was the sound of a bugle blowing on the walls of heaven, announcing that Vayu was flying back, and the gods rushed out onto the verandah and saw Vayu coming towards them waving his arms and shouting for joy. And the gods thought 'What is it, what can be the news he brings?'

And Vayu flew down to where they were standing and, panting for breath, said 'Gods and goddesses of heaven, I have found out a great secret. Krishna the cowherd is no mortal at all, but come down to earth again to help us, he is lord of the universe: the mighty Vishnu himself.'

The gods cried out and embraced each other, they were so happy, for when Vishnu came to earth all things were well, and an age of great peace and universal grace was come. But Indra and Agni were not pleased. And Agni's flames dimmed and darkened when he heard the news, and he turned away, glancing backwards evilly, and slunk off and dived into the air of the world.

But Indra cried in an angry voice 'Let Krishna be who he will. They were my words, and my word I keep. I shall not help such a little prankster. Let the dragon Vritra eat him. I care not.' And in high rage he left the chamber and went up into the heights of heaven, and sat on a great peak looking out into the purple sky. And he nursed his anger, and would not speak to anyone.

But in heaven the news that Vishnu had come to earth was spreading like happy fire from house to house. The little gods shouted it to each other on the balconies and rooftops, and the bugles rang gladly in the streets of heaven. There was a sound of laughter and cheering, and the very flags seemed to writhe with joy.

And the gods were happy, and Indra's wife said, as they smiled at each other, 'Vayu, our thanks, for you have brought us peaceful minds. If the Lord Vishnu is among us, we have nothing to fear. In time Indra's anger will cool, and he will join with us in helping Krishna. Until then we must wait and see what the coming days bring. For this time at least our searches have a happy end.'

And the gods feasted again, and forgot their cares a while, in the draughts of amrita, and the music of Kubera's court.

Then, in highest heaven, Lord Vishnu himself smiled, and looked on his wife Lakshmi, who was weaving a garland of lotuses, and he said 'So, you have given me a place in the story, and cunnningly, my dear, have you answered my question. And now, come and kiss me, since the gods are friends again.' And he stretched out his hand to his wife.

75

But Lakshmi drew back and said 'Not all the gods are friends, and there is much more to come, and sad days too, before we can break off our tale in kisses.' And Lakshmi slid down the fifteenth lotus onto the thread of the garland, and said 'When the last lotus is in place, you may kiss me then.'

And Vishnu said 'Then you will no doubt keep me waiting until you have woven my conch, my mace, this golden lotus, all into the tale. And the serpent I lie on and our white bird too?'

Lakshmi did not speak, but smiled as if to say 'All have a part in the story.'

PART III

Radha's Temptation

Book Sixteen

Kamsa Plans a Massacre

King Kamsa now grew even more wicked and horrible, for his armies were everywhere, and he thought he was ruler of the world. And when people think they are very important, they grow annoyed and angry with every little thing, because nothing can ever be as good as they think they deserve. And all the people of Mathura had to bow down to him to the ground, and no one was allowed to disagree with anything he said.

Kamsa knew that Krishna had been sent into the desert by the man who calls up spirits, and he thought that by now Krishna must be dead, so he called once more the holy man who could see into the coming days and tell what would happen. And the holy man came in, and he had a long white beard, and wore long yellow robes, and carried a tall wooden staff with a fork on the end, called a trident.

And King Kamsa said 'Tell me, O holy man, is Krishna the cowherd dead, and shall I rule now as an almighty King?'

But the sage did not answer at first, but stared out of the window. At last he said 'Krishna will live in the hearts of everyone, and the days of King Kamsa will soon be done.' And with that he turned and walked straight out of the hall.

And Kamsa grew so afraid at what he had heard that his mouth fell open and his eyes grew larger and larger and he shuddered, for the thought of Krishna was like a pit in the ground that kept opening and opening wherever he stepped.

But then he jumped up and thought to himself 'If Krishna lives in the hearts of everyone, then the hearts of everyone must be closed so that he shall die.' And on fire with this plan, he strode out of the hall, and his courtiers bowed low and touched their brows on the floor, and not one of them knew what was in King Kamsa's mind.

But King Kamsa left the palace, and went in the narrow streets to where the man who calls up spirits had his house, in a gloomy square next to the prison and the slaughterhouse, and he banged on the door with his mace and was let in. And Kamsa said to the man 'Great things are to be done, and you are to do them. Call me up not one demon, not two demons, nor three demons, but a whole army of demons, and send them into the land of Braj. There let them kill and bully as they may, for the people love Krishna, and I shall close their hearts against him.'

But the man said 'King Kamsa, I have called up demons enough for you before, and for your good also I have got rid of Krishna. But to get rid of Krishna you did not command me, a god in my sleep did that. An army of demons though is a terrible thing, for he who calls up demons cannot always put them down. If I call up a hundred demons to this earth, they may kill and burn all Braj and Mathura, all India too, and you and me also.'

'Call them up!' said Kamsa, 'And on my head be it.'

And the man looked at the King for a long time, as though in evil thought, and the man said 'It cannot be done at once. But leave me a little time to my books and charts, and I shall call you up a gang of demons such as this world has never seen. There is a great well, waterless and not used now, inside the prison walls. The air is cold that comes out of it and deep is its base in the rocky earth. Meet me there when the sun goes down towards evening, and I will work you what mischief I can.'

King Kamsa's eyes sparkled for joy, and he left the man and walked back to his palace, impatient till the time the demons would come. In his heart he hated Krishna and the cowfolk, and longed to make them suffer and curse their fate.

Book Seventeen

Radha Sees the Palace

Radha and her brother meanwhile came on to Mathura as prisoners of the King, and in the evening light they neared the city, and saw far off in the dying sunset the ruddy glow of the city walls. Radha said 'See, brother, the sandstone walls of Mathura. I wish we had never gone there first to plead with King Kamsa, for since that day all these evil things have come upon us. Look, how in the sinking light the walls glow bloodily and call us to our doom.'

But the brother said 'Have courage, Radha, for we do not know what end awaits us, and Mathura may yet bring us luck.'

And Radha said 'No, I see my death approaching. The city gate, like the jaws of fate, yawn to swallow me up, and here I shall not pass again, until my soul has gone to the depths of hell.'

The ox-cart went in under the echoing gateway, and they came to the city. And all overnight they were kept in the King's armoury among the spears and shields.

But when the morning came, the wicked priest went to see the King, who, as it happened, had just then got back from his visit to the man that calls up spirits, and Kamsa's mind was afire with the thought of the demons, and restless longing for that dusk to come when the man would call them up and send them on to Braj.

But the priest approached the throne where the King sat and said 'King Kamsa, Raj of Mathura, Ruler of the World, I have brought to the city Radha and her brother, as you had asked me. They are both my prisoners, and Radha had been tried by a lawful court for unfaithfulness, and condemend to die. But it is well known, O King, that you can save a woman from her death. Shall I bring this Radha to see if she will please you?'

'Build up a bonfire, and throw her on it,' said King Kamsa. 'And as for her brother, fling him in jail.' And with that he sent the priest away, and returned to his thoughts of the fiends.

And the priest went, astonished at Kamsa's change of mind, and sad that he had not been able to please him nor earn honour from his deeds. He ordered slaves to bring sticks and wood to the market-place, and build up a fire. And he had Radha's brother thrown into jail, and Radha brought to the square in chains, and put up on top of the fire, and tied to a stake. Then the slaves came with flaming torches and got ready to light it.

But Kamsa was a crafty King, and though he had told the priest to burn Radha he did not mean to let this happen, for he planned that at the last minute, when the flames were about to take her, he would pardon her and save her from the fire, and in that way he hoped to win her trust and thankfulness. So when he saw from a window that the burning was about to start, he called down and stopped them, and went to the market-place himself.

When he came to the fire Kamsa pretended to look surprised, and he turned to the wicked priest and said 'This is the woman Radha, whom I summoned with her brother to my palace. How dare you treat a guest of King Kamsa in this way? Let her come down at once, and bring her to my court.' And before the priest could answer or exclaim in surprise, Kamsa turned and left.

The priest felt afraid, because he seemed to have angered Kamsa, and he went then to the man that calls up spirits, to ask him what he thought of these things. But both of them were soon to be wound up in the net Kamsa was weaving, and even before the dawning of the next day they would be dead.

Meanwhile Kamsa received Radha in his lofty apartments, where he lived with his wives, for he had many wives and the part of the palace where they lived was called the harem.

When Radha was led to the harem she felt sick and faint with fear, for she had thought she was going to die by burning, and the smoke and flames had made her afraid. The smell of the smoke she could smell wherever she went, and she was shaking from shock and horror. But now she trod the silky carpets on the marble floors, and glinting around her were gold and silver lamps, and by the walls were divans strewn about with cushions and embroidered bolsters. And she was brought to King Kamsa who sat cross-legged on a low jewelled throne.

Kamsa waved his hand so that the guards went away, and he spoke to Radha saying, 'Radha, come here. Sit down. Rest. A terrible fate was nearly yours: an agony of burning and a miserable death. Had I not looked out of my window at that moment you would have perished in the flames, have choked in the fires, and gone burning to the land of the dead. But now you are safe in my palace, you have me to protect you, and everything here is kind and wishes you well. I wish you well, Radha, I who saved you from death.'

He looked at Radha, but she did not speak, for she knew he was only pretending to be kind and guessed that all the time he had planned on saving her from being burnt. So in silence she waited to hear his true thoughts.

And Kamsa said 'For a long time I have watched you, and thought of you. Now I want to ask you a question. You are such a beautiful girl, that I do not like to see you wasting yourself on the stupid people of Braj. I wish you to live here in the palace and become one of my wives. My harem is greater and more lovely than that of any King in the world, and you would be its chiefest jewel.'

Radha looked at King Kamsa, and her heart was afraid, for she had dreaded he would wish this. Yet she feared angering him, for her body still shook from the shock of being so near to burning, and so again she just looked at him and said nothing.

And Kamsa said 'Come, my dear, let me show you my palace, and afterwards you may give me your answer.' He took her arm, and Radha felt that his touch was sharp and full of hate and anger.

As Kamsa took Radha round his huge palace, everywhere they went slaves bowed down silently to the ground. He showed her great council-chambers, hung with branching lamps, and rooms piled thick with rich carpets, and strewn with dishes of gold. White peacocks yelled on the verandahs, and tame panthers scratched their necks on glossy floors.

Kamsa showed her fountains, and cool couches, and rooms where scented water ran through in channels in the marble floor, and he showed her gardens ranked with rose-beds and marigolds, and full of bowery dells. And at last he took her to a small room that was his own where he slept, and the room was dirty and stank.

And Kamsa threw off his crown, and rich robes, and lay down wearily on a low couch, and he said 'Come then, let me make you my wife.'

And Radha looked at him with disgust and said 'Fetch your firewood, King, for I would sooner go again into the flame than into your harsh embraces.' And with that she walked out of the chamber and into the sunny air.

Then Kamsa scrambled up, and pulled on his rich robes, and hurrying from the room, with one hand stuck his crown slanting on his head, and he shouted to the guards who stood about with their spears watching 'Seize that woman, you brainless apes! Haul her off to prison, and stick her in the darkest, dampest cell, or I shall have your throats cut all!'

The guards took Radha to prison, and Kamsa went back to his room and raged so that he smashed his cups to the ground, and kicked and tore at the dirty carpet. Long it was before he returned to his senses, and then when his rage had left him he yearned fiercely to be revenged on Radha.

Book Eighteen

Kamsa Calls the Fiends

Meanwhile the priest had come to the man that calls up spirits, and
he found him deep in his charts and spells, and he said 'What are you
doing, man that calls up spirits, that you work so fiercely at your
books?'

But the man said 'Hush. Towards evening will you see my work,
when I shall call devils enough to pull the gods from heaven, for
Krishna lives in the hearts of people, and I am to close their hearts
against him.'

And the priest stayed and helped the man, for he still yearned to
get honour from King Kamsa.

But the King meanwhile went back to his court, and a soldier
greeted him, who had waited long to see him, and the soldier's
armour was hacked and he had wounds upon him. The soldier said
'Hail, King, I bring you news from the North. The tribe of the Kurus
have slaughtered your troops, and our armies have been pushed back
into the land of Braj.'

And the King raged and struck the soldier, and said 'You dog, how
dare you bring me such news? I will brook no defeats. You are all
weaklings and fools to be pushed back! You should have fought,
fought and died. Dead you should be all, not bringing me such news!'

And Kamsa raged and struck out at his councillors and guards,
and knocked old men down and sent helmets rolling, and all the
councillors were afraid. But fearful though they were they dare not
leave the chamber and avoid his blows, for a blow given is soon over,
but the special hatred of Kamsa is death. But Kamsa grew calmer at
last, and came to the window and looked out at the sinking sun. He
thought of the demons, and to himself wearily he said 'Ah, my
demons, you will do me more good than cowardly soldiers!'

And he turned and shouted to his courtiers and guards 'To the
great arena all of you. I will show you a better army than this scum
and tribe of geese.'

The hour came for the demons to be called out of hell, and the priest and the man that calls up spirits went to the prison and stood on a watch-tower, above the dark well, and Kamsa with his courtiers went to the pavilion in the new arena to review the demon troops.

And the man on the prison watch-tower began to recite his spells and said 'Dark and fiery devils, demons from the earth's very centre, rakshasas and dasyus, vampires and tusky vetalas, powers of the dense darkness, goblins of thick dissolution, throng to the great Kamsa and be his thunderous army!'

Here there was a rumbling underground, and the earth shook so that the sand fell off old towers and crumbled walls, and then the earth seemed to bellow like a murdered ox. Smoke came out of the pit and with it a strange hollow sound of roaring and cursing, a noise of chains and gnashing teeth.

And a great dense pack of red fiends leapt out of the hole, like a boiling lump of lava, and teemed all over the prison as if they were a swarm of hornets. Some ran up and down the walls of the prison, and some climbed over the walls and fell into the street outside, and as the fiends cooled they grew darker and then began running in the road, so that the sidestreets echoed with wails like a dark tunnel underground. And another mass followed, and another.

King Kamsa meanwhile with his courtiers in the pavilion heard far off the strange wailing and cursing of the fiends, and they looked at each other with awe and fear. And the fiends when they had rioted for a while cooled down in their passion of joy at bursting upon the earth, and obeyed the man's summons and went to King Kamsa. They came in a dark troop to that sandy circle, and Kamsa watched them enter in their ranks with vivid eyes.

There were goblins, some with many heads, marching and pushing in the vanguard; there were fiends like gorillas, and some like dwarfs or serpents, and some were women with hairy bodies and with tusks not teeth; there were battle fiends with cruel hooks and clubs; there were drought demons with fiery mouths that sucked and dried all life; flying fiends there were and fiends that rolled, fiends that slid there were and fiends that jumped, all manner of evil things that have been since the world began. There were naked ghouls with wounds on them, and hands and feet lopped off, who hobbled and crawled along, sometimes falling and writhing on the ground, and there were vampires and werewolves, blood dripping from their teeth, and rotten limbs and heads swinging from their taloned hands. And the

86

fiends all roared in a strange sound that seemed to say 'Hail Kamsa! Hail Kamsa!'

And Kamsa spoke to them and called out 'Fiends of all parts of Hell, welcome to earth! Pledge your faith to me, and all earth shall be yours to sport with. Up then. Sharpen your teeth. Run to the land of Braj. Surround the village there, and settle, camp in a great ring about it, and do not let anyone out. Rejoice this night. Tomorrow I shall send you word what you are to do.'

And now the fiends were glad to have some mischief, and raged with delight and surged out of the arena. So great was their joy that they stole things and fought with one another, and they ran through the streets of the town throwing stones at the houses and pushing over carts and stalls. They went rioting to the walls, and poured out of the gates of the town. But when they came to the clear vast spaces of the plain they stopped in wonder, for Hell is thick and close, and it had been long since they had known spaces like these. And their hearts were quietened, and for a while they felt peace, and they made on softly towards the woods and fields of the fair land of Braj, stricken with wonder, and forgetting who they were.

Book Nineteen

The Great Temptation

Radha meanwhile in the great sandstone prison sat thinking of all that had passed, and said to herself 'Now what is to become of me? I have been saved from a burning death, but now King Kamsa wants me for his wife, and that would be worse than burning or death. And here am I in a tiny cell in prison, shut away in a dark hole with nothing but straw to lie on, and who knows what worse comforts await me? And my brother, where is he? And what is to become of him? O how I wish that time could be put back, and we were all free again in Braj, before these evil days of the tyrant came upon us. O how I wish I had known then how happy I was! O Krishna, Krishna, where can you be? You said I had only to call and you would come. O how I would like to call you, and have your strong arms here around me, and your kind face to give me comfort.' And while Radha lamented in prison, the night came down, and brought stillness to the noise of shifting chains.

King Kamsa in his palace meanwhile was full of joy at the demons he had made obey him, and he thought that his kingdom would soon range over heaven and hell. So powerful did he feel, and so full of himself, that he decided to call at once on Radha, at the dead time of night, and force her to be his wife. And he summoned the priest and the man that calls up spirits to come with him, and together they went through the silent streets of the town.

And when they came to the prison, King Kamsa said 'I doubt not that this woman will gladly be mine, and I will go to her alone into the cell. But if she does not submit I shall threaten her with my demons, and then I shall have need of you both.' And with that they went into the prison.

Radha was in a cell that led off the courtyard where the pit was that the demons came from, and King Kamsa commanded a jailor to open the door and put a torch in the bars of the door to light them, and he went in alone to Radha. She looked up at him against the light, startled by the jangling of keys from a fearful dream.

And Kamsa said 'It is I, the King, Raj of Mathura, ruler of demons.'

And Radha said 'You! Have you come to plague me more to be your wife? Save your breath for your crouching courtiers. You'll get nothing of me.'

And King Kamsa scorned her and said 'Very easily I could force you to be mine, O proud and foolish woman, and easy would it be to teach you with torture how to treat a King. But I scorn the trade of a common jailer. With my will alone I shall make you be mine. With my will, that has sent forth soldiers over all India, and has commanded fiends from the depths of Hell.'

And Radha said 'O mighty mole to cast up such a mountain!'

But Kamsa said 'Come now, scornful, you have had a taste of dirty cells and stale water, will you not sell this for a life in such a palace as you saw? This night is the first in a long parade to death. Will you spend that procession languishing in a world like this? Come now, think sanely. Let me take you so, and lead you back into pleasure and wealth.'

And Kamsa reached forward and took Radha by the arm and then by the waist. She struggled against him and hit him with her fists, and she sent the torch flying so that they were plunged in darkness. And Kamsa grabbed her by the hair to tear her from the cell by force.

And Radha said 'My Krishna will take you by the hair soon. My love will avenge me.'

Kamsa let go Radha, and snatched away his hand with horror as if he had taken a snake, and he turned round and hammered on the door to be let out. And he ran out into the courtyard and the door clanged to after him.

And Kamsa shouted 'She speaks of Krishna. Which of you told her this? How does she know to speak of Krishna?' And he raged at them, and his eyes rolled madly in his head.

And the priest came forward, and bowed low to the ground, and said 'Kamsa, great one, Raj of Mathura, no one has told her to mention his name. I can explain all. Have no fear. You will see rather that I have done everything in my power to obey my King's word and work for his desires. This is the woman you told me to bring to your court, and to work a lawful way that she might be your wife. When I came to the land of Braj I found she had been taken with Krishna in the woodland, and I charged her therefore with unfaithfulness, and by a lawful trial she was sentenced to death. Now I remembered well that the King has power to pardon all condemned, and I brought this woman to you therefore as a lawful prize, meaning that you should pardon her and her life would be yours to do with her as you desired. In this way I had obeyed you and made it so that she was your own. Strange it seemed to me, O King, when you ordered me to burn her, but I obeyed, as always. But you see now why she calls on Krishna, for he was the very means by which I took her for you.'

And Kamsa stared at the priest with hatred gleaming in his eyes, and he said 'All the time you knew of this, and told me not.'

And the priest said 'My King, I wished to help you to your desire.'

And the King called the guards and said 'Guards, seize this traitor of a priest, and take him to prison. Hanged shall he be for knowing better than his King.'

But the priest cried out and begged the man that calls spirits to help him and tell the King he worked only for his good, but the man shrugged and spread his arms as if to say 'Forgive me dear friend, there is little I can do.' And the priest was lead away to death.

And Kamsa cried 'Now jailers, fetch your instruments of torture. This woman shall not live in peace until I have ground her to my will.' And the jailers hurried off, fearful of the King's rages.

And Kamsa said 'And you, O man that calls spirits, have you no furies that can hound this woman?'

And the man said 'Indeed my lord, this woman's heart is within, and your screws and racks are but bodily torment. The fiends of Hell work in the mind, and have tortures a thousand times more sharp than these.'

And Kamsa said 'I'll have them all, all.' And he turned to the guards and said 'Fetch out the woman to the courtyard.'

So Radha was brought out to the courtyard by the pit that leads into Hell, and Kamsa looked at her long, and said 'Krishna lives in your heart then, woman? It was an unlucky day you fell into my hands, for I shall not stop my work until Krishna is rooted out of that place and your heart is shut against him, and then he will die and trouble me no more. Sweetly I have spoken to you and asked you to be my wife, but now is the time for harshness and compulsion.'

And the torturers brought their instruments, and Kamsa said 'Do you see these racks? To them will you be given for your body's torment.'

And Kamsa turned to the man and said 'Do you see this man? From him will come fiends to attack your soul from within.'

And Kamsa laughed and held out his hands and said 'Do you see these arms? To these you will fly for an end to all your pain.'

Then Radha looked at him and said 'Tell the Jumna to flow in the gutter. You are but a boy playing with banks of mud. What care I for your baby toys?'

And Kamsa struck her across the face and said 'Is that a toy?'

Radha said 'Such is the blow my Krishna will give you. He is watching from the ocean of my heart.'

And Kamsa raged and said 'Fetch me her brother here. Him will I torture and kill and have the devils come and seize his soul. Then we shall see what is this thing called heart.'

And Radha called out 'What has my brother done that he should be tormented? What has he done that he should be in prison? Leave him alone, King. He is nothing to you.'

But Kamsa was pleased to see her distressed, and knew now he had a way to have power over her, and Radha's brother was fetched from the cell and held by the guards before him. And Kamsa said 'Now, Radha, will you see your brother tortured and put to death, or will you give way to my will and become my wife?'

And Radha's brother shouted to her and cried 'Do nothing because of me. This is an evil King and shall not have his way.'

'Summon your fiends,' then cried Kamsa to the man, 'and we shall see this mischief work,' and Kamsa stood back so that the man might call up his spirits.

And all was quiet then as the man that calls up spirits walked slowly towards the darkened pit. He drew out three long strands of leather, which had wide collars at the end, and held one end and threw the other over the pit's side. And the man closed his eyes and began to recite his spells.

And the man said 'Furies of harsh Hades, furies that are torture to mortals, rise from this pit and on this leash come as hounds to the slaughter.'

There was a sound of howling in the pit, like wolves that bay at the moon, and then a sound of snuffling, as of hounds that follow a trail. And looming up out of the pit, three tall fiends appeared. They were like men and like dogs, for they were tall and stood upon their hind legs but had faces as sharp as dogs, with long jaws, long teeth and long tongues, and they were on the three leashes held by the man, and stood still and silent.

And Kamsa said 'See here these torturers that will bring your death, and see here your marshals that will bring you after death to the tortures of Hell. Let us see now if the woman will bear your torment.'

And Radha cried 'O my brother, my brother, what shall I do? I shall not bear to see you tortured or tormented. O Krishna, Krishna, why did I ever love you? All this trouble has come as you made me love.'

But Kamsa shouted 'Call not on Krishna. If you want your brother to be spared, cast Krishna out of your heart.'

And Radha shouted 'How can I cast out of my heart what my heart has become? My heart is Krishna, and Krishna speaks in me. O my brother, forgive me, for what I cannot help.'

Kamsa cried 'Come then, you torturers, pinion this man, and let us shut fast that great heart of hers with the sound of a brother's screams.'

But Radha's brother stood firm and shouted 'Krishna shall avenge all these acts in the coming days, and tumble you into Hell, tyrant, where you belong, and all Mathura will rejoice, which you have ruled badly like a petty child, and the people will be free of you and the land will smile and Braj shall rejoice again, and all things will laugh as if you have never been—aye, never more than a speck of burnt dust on a mighty plain.'

But Kamsa was so enraged with this speech that he drew his dagger from the silk sash round his waist and went to Radha's brother and plunged the dagger in his side, and the brother sank to the ground wounded and bleeding his life away.

Then Kamsa turned to the man that calls up spirits and cried 'Let loose your hands!' and the man dropped his hands so that the leashes that held the fiends that were like dogs fluttered down to the ground. And the fiends ran over and waited by the brother to catch his soul when he should die, and they snuffled and whimpered as hounds on the chase.

But Radha was stricken with horror when she saw what the King had done, and how the fiends waited for her brother's soul, and the hairs on her head stirred and rose up and she wanted to run away.

But the sight of her brother bleeding on the ground overcame her with pity and anger, and she ran over to the fiends and lashed them like hounds and cried 'Away from my brother, hell-hounds! Away!'

The fiends attacked Radha with baying and roaring, and all was thrown into confusion so that it seemed Hell itself had come onto earth. Kamsa shouted to the man to call off the fiends, but the man could do nothing, and the fiends struggled and tore at Radha all round the courtyard. And Radha's brother heaved himself up and caught Kamsa by the ankle to pull him down, and Kamsa fell on him, stabbing and hacking him with his knife, and her brother fell back dead on the dusty floor.

And the fiends were tugging Radha by the arms, one on each side, and the third hailed her by the hair, and dragged her towards the pit, but Radha fought against them and would not give way, for as long as her heart was strong with pity for her brother the fiends could do nothing to gain her soul.

But when Radha saw her brother dead on the ground she fainted and fell back into the arms of the demons. They were all so near the pit the fiends leapt into the air with her, and Radha and the fiends fell into the pit and were swallowed in the darkness, and the courtyard became silent, because the devils were all gone.

Kamsa was astonished and stood silent for some time, but then he said 'Where is she gone?'

And the man said 'The fiends have taken her bodily into Hell.'

And Kamsa said 'How can that be?'

And the man said 'Grief for her brother's death halted her heart. She was dead for the instant and the fiends could take her.'

And Kamsa said 'But the fiends were called to take her brother's soul. How can they take the woman who was my prize?'

And the man laughed and said 'King Kamsa, the fiends come not because you or I have called them; they are not subject to our wills or power: they come because we think of them, and make ourselves fiends. You cannot grieve when they act in their own way.'

And Kamsa said 'And in her soul then is Krishna still alive?'

And the man said 'You heard what she said: her soul has become Krishna.'

Then Kamsa raged and cried 'You have betrayed me, man that calls up spirits, and your devils have disobeyed the word of their lord, and now you have betrayed my plots and Krishna lives for ever in the soul of that dead woman, for she is dead and in Hell and can never more be tried by my will. Wretched man, this is all your work. Take your reward then for your treacherous scheming against me!'

And Kamsa seized a spear from one of the guards, and he ran at the man with it, but the man ducked and ran away. Kamsa pursued him and caught him in a corner against a wall and ran him through with the spear until its point scratched and grated on the wall behind him, and the man slid down against the wall to the ground, dead.

And Kamsa threw down the spear and went to the edge of the pit, and looked over into the cold darkness and said 'Is she gone down there to be the guest of Yama? And will the fiends come up again to help me? And will the others that are out now turn against me?'

And he swung round and looked at the dead body of the man that calls up spirits and said 'I should not have killed him in my wrath. Who will now tell the fiends to save me from Krishna?' But then he looked up at the sky and said 'Why, I shall command the fiends.'

Now the grey dawn was beginning to come forward, and the painful day seeped into the open sky, and the colour of morning grew. Kamsa looked at the sky with horror and said 'Look, look, the light! He comes now, he comes now!' and he ran out of the prison court-yard and into the road outside. And he ran down the grey streets in the dawn, looking backwards over his shoulder at the sky, fearful, as if a great eagle were after him. As it grew lighter he cried 'He can see me. He can see me. And blue is the colour of my doom!' He came to his own palace and ran indoors and shut himself in his own small, dirty chamber in the darkness, and sat there shivering and gnashing with fear.

Book Twenty

The Gods Seek Help

In Braj now, when at evening they saw the fiends coming across the plain, the cowherds were frightened, and did not know what to do. The soldiers who were guarding the village also wondered at it, and went to the bounds of the village, gazing. And the fiends in a mighty army stopped far off, like a vast long cloud hovering on the sand, and there was a sound like the creaking of wings, which was the babble of their voices and the sounds of their laughter.

The crafty Akrura, whom Kamsa had sent to Braj with the challenge of the tournament some days before, had come to the village to talk with the captain of the soldiers, and he looked on the fiends also, nor did he know anything about them. And the captain sent a messenger out to ask the fiends what they wanted, but they would not speak with him, and sent him back, laughing still and throwing at him the pebbles of the plain. And then as dusk came on the fiends drew out their legions and came round the village, so that wherever anyone looked out, North, South, East, West of the village, they saw the pastures and the sand, and from horizon to horizon the dark and teeming line of fiends.

When night came Akrura and the captain made the soldiers stand guard round the village and light fires to see the fiends by, and when darkness had come the village was surrounded by a ring of soldiers' fires. Out from the darkness came the babble of the demons over the empty air.

And in the night the villagers grew afraid and went to Nanda and Balarama and said 'Nanda, we are afraid of these strange creatures who are waiting beyond the crossroads. Let Balarama go to them and drive them away, for he is a great slayer of unknown things.'

But Nanda said 'Away, you dogs! It is because of your jealous hearts that they have come, for demons can scent hatred even from Hades and the hounds of Hell are quick to come when there is any evil brewing. You have waked them. Peace is fled your country. Reap the bitter fruit then. Trouble me no more.'

95

The villagers went away sad and fearful, and thought 'We should never have stirred up such trouble against Radha, but in those days life was idle and it was easy to be jealous. Now we are alone, we should always keep together. O Radha, when this is over come back to Braj and give us your forgiveness.' But they were not to know when they thought this that Radha was already gone upon her journey to the land of darkness.

In the morning when the sun rose coppery, and burnt the fields from a parching sky, the demons were seen walking round the village in their packs, grumbling and quarrelsome at being kept so idle. Soon when the day grew hot they began to look towards the village, for they were hungry too, and the ranks of them yearned food.

Near the boundary of the village on the South side was a pen where a herd of cows were kept. The fiends soon smelt this out, and one or two of them raided it and carried off a lowing heifer, and the others of their troop fell on it when they got back, and tore it apart, running away to lonely spaces each to eat legs and haunches. They ground up bone and all with their teeth, and one there was that ate the horns.

And another troop saw this, and out of jealousy raided the cow-pen themselves, broke down the fences, and drove the whole cattle herd onto the plain, and they fell on the cows, biting their backs and maiming them, and spurned the maimed cows with their feet and laughed. As there were more cows than they could eat, many carcasses were left for the birds, and the ground became littered with red limbs and entrails, and vultures began to flutter and hop about the sand.

The man whose cows they were ran out at them and was killed, and his wife was killed and his children. And another rank of demons, who had scoffed at their fellows for eating cows, began to eat the children. They crouched down and crunched them with their teeth, and brandished their corpses in front of the others, taunting.

Now Akrura spoke with the captain and said 'What these are, or who sent them, I do not know, but they are certainly from Hell, and shame us all. For our own safety then we must guard ourselves. Therefore send your soldiers to guard all the ways into the village with extra force.'

But another rank of fiends had come up, and were afire to kill children for themselves, and they came and broke into the camp where the soldiers had not yet come. They raided the huts of the

96

cowherds, and carried away many young boys and girls, while the mothers shrieked and cried to heaven and went lamenting about the village.

And the fiends began to quarrel over the bodies of the children, for even those that were full did not like their fellows to eat too, and they fought with them and tugged the bodies this way and that. And they ran and tore scales and bristles from each other, and threw the carcasses of the cows about. Then the commanders of the fiends came up to stop the quarrel, and some of them slew their own men, and some others.

But the day grew hotter and hotter, and the demons became crammed with food. Soon they broke off fighting and sat down, sneering and groaning on the sand, and as they were full they belched up blood and chunks of flesh, and struck out lazily at the vultures who were hobbling round them. The crows also came down in swarms, and whizzed in the air overhead, crowing and cawing.

And in the village the parents of the children were heartbroken, and wept and lamented, and the cowfolk were speechless with horror, and even the soldiers also. And Akrura stood amongst the weeping villagers and said 'If King Kamsa has sent these fiends to do this, then I will turn away from him, and work against him with my craftiness, for soldiers and conquest is all well, but these fiends will devour us all and bring the world to ruin.'

Now when the gods heard of what the fiends were doing in Braj, they were horrified, and met together in the council-chamber to decide what to do. Some blamed Indra for what had happened, and some blamed Agni, and some said that Yama, King of the Dead, was trying to take over the earth, but none of them knew what to do.

So they went in a group to the high peak where Indra sat, and Indra's wife spoke to him and said 'My dear lord, the country of Braj, where you used to live, is sorely troubled by a pack of fiends from Hell. We beg you to forgive them for the past, and come down and chase the demons from the land, for if something is not done quickly the whole earth will fall into the power of Hell.'

Indra turned to them and brought his eyes from gazing at the plain of India, and he spoke to his wife and said 'My dear, I have been watching the land of Braj, with sad remembrance, and I have seen the suffering of these people, but I am afraid what they suffer is

97

brought upon them by their own sins, and fate has willed it so. But I have sworn to Yama never to harm his kingdom, and so I am unable to drive off these fiends in any case. We must leave it to time, I am afraid to say, and they must suffer it out.'

And all the gods were saddened at what they heard, and many of them were angry with Indra for being so stubborn, for they knew that it was pride and stubbornness alone that kept him sulking on the peak, and none of them knew what could be done.

But then Ganesha, the little elephant god, spoke and said 'Let us all go to the wise Varuna, that lives in the Western Ocean, for he is an all-seeing god, and he will know what to do.'

And the gods agreed all with this plan, and left Indra's peak. They came down from the lonely crag and walked again in the lovely streets of heaven. Then the gods got ready, and put their houses in order, and at a signal from Indra's wife they flew up into the air. High above the clouds in chariots and on glittering wings, they flew in the thin sunlight towards the Western Ocean.

And Varuna sat in his watery kingdom, a great god with a green body and snaking hair of azure blue. He sat on a great shell with a curly rim like a clam, and round him played white horses with manes of waving weed. And when Varuna saw the gods coming he jumped up happily, and made them welcome. He sat them round on the colourful rocks and coral of the sea floor, and he had sleek-bodied maids bring them shells full of sea-nectar.

And after they had drunk, Indra's wife said 'My dear Lord Varuna, we gods have come to your watery kingdom to ask your advice, for things on earth have become so troubled that we fear for the fate of man, and do not know what we can do to help him. Let me briefly tell you what has happened.

'Firstly, my Lord Indra has quarrelled with the cowherds of the land of Braj, and in rage he has sent away his cloud-warriors, who are now nowhere to be found, and the time for the rains is past, the land is parched, and all are nearly dying in the drought.

'But worse than this, and far more terrible, the King of the land where the cowherds live has sent out his soldiers in conquest over all India, and is ruling the people harshly, so that they are all miserable and downtrodden, and the happy cowherds are now his slaves. But now, maddened by his own pride no doubt, he has done far worse things, for he has summoned up an army of demons, and has sent

98

them forth. They are plaguing the cowherds, killing their cows and their children, and making the earth a charnel house and a hideous mirror of Hell. Such a state of things is almost like the ending of the world. O Lord Varuna, help us with your wisdom, for we do not know what to do. Find a way out for us, and clear these troubles from the land, or else we fear all India will sink into an age of burning and death, and the gods will no more be honoured in that shining land.'

The gods looked at Varuna, hoping he would know what to do, but Varuna smiled and turned aside and called to him a snake from the ocean-bed. This was Kaliya, whom Krishna had saved.

And Varuna said to the snake 'Come, my friend Kaliya, and settle this problem for us with one word, for things are never as bad as they seem. Tell the gods who it was that saved your life and sent you and your wife and children to my peaceful land. And you gods listen well to his answer, for in this word lies all your hope.'

And Kaliya bowed to them and said the one word 'Krishna.'

Varuna laughed and said 'My dear gods, I know all about the woes that are rife in the land of Braj, for my friend here has told me of them all. But have faith all of you, and all things shall be well, for Krishna is here among us, who has come to put all right.'

The gods looked anxious at this, and Vayu spoke up and said 'But Lord Varuna, it is not quite as you think. Krishna has been punished by Lord Indra, so that he does not know who he is, and he has been cast out without memory into the hostile desert. None of us knows whether he is alive or dead. How can he then help us, when he is miles away, lost among the flints and stones and the unfriendly creatures of a barren desert?'

And Varuna said 'Krishna shall help by finding ways out of all such deserts.'

And Vayu said 'But how can he help when he wanders alone, and he has no memory to tell him of Braj, and there is no one to help him and tell him who he is?'

Varuna said 'Krishna shall help by finding out who he is.'

And Vayu said 'O, how can anybody help when the world is plagued in such strife and trouble?'

And Varuna said 'Have faith.'

But when Varuna saw that the gods were still troubled and sat looking gloomily with wrinkled brows, he said 'If you are worried by doubts still, let Vayu go out himself to find Krishna and bring him quickly to our peaceful kingdom. Then perhaps you will be comforted when you see your saviour with your own eyes.'

The gods agreed to this plan, and Vayu was willing to go again on their errands. Without further talk he set off from the ocean to look about the earth for signs of the wandering Krishna.

But the gods were cheered now by Varuna's confidence, and putting their trust in his wisdom they relaxed, and stayed with him to await the arrival of Krishna.

PART IV

Krishna's Journey

Book Twenty-one

From Desert to Jungle

Now when Krishna was left in the desert the man that calls up spirits sat him down among the stones and sand. And when Krishna was alone in the waste he shut his eyes and thought, and put his hands over his eyes to shut out the glare of the desert and wondered who he was, for he did not know who he was because of the potion that the man had given him to drink, yet he knew even so that he did not know. So he sat for a long time in thought.

And Krishna was aware of the blackness in his head, and he thought 'I must be this blackness, for this is all that is left, when everything else has been shut out. I shall call myself blackness, therefore, and black shall be my name.'

And it so happened that in the language Krishna spoke the word for black was Krishna, and so he had without knowing it called himself by his own true name.

And Krishna then was aware of a fluttering that he felt was a sound. He took his hands away from his eyes and it became light, and he opened his eyes and saw a white bird before him on the sand, pecking and pulling at a worm. But once Krishna was aware of this it flew away with the worm in its mouth.

And Krishna saw before him a vast white plain of burning sand and rock, and above it the sky glowed yellow as if on fire. Krishna looked in front of him, where the bird had flown, and got up and began to follow, for he felt that the bird would lead to better things than were already behind him.

He passed over red and grey plains that swirled with dust and sulphurous gases, and among tall rocks that were gnarled and full of holes, and he went through a country of canyons and strange pillars of sand, eaten by the winds so that they looked like teeth. Amidst the hills the sun flashed on metals that were like veins in the ground.

So he came to a broad river that swirled in the desert, tumbling the golden silt towards the sea, and went down to the river to drink. But just as he reached the water's edge and the river stroked his ankles, a water-snake appeared, rolling and waving in the chalky stream, and opened its gleaming mouth and shot out its red forked tongue. Krishna was about to fight the serpent when a white bird called an egret swooped over his head and caught the snake by the neck and flew with it to the other shore. The snake coiled round the beak of the bird, twisting and striking, and the bird flew off with it in the direction Krishna was going.

And after the snake had been snatched from the water Krishna felt slimy things tickling against his feet, and he looked down and saw in the silty water a thousand little creatures thrashing their tails and thrusting like shrimps and eels. And he saw molluscs and crabs and snails that tumbled along, with all the colours of the rainbow glinting on their curly horns, and Krishna thought 'Now the snake is gone, this water teems with creatures. I will name this water the River of Life. It comes from the mountains, washing gold, and suckles with its milky torrent a million little sons and daughters. O precious stream, that leads this country on!'

Then the blue Krishna leapt into the sandy river and threw up its spray, making rainbows in the sunlight, and the little shrimps and fishes played with him, and laughed and romped in the kindly waves. And when Krishna had bathed he got out on the other side of the river and followed the bird's path once more.

But then Krishna began to doubt the way he was going and said to himself as he went along 'Is this the bird's path?' Once he had begun to think this he thought 'Why do I follow this bird? Why should I feel it would lead me to better things? What is the use of going forward when I do not even know who I am?'

And Krishna turned round and looked over the ground through which he had come, and he saw the shining river and beyond it the ruddy plain and the gnarled rocks, and he thought 'Behind me are sad and happy things. The plain was dreary but the river full of life. Should I go back to them again, and leave my journey and relish what I have?'

Then he thought 'The bird that led me here awoke me from my thoughts by the rustling of its wings, and it killed the worm. Then did it lead me to a river, and it killed a snake. So better things and worse lie ahead of the old. But who is this bird? And what are these serpents? And is it true that I am nothing more than blackness? O,

104

to answer these things I must go on ahead. Forward then, Krishna, follow the white bird on.'

And so Krishna thought, and decided to go on again. He came then to a land of ripened greenery. Palm-trees and ferns in the steamy heat of a decaying wood shaded the balmy air with horsetail trees. Krishna felt his feet squeak on the juicy reed, and the damp ground was plump and rosy with hairy moss. He smiled to see such lushness, and reached up and from some sulphur-yellow leaves plucked a flower, pink-veined like cockle-shells, smelling of lilies of the vale.

Krishna became drowsed and dreamy with the perfume of the flower. He stretched out his blue arms and tangled them among the milky leaves and blooms, and the golden pollen shook itself on his face. And dappled fawns came nuzzling in his hands for food, and horses blotched with rose rubbed their sleek flanks against him, and bees and butterflies in speckled clouds thronged round his ebon hair. Then Krishna lay down on a sanded bank and lilies twined about his purple arms and magnolia, smelling of mangoes, and swooning jasmine in the warm wind rained from the blue forest on his sweating breast. And before him danced the lyre-birds and the birds of paradise.

But then moving among the dusk he saw a lumbering dragon, long and fat and grey, with a slimy body and a small sleek head. It saw Krishna and came towards him, its mouth open wide, so that he could see its pink tongue. Krishna stood ready, and when it lurched at him he ducked under a horsetail tree, and the dragon missed him.

But just as it was about to strike again the air darkened as a huge bird came down. Just by Krishna it landed, with red legs thick as tree-trunks. And the bird struck at the dragon and caught its head in its beak, then strode forward, tugging the dragon out of sight among the cloudy trees.

And as soon as the dragon and the bird had gone, Krishna heard voices, and among the trees then he saw brown men with spears, looking at the flattened trees where the dragon had been pulled, and gabbling to one another. And Krishna ran forward to greet them, and they were astonished to see a man of the colour of blue. They gazed at him with open mouths, and looked back on the track of the dragon and back again on Krishna and his blue limbs. And Krishna pointed after the dragon, and then pointed to himself, and then shook his fist as if to say 'I made the dragon run away by fighting it.' And the people looked at one another, and then they all laughed and shook his hand, and took Krishna back with them to their village.

The village was a small group of houses made of bamboo and thatch and set up on stilts, and when the people shouted to their fellows they all came running out. And the brown men had stripes of paint on their faces, and snaky tattoos over their chests, and in their nostrils they wore the copper-gold feathers of the birds of paradise. They were friendly, and smiled and wagged their heads at Krishna. And the women came out also from the huts, and were shy at first of looking at Krishna, and their children were shy too and hugged their mothers' knees and hid their faces. But soon all the people sat around in the grassy clearing, chattering loudly with one another about what had happened, and their gabbling voices echoed in the gloomy jungle.

Krishna could not understand a word they said, and was left alone, even though they spoke about him, and Krishna began to think again, and wonder about these things. And he thought 'Again a worm or dragon has appeared, and again a white bird has killed the dragon and flown on. And the first time after the bird had killed the worm I awoke to see a plain of rocks and sand. And the second time after the bird had killed the snake I was aware of teeming life within the river. And this third time after the bird had killed the dragon I met a whole tribe of people living in the forest. Each time the dragon comes the bird attacks it, and I go on into a richer life. What is the meaning of this worm and bird? Still I do not know. And still I do not know who it is that I am. O, I long to answer all these questions, and satisfy this restlessness within me. Well, I must wait, and see what time will bring.'

Just then some of the tribe of people who had been hunting all this time came back bearing with them a great black boar. And the people rejoiced and skinned the boar and cut it up into portions and set them to roast over a crackling fire. Then they made merry and danced around the fire, making magic for a good day's hunting the next dawn. The women brought mead for them to drink in cups made of gourds, and Krishna was given food and drink, and he joined in their songs, and made them laugh as he garbled their natural words.

Evening came upon them, and the smoke of the fire floated into the gloomy trees, and the warm night came in, pierced by the calls of peacocks and bubbling with the parrot's song. The crickets whirred

106

among the dusky leaves, and Krishna went to sleep on the rushy floor of the grassy huts, safe from the snakes that hung above and the beasts that prowled beneath. He sank once more into the blackness of sleep, and found an end to all his questions.

Book Twenty-two

A Cycle of Asia

In the morning Krishna bade farewell to the people of the forest and made on again in the bird's path, wondering where it would lead him. And soon he found he was climbing hills, where the walking was difficult and he was unsure of the way. He climbed up a grey-limbed tree onto its bouncy branches to look out, and he saw green hills, and beyond them grey mountains that looked as they might never be climbed. And Krishna got down from the tree and wondered what he should do.

And a voice from beside him said 'Fear not for the way forward. I that have brought you so far will lead you further on.' When he looked up, lo! the great white bird was beside him.

Now Krishna was astonished and said 'You are the bird I have been following in the forest, and it was you that killed the dragon that attacked me. Who are you? Where do you go? Why have you come to me now?'

And the bird said 'Krishna, you have come a little way on your journey, and have crossed deserts and streams and woods by foot alone. Now there are continents and worlds for you to travel, and you will need more than your legs to get you so far. I have been sent down by a mighty power to be your guide, and on my back you are to fly over mountains and far-off lands, for it is time now that you gain knowledge both of yourself and the world, for the whole world lies waiting for the wisdom which can be yours.'

And Krishna was astonished and said 'Is it me you really mean? Though you have guessed that I called myself Krishna, I do not really know even who I am.'

And the bird said 'Then your mind is a fit blank for the lessons it shall receive. Come then, let us not idle in empty talk, for there are visions for you to see, and speaking signs. The vast progress of the world is to be shown you, and your travel is to take you even to the ends of this huge universe. And all your questions are to be satisfied.'

Krishna looked up eagerly at this, and said 'Then will you even tell me who I am?'

And the bird said 'Who you are, and the earth, the world, mankind, the stars, all shall be told in time, for I will lead you through man's history, and through the history of thought and mind. I will tell you secrets of yourself, and secrets of the universe entire, and show you all the ways of the bright stars and all the fields of heaven and the earth.'

And Krishna was astonished and opened his mouth in amazement, and he said, as if to reassure himself 'And you will even tell me who I am?'

And the bird looked angrily at him and cried 'Have I not said?'

And Krishna jumped immediately onto the bird's back and held tight on his silky plumage, and he felt the bird lean forward and the muscles of the bird moving below him, and the bird stirred the air with its wings, and crouched and leapt. Krishna's heart hopped as he felt the bird suddenly lie on the hot air, and the wind flew into his face and streamed his hair, and he could feel the bird swimming on the breeze, and climbing upwards towards the burning sun.

And so they began their journey, flying in the winds, and casting a great shadow. Soon they were winging over hills and woods, and down below the bushy trees looked like moss, and the muddy rivers flashed in the sun, meandering like lizards in the green. Soon they were in the keener air of the grey mountains, and the passes and ranges were like creases in the solid earth. And Krishna laughed with joy to be so cutting through the air, and jumped up and down on the bird's neck, as if riding a horse.

And when they had gone over the mountains, they flew on through the world of man, and passed Bhutan, and the plateau of Tsinghai. They crossed the snaking wall that keeps Nan-Shan within, and the great Gobi void of life, and they came then to a lower land. And soon they were flying over a country of vast plains of rippling grass, and there was nothing to see but the lonely steppes and the sky.

And the bird shouted to Krishna through the roaring wind 'What did you seek, that you have become a traveller?'

And Krishna said 'That I cannot tell you, for I found myself in the desert, and could not at all remember what I was to do. I tried to search in my mind to find out this fact. I tried to think who I was, but

I could not. The only thing I knew when I looked inside was blackness, but I do not know if that is really who I am.'

And the bird said 'Let us search the earth then, and see if there is anyone to tell you.'

And with that he glided downwards and flew close to the plain. And soon Krishna saw sheep grazing on the grass, and herds of goats with them, brown among the white, and there was a shepherd guarding with a curly crook. They passed over the black tents of the shepherds, and saw camels tied outside, and some there were who rode grey horses, racing them over the vast steppes. And a raiding party came and slew the horsemen, and cut down the tents, and rode off with the shepherds' sheep.

And the bird said 'They are the Mongols with their sturdy steeds, and fighters, as you see. Do they remind you what you might have been?'

And Krishna said 'No. For sure I did not look after herds.'

And they flew on and veered then Westwards from Ulan-Bator, across the Altai, and towards Tashkent, and so they came next to a land where there were fields of summer wheat, white-eared and rippling in the sunny air, and among them were farmers reaping corn, and waggons loaded with the golden sheaves. And by them was a village, and the houses were of mud and on their flat roofs carried haystacks.

The bird said 'These are the fields upon the Oxus, with all their ripe-eared grain. Do they remind you of what you were?'

And Krishna said 'No. Surely I did not live near a plain.'

And they flew on a little way towards the hills, and came to a sparkling city, walled round with battlements and towered gates. Among the merchants at the market, the camels with their load of blood-red carpets, silks and spice, were sandy buildings bearing towers of gold, and domes that glinted in the slanting sun.

And the bird said 'Yonder is the glittering city of Samarkand. Does this remind you where you might have been?'

And Krishna said 'No. Surely I never lived near a city.'

The bird wheeled round and circled the city, and they saw soldiers on horseback with glinting scimitars spurring in masses towards the city, and the soldiers raided the city and overthrew it, and the city was lost in plundering and fire. The white bird flew away and left it, the smoke billowing to the sky, and Krishna craned his neck and looked

110

behind, watching the ruin of the city until it was but a speck among the hazy hills.

And when Krishna could see it no more, he turned to the bird and said 'Tell me, O great white bird, we have flown over herdsmen and farmers and citizens in a great city, and the city was attacked by vandals and overthrown. What is the meaning of this that I have seen?'

And the bird said 'Such has been the pattern of human life. In the wilds on their horses men became strong and lords over all that could assail them. But in the plains with their crops did men learn to build cities, and glory in the arts of peace. The riches of these men proved a lure to the others, and the wild tribes sacked the city and the city fell. And so shall be the story throughout all history, until all men are wealthy and children of a single city.'

And Krishna said 'What! Who would live in a city, when the woods and hills are about him still?'

And the bird said 'The men that build cities shall come to think as you. But they must on. And on must we. See, there are the mountains of the Hindu Kush. They are the Western range of those we crossed first at Bhutan. We have flown now the half of a circle, and now we are to make the ring complete.'

But Krishna was not satisfied by what he had heard and said 'But why, O bird, do you bring me all this way? There is nothing here to tell me who I am. And still I do not really know who you are, nor why you came before me on my journey and killed the dragons that I found? Now tell me, bird, what is the meaning of all that I have seen.'

And the bird said 'The time will come for explanations. Sit back, and let us fly on with our journey.'

And Krishna said 'No, I shall not sit back, but I shall jump off your back this minute into those mountains unless you tell me who you are, where you go, and what were the dragons you killed on the way.'

And the bird laughed and said as he flew 'Very well, my Krishna, I shall answer your questions, for it is indeed time you knew a little of the journey you have gone. I am the bird that flies ever forward, and some there are that call me Time. I fly in the world of matter that you see, and the world I lead on from age to age. The first time you met me you heard first the fluttering of my wings, and the fluttering came

111

in the blackness of your mind. This was the way the world began, with a little sound, brought forth by time in the blackness of eternal space. Now when you opened your eyes at the sound of my wings you saw before you all shapes of matter, sands, rocks, metals and gases, all the elements that make up the universe. Such then was it in the beginning of time, when the barrier between blackness and matter was broken, for once there was nothing, and then after time there was matter, and the barrier between nothing and matter: that was the worm which you saw me devour. Do you follow me then, my little Krishna?'

And Krishna said 'Indeed I do. The adventures that I had were all but a picture, and the picture showed me the beginning of the world. But what happened then, O great white bird?'

'Next you came to a river of water, and such was the earth a long time ago: land and water and sky and nothing else. The snake was the barrier between this and the beyond. And what was beyond this matter but life? For the land and water and sky were all matter, but as yet there was nothing living made up of these things. When I killed the snake the barrier was gone, for millions of little creatures appeared in the water. Do you follow me so far, my little blue Krishna?'

And Krishna said 'Yes, bird, indeed I do. The adventure you talk of was the beginning of life, for life began in the waters, and was a new thing on earth. But what happened next, O great white bird?'

'Next you came to the teeming forest, and such was the earth a little while ago: plant, fish, fowl and beast, and nothing else. The dragon was the barrier between life and the beyond. And what was beyond life, but mind? For the plant, fish, fowl and beast were all life, but as yet there was no thinking thing made up of these things. When I killed the dragon the barrier was gone, for hundreds of forest people appeared to greet you. Do you follow me so far, my little blue intelligent Krishna?'

And Krishna said 'Yes, O white bird, indeed I do. The coming of man was after the creatures, and yet man is a creature except for his mind. The coming of life was after that of matter, and yet life is matter except for its growing. And so man's mind was a new thing on earth. But what happened then?'

And the bird said 'For that you will have to hold tight and see.'

And they flew on a while, and then suddenly before them, flying

112

over the mountains like a bank of cloud, was a huge dragon, greater than any they had seen. And the dragon roared at them, and shot flame towards them out of its mouth, and it coiled its scaly body which flashed in the sun like fire or sunset clouds, and made at the bird with black curled talons. The smoke of its mouth made Krishna choke, and he held tight as the bird flew straight at the dragon. As the bird touched the writhing body of the dragon with its beak, there was a deafening clap of thunder, and Krishna felt inside him a sudden flash, as though he had woken up from a sleep beside a fire in winter, when the snow comes down outside. He looked in front of him and the dragon had vanished like cloud.

And the bird flew on and said to Krishna 'Such is the next step from mind to self.' And he said no more, but winged on his way, over the pine-covered peaks of the winding mountains.

Book Twenty-three

Buried Treasure

And they flew on and came to a high plateau, full of glassy lakes and fields of yellow mustard, and ranked about with the pale poplar trees. This was the land of Kashmir. And they saw a city below full of shining canals. and the shingled roofs of houseboats clustering on the water.

And the bird said 'Behold the city of Srinagar in the land of Kashmir. Now we have crossed the barrier of the mountains, go down and see if there is any there can tell you of yourself.'

The bird landed on a grassy pasture on the riverbank, and Krishna went among the people to see what he could find. He came to a mosque, and marvelled at the tiles of mauve and turquoise that were set between the sandy stone, and he passed under an arch of purple honeycomb into a wide courtyard with a pond of water, and in the pond was reflected the full dome's emerald green.

And there was a man sitting among the alcoves praying, and he had on his head a curly sheepskin hat. Krishna went to him and said 'Is there any here can tell me who I am?'

And the man smiled and said at once 'You are what all men are: the friend of God.'

And Krishna said 'And who is God?'

And the man smiled and said 'The one you love.'

And Krishna thought and then he said 'How can I know if I love anyone?'

And the man said 'Pray and seek and you shall find,' and with that he returned again to his prayers.

And Krishna left the man and went back to the pasture where the bird was waiting, thinking of these things. But when he reached the bird on the grassy pasture by the river he found a huge crowd of people all in sheepskin hats crowding around the bird and chattering. They nodded their heads, and lifted up their children to see the bird, and pointed for each other at its great gold beak. And when the bird saw Krishna coming, it cast up its eyes to heaven as if to say 'See what

114

I endure for this little one!' And Krishna leapt on its back, and to a great gasp of wonder from the people it flew off over the mountains.

And they flew down to the parching plain of India, where the drought was, and the hot air buffeted them as they sank through it. And the bird landed by a river on the plain.

The bird said 'This is the river Jumna. Do you know this sacred stream?'

Krishna shook his head and yawned.

The bird smiled and said 'Yonder is a city on the banks of this river, and this is the gloomy city of Indraprasthra. There live the Kurus who have ousted their cousins the Pandavas from the throne. Go into the city and seek for a holy man in a temple, who you shall know by his orange robes. Ask him your question, and see what he says.'

And Krishna went through the sandstone gate in the walls of the city, and walked its thronging streets to a darkened temple. And the temple had a tower like a pine-cone, layered with eaves and sculpture of smooth girls, and a yellow flag fluttered in the hazy air. Krishna went in towards the whining music, and stepped around the sleeping forms of cows.

And there was a holy man sitting in orange robes on the glossy floor, and Krishna went and sat among the marigolds that littered the ground, and said to the man 'Who is there who can tell me who I am?'

And the holy man looked up and laughed, and said 'Such is the quest which all men come to. No one can tell you this but yourself.'

And Krishna said 'But how can this be when I do not know?'

And the man said 'No man knows until he seeks.'

'But how can I seek?'

'There are a thousand ways. But you must seek within rather than without. And when you have found the self within, then have you found the self without, for you are the self of all things and of the universe entire.'

And the man's eyes went blank, and Krishna could see he would not speak any more, so he left him and went back and told the bird what he had said.

And Krishna said 'These people do not agree with each other. One man told me I am the friend of God, and another man tells me I am

115

the self of the universe. Are there any more who can tell me of this? What do you think, O great white bird?'

And the bird said 'You are my master. That is all I know.'

And Krishna said 'But what is the meaning in the words of these men? If man has come so far, building with his skill such great cities, and gaining such power, are riddles like this the sum of all his wisdom?'

The bird said 'When you met the dragon in the forest, did you think you could overcome it, or were you frightened by its power?'

Krishna laughed and said 'I was not frightened. Such dragons and goblins are only make-believe. If you face them with courage, they will soon run away.'

And the white bird said 'There you have great wisdom, little one. It is so indeed. For the dragons and serpents and worms and all demons are but the line between one state and another. The demons of men we think of as brutish beasts, because they are what we become when we fall below our human selves, and into the life of the beasts we bodily are. The line between mind and life seems real, because the states of life and mind are on different planes, but how can a difference be a thing of itself? The lines of difference are therefore an illusion, and you have seen wisely that you know them so.' And the bird tapped with his beak on Krishna's wrist and said 'What is this bracelet on your wrist, this ring of silver?'

And Krishna looked at it and said 'I do not know.'

And the bird said 'You must have found it when you were a child in the forest, or in a cave perhaps. It is this ring which gives you this wisdom. For this is the disc of discernment, and he who wears it shall see into the truth of all things.'

And Krishna was astonished and said 'How did you come to know this? What is this ring then? How does it have magic powers?'

And the bird said 'Settle yourself in comfort, Krishna, and I shall tell you the story.' And the bird looked out over the hazy plain a while, and in the distance he could see the blue mountain of the land of Braj, and the very country which was Krishna's true home, and then he preened his feathers and began his tale.

'Once upon a time, when man had come on earth, and mind was created, the mirror of all things, Vishnu, the great preserver of the universe for man's good, sent down treasure to the earth. The god Kubera had made it for him many years ago, and it was a great hoard of golden treasure, among which were four precious things. And these precious things were a mace, a conch, a lotus and a ring, and each of these things had a magic power. With the mace will came down to man, with the conch skill, with the lotus love, and with the ring wisdom. The man that found this treasure would be the greatest of all. But the treasure was buried in a lonely mountain, and the nymphs of the hills and the fays of the forest guarded it in their gloomy caves.

'But one year there came a terrible drought to the land, such as yet the world had never known, and in this drought all things were near to death. And men with fear and thirst became as beasts, and the beasts through lack of water died and became dust, and it seemed that all things were resolving into the lower fabric, and life and mind were nearly gone from the earth. And in this drought thus the lines of difference drew near, and serpents and demons began to plague the earth. And at last the earth became so evil and low that the greatest of all demons, the dragon Vritra arose, Vritra the dragon of earthly dissolution, with his breath of fire to burn up life and mind.

'And Vritra thus stole the treasure that was in the mountain, and he shut up all the nymphs and fays in the deepest caves, and began to take the treasure back into the desert, to hoard it for himself in his cave of darkness. And first he took the gold that was piled in the mountain, and all the precious cups and dishes that Kubera's dwarfs had made, and because he was greedy for gold, and thought that the most precious, he did not at first pick up the conch, the mace, the silver ring and the lotus. But the gods, knowing of the power of these things, swooped down when he was gone to save them. Kubera took the lotus, and Varuna the conch, but the dragon came back and seized the mace, and the ring was lost among the dry leaves of the forest.

'Now when Vritra had the mace, he had the will to overcome the world and rule it, and he became then so powerful that his breath burnt up nearly every living thing, and he grew and grew in size until he was ready to open his vast jaws and swallow the whole world.

'Now Indra all this time, who was the King of the gods, had not stirred himself to help the world of man, but when the other gods saw what was happening they ran to him and begged him to come and help. And Indra looked down and saw the dragon, and decided he would like a fight, and so flew off to the sea. And out at sea he

117

summoned all his warriors of the clouds, and got them together and then came rushing inland. The black clouds came and the thunder roared, and the warriors threw their spears down on the parching earth, and the dragon Vritra roared and reared up to bite them. But Indra meanwhile, at the feasting of battle, had drunk a huge sea of soma that gives him great power, and he threw himself on Vritra and fought him with his hands, and nearly throttled the dragon and drove him from the land. And the rains poured down on the hot and burning earth, and all things were revived from the terrible drought, and Vritra slunk off home to brood and plan more evil from his gloomy cave, although from that day to this he has not ventured out again.

'Such then is the story of Vishnu's buried treasure, and this is how it came to be scattered all over the earth, until one man shall come and bring it home again. And so Vritra the dragon still has the mace of will, and he guards it with the treasure in his parching cave. The lotus and the conch are still yet to be discovered. The ring you have with you, glinting on your wrist of blue. Now you know how I had heard of the ring, and now you see how it gains its magic power.'

And Krishna said 'Indeed I do, O great white bird. I thank you for a tale well told.'

The bird got up and seemed ready to fly, but Krishna said 'Still you have not told me of the words of these men. Why cannot I see their meaning if I have the disc of discernment?'

And the bird lifted up its feathered eyebrows and said 'O Krishna, will you still be asking questions? It is not yet time for you to know of this. There is another journey we must make before then. Climb on my back, then, and let us be onward.'

And Krishna climbed on his back, and the bird was about to fly when it stopped and said 'There is one thing, though, that you ought to know. Of the treasure of Vishnu, which you have heard tell, the greatest pieces are the lotus and the ring. When these two are united, the rest will quickly follow, and the man that has them will be master of the world.'

Book Twenty-four

Krishna Comes Home

And so they began the last of their journeys on earth, Krishna and the bird, flying in the sultry air. Once more they left the plain and headed towards the mountains, and while they were yet a long way off, lo! in the hazy distance, high in the blue air, the white horizon of the snowy peaks called them ever forward.

'There is the land where we go forward,' said the bird. 'See how from far its snows call travellers on. From the plain of man it lures us to the land of gods.'

And they came to a land of rolling hills, green with the untidy jungle and terraced neat with fields, and tall trees grew red orchids in their mossy branches, and the earth was rusty below. And they flew over a great ridge with pines and cedar trees, and streams and waterfalls went greyly tumbling in the jagged rocks. And they flew on, and lo! again the mountains, like a great crown that hung in the sharp air, the glittering land, the golden snows, the mighty Himalayas, and to the East far in another country they saw Chomolunma, which is called Mount Everest. And as they flew the sun was sinking, and the terraced hills grew pink, and the sky glowed orange, setting the snows afire.

The bird then flew down into a plateau, where there was a city, and said 'Below is the city of Katmandu in the country of Nepal. Let us go down there, and you will find a man with shaven head, turning a wheel, and him you may ask your one fine question.'

And they sank down over the city, and Krishna saw below the narrow streets and balconies, and a square set round with tall pagodas that had roofs of many storeys, eaved round with red-hued beams. They glided to the outskirts of the city where a nest of temples clustered by a brawling river, and Krishna heard great booming bells ring out. And the bird then landed by a huge white-washed mound, which was called a stupa. On its top was a gold tower, painted with eyes that looked East, North, South, West.

Krishna went and found a man with a shaven head, dressed in

119

russet robes and turning a prayer wheel, and he went to the man and said 'Is there any here can tell me who I am?'

The man let the wheel run on and said 'Why do you think you are anyone at all?'

And Krishna went back to the bird, and said 'This man thinks I am nothing at all.'

And the bird laughed. But then he stared into the distance, and they sat together silent for a while, a little way from the stupa, and near the stream that whispered through the mountain land.

And Krishna said 'I do not know what to make of all these puzzles. This man baffles me with thoughts that I am not. That man sets me seeking what I already am. And the other makes me wonder who he is that I am such a friend of. And if as the second man says I am the self of the universe, then surely that self must be none other than God but if I am the friend of God how can I be the friend of myself, and if I do not exist how can I have a friend at all? O, these people merely think up riddles to make us think. They have given me no answer to who I am.'

And the bird turned to Krishna, and took his eyes off the distant snows, and said 'You play with these thoughts as a child with toys, seeing how they balance on top of one another. If you would find out their meaning truly, you must turn them over in your very soul, for these are the thoughts that satisfy the deepest meditation.'

And Krishna said 'Very well then, wise one, what is it they mean to you?'

And the bird said 'When you are a man, the way forward is as a razor's edge, along which you must tread, neither falling one way into hate and lust, nor the other into fear and despair, and you must pass up through many regions of riot and misery. First there are the images of anger and fear, which throng like demons luring and routing. Then there are the pictures of like and dislike, the phantoms for which you plunge across deserts, and flee over icy plains. Then there are the symbols of love and grief, and these are the highest leading you from and towards. And in all these regions, the heart and the brain, these are your method of travelling on, for the heart is the horse of the chariot and the brain your guide.

'But there is an end of all this progress, when the mind is stilled and you become free. The man who told you you are the friend of God leads you forward by the heart in all its purity, for in loving God the three regions are crossed, and the goal is reached in bliss, and you come home. The man who told you you are nothing at all drives you from this floating world by giving up all desire, so that fleeing from phantoms you cross the three regions, and the goal is reached in renunciation, and you come home. The man who told you you are the self of the universe, in a single stroke of wisdom, lures your mind to the truth, and the three regions are crossed, and the goal is reached in wisdom, and you come home. Your ring gives you wisdom. You should understand this now, and the lotus when you find it should bring all home within you.'

But now the evening came on, and the sun went down behind the Western mountains, turning the Eastern snows to the hues of rose-leaves, and above them in the deep sky a forest of stars came out. And Krishna forgot all his puzzles to rejoice in the dusky air.

But then the bird stood up, and stretched its neck and shook itself, and it flapped its milky wings and said 'Come, little blue one, you are refreshed? For the night comes, and the stars call us forth on a greater journey. Are you ready, my friend, for another quest?'

And Krishna said 'I am ready to go wherever you will lead me. For you are my guide, and I have put my trust in you. With you I have seen the great cycle of earth, and tried the answers of its stores of wisdom. Another flight, another journey, my heart is eager to go flying forward, for before us lies the great plain of unknowing. I cannot rest until its secrets are all mine.'

So Krishna leapt upon the white bird's back, and the bird sprang up on its ruddy legs and soared with thunderous wings into the dark night sky. Like a comet in winter that leaves a shining furrow in the East, so did the bird soar into the stars. And the half-set earth with lands of brown and seas of misty blue soon shrank with its swirling clouds to a size no bigger than the moon, and the bird and Krishna came to the land of the burning spheres.

Krishna was amazed now to see all the planets of the sun floating past them like the moon in a village pond. And the moon was the first they passed, and this had silver deserts and huge peaceful seas of dust. And next they flew past Venus, the evening star, and this planet was covered in mist and fog, and as they went by they choked in the dust that billowed up in clouds. And next they went by little Mercury, and Mercury was scorched and had a crackled face, for the looming sun grew huge and ever nearer, and the heat made the bird turn course and circle it. As they flew round the massive sun they were quite dwarfed by its blazing, and seemed but tiny specks of shadow on its flaming face, and leaping flames of gas flew out like giant tongues and almost licked them in towards its dazzling surface. But when they came round on its other side they soon relaxed and felt cool again, and flew on towards the empty darkness.

And then they passed the ruddy planet Mars, and Mars had a marbled face, and snowy poles. And Jupiter they passed, streaked like a bloodstone, and thronged with a large family of moons. Saturn they passed, swirling its banded disc like a juggler with a plate, and Uranus, cold, and Neptune, green, and Pluto, smallest of them all, and circling far away, cold and forgotten by its grander brothers. And so they left the round fields of the sun, the dancing spheres that warm themselves against his huge bonfire, and came into the region of the stars.

And then they saw a shining river before them, winding a lazy way through the vast darkness of space, and the bird looked towards it and said 'There is the place we must hasten towards. There is our goal, the glorious, endless river.' And Krishna held tight as they flew onward towards the stream.

But as they went, they caused the denizens of heaven to wonder at them and turn round with marvelling gazes as they fluttered by, and all the creatures of the stars came gathering closer, so that heaven itself seemed to shrink for the travellers. Orion, the great hunter, strode forward, dangling his mighty sword, and his little dog Sirius barked at them from his master's heel. The great centaur, Sagittarius, dropped his bow with amazement as he watched them, and pawed the ground with his horse's hooves, and stamped on the dragon's tail. The twins laughed, hugging each other, and the bull shook his horns. But the Plough went by in the darkened fields, too intent on his work to notice, and turned up from the blackened earth the further treasure of a trillion stars.

And all this while the glimmering river led them onward. But then the bird stopped and said to Krishna 'Now we are in the centre of that river, and it is time for you to know who you really are.'

But Krishna looked puzzled and said 'How can we be in the centre of the river, for, look, the river is before us still. And see, there behind us also.'

And the bird said 'Thus we are in the centre, for the river is like a snake, and winds round and round within itself, so that it seems to go on for ever. But we who are in the centre of the coil see only outwards, and the body of the snake.'

And Krishna said 'But there and there you see the river: it has a thickness and a density. Here where we are is nothing but space and darkness.'

And the bird said 'It only seems so, because we are so small. To see the river truly we must change our size.'

And the bird explained to Krishna what he must do, and said 'When in the desert you sat down, and covered your eyes to find yourself, you saw nothing but blackness. This space you see above and beneath you is the blackness that you saw. Try now again to go within yourself. Let us see this time what you seek and find.'

And Krishna on the bird's back closed his eyes and searched as he had done before, shutting everything out from his mind to discover what was left, and when he had done that the bird said 'What do you see?'

And Krishna said 'I see blackness.'

And the bird said 'You see blackness, therefore you cannot be the blackness. What further do you see?'

And Krishna looked and said 'I see a space between me and the blackness.'

And the bird said 'That is a greater blackness than the blackness itself, but still it is not yourself, for you see it. Now tell me, for the last time, what it is that is aware of the space between you and the blackness.'

And Krishna looked, and thought, and was, and said 'That I am.' and lo! he knew himself and was released from all his searching.

And the bird spoke to him again and said 'Do you also see that you are my master?'

And Krishna felt within himself, as if they were children cradled in his arms, a blue man lying upon a snake coiled round, and the great white bird was there also, and had just spoken the words that he had heard. And Krishna opened his eyes with surprise, but found that he was still on the bird's back, as he had been before, and he said to the bird 'Who was the blue man you were with on the sleeping serpent?'

And the bird laughed and said 'That was Vishnu, Lord of the Universe, whose servant I am.'

And Krishna said 'Then who are you, and who is the serpent?'

And the bird said 'I am Garuda, King of Birds, I fly forward throughout the whole of creation, and bring about the ripening of the soul within. The serpent is Ananta, Coil of the Universe, and he is the channels in which I fly, for round and round on ourselves we go, building upon the past and the matter that is behind us, yet not flying far, but coiling within ourselves.

'And such is the journey you have been on, Lord Krishna, voyaging through earth and heaven towards fulfilment, from self to matter to life to mind, and again to self which is the home of all our seeking. At each circuit of that vast circle we found ourselves inward of the path we took before. And the lines that seemed between us and our forward selves were the sides of the serpent, coiling ever inward. Such were the snakes and dragons you encountered. But now, my master, have I brought you well on? Do you now know who you really are?'

'I am,' said Krishna. 'That is all there is to say. Why could not those sages have told me this at once?'

And the bird said 'Come now, Krishna, was there no truth at all in their words?'

And Krishna said 'Nothing I am, because I am not anything in this universe. The self of the universe I am, because all this is in me. And because I have now all this and myself, I am the friend of God, which is myself.'

And the bird laughed and said 'You are a good pupil, for you have quickly become your master's master.'

And now all the stars in heaven had gathered round listening to their talk, and when the white bird laughed, they too broke into peals of tinkling laughter, and all heaven rejoiced at Krishna's realisation. It was a sound as of a million bells, and all the pageant of the constellations wheeled round making the music of their spheres, hunter and archer and ploughman and maid, and the lyre twanged its rainbow notes, and the triangle its silver rings. And the rustling of the nebulas roared and fizzled in the festive air, and the doom-like gong of silence rang from her bronze containing all.

And the white bird said 'All's done, my master. All is fair and well. Your searching is over, and your spirit is home. Now, armed with the knowledge of the thing you are, no further trial or grief can come your way. You have snuffed out the fire of your desires. You have become that in which all things are. You have met the friend. And now farewell. Return to earth, and fulfil there your appointed destiny.'

And Krishna smiled and said 'Thanks, my dear friend, for leading me so far. May all men bless you that lead them ever forward. I am content to go where my fate now shall take me.'

And the white bird said 'The stream we have pursued into this centre is the snake Ananta on which Vishnu lies, too vast and mighty for us now to see. It forms the galaxy of stars which men on earth have named the Milky Way. It winds its path across the floor of heaven, and falls to earth in misty cataracts on the snowfields of those lofty Himalayas, where it becomes Ganges the sacred stream. Leap off my back then, Krishna, and you will find yourself soon at that juncture of heaven and earth. Go. Farewell. For you are free for ever.'

And Krishna leapt from the back of the white bird, and like a sledge that skelters down an icy hill, so did he slide down the winding river of the Milky Way. And past the stars he sped, and past the planets, great Jupiter, red Mars, and soon he saw, hurtling towards him through the depths of space, the fair-faced earth, smiling with sunlight, and welcoming him to her mother's arms.

And he roared into the atmosphere like a meteor, burning a sparky trail, and fell like a stone through the jangling curtains of the Northern Lights, and plunged through the clouds, which he tried to sweep up in his arms, but as he reached forward he twisted himself a little from the course of the falling river, and he fell alone towards some peaks away from the Ganges' source.

And he landed with a thump in the heaven of Kubera, right in the middle of his splendid court. When they saw Krishna crash through the roof the girls and nymphs of the court screamed and backed away but Kubera was delighted when he saw who had dropped in, and the girls were too when they saw that it was Krishna, and soon they were all friends, chatting merrily about Krishna's adventures, and feasting and drinking in that heaven of delight.

And the girls said 'How did you come to fall through our roof?' and 'What were you doing to be so high in the air?' and 'What brings you here to heaven in the mountains?'

And Krishna said 'It all began when I was in the desert, and I saw before me a worm and a bird. But the story is too long to tell you here. You would all be asleep before I reached the end.'

125

And Kubera said 'Krishna, we gods in this heaven are idle souls. In painting and music and poems are our delight. The other gods care for men and dash about, and are probably all now plotting some urgent scheme. But we have all time, and love to hear stories. Tell us your travels, and take as long as you like.' And the girls all agreed with this and begged him to do it.

So Krishna looked about, and filled his glass, and then he began to tell them of his journeys, and back in the desert he started with the worm and the bird.

And all this time Vayu had been searching for Krishna over the deserts and mountains, and began to despair of ever bringing him into Varuna's kingdom, where the gods all waited for him to come and save the world. But for all his puzzling as to where he might be, he never thought he was in the heaven of Kubera, or that before getting there he had circled all Asia, and thrice had crossed the vast Himalayas, and even had been to the region of the stars, and seen Vishnu himself on the endless milk ocean.

PART V

The Battle of Fiends

Book Twenty-five

Indra Takes Notice

And as Krishna feasted in the court of Kubera, the dwarf god, the other gods were feasting in Varuna's kingdom below the waves. They drank nectar together from the little shells, and were happy, and all of them looked forward to the time when Krishna would come with Vayu and set about the redemption of earth.

And Ganesha, the little elephant god, said 'I wonder if Vayu has yet found him. He should find him soon, and Vayu will, whether he is on the seas or on the earth or in the gloomy mountains. I long to meet this blue cowherd, for as all we know he is really the god Vishnu in disguise. And soon he will be with us, and routing the fiends.'

And another god said 'And when Krishna comes the drought will be lifted, and all things on earth will live again and be green.'

And the gods smiled and drank to this happy thought, and each one dreamed where Krishna might be, although no one thought of him in Kubera's heaven.

But Indra's wife could not be gay. She kept thinking of her husband on his gloomy peak in the mountains, and wishing he were here. At last she turned to Varuna and said 'Lord Varuna, it is not right that my husband Indra is not here, waiting with us for Krishna the cowherd, for he is leader of the gods, and we should not do things without him, foolish though he may be. Let me go and persuade him to leave his peak, and come.'

But Varuna shook his head and said 'My dear goddess, leave things as they are. The world has reached a crisis, and one small impulse of Vishnu will quickly set all to rights. You will see: all shall be well.'

But the goddess still looked unhappy, and said 'But what of the Maruts, my lord, the warriors of the clouds? Lord Indra scattered them over the face of the earth, and they are gone. How shall Krishna ever find them and call them together, for if he is to bring the rains it is they that must call the clouds. Let me go and tell Indra to recall his warriors, and all shall be ready for when Krishna arrives.'

But Varuna shook his head and said 'It is not necessary, dear goddess, and as for your lord do not worry about him. Though he may be sulking on his high rock, yet things will soon happen to fetch him from that place. No man can keep silent when he sees his old enemies returning to the fight. Leave all alone, and he will come to us.'

And there was such conviction in Varuna's words that Indra's wife became persuaded, and she believed that soon Indra would come down to them, and all things would be well. So she joined again in the feasting, and all was merry once more. And the deep-sea monsters that slid by with phosphor lights, lighting their way in the darkness with fizzling antennae, listened once more to the strange sound of laughter, never heard before in their gloomy realm.

Meanwhile, in the land of Braj, Agni was at work again. And he brought up more fiends from Hell so that the whole plain of Braj was swarming in them. It was like a battered island in the Arctic where the seals live: the rocks cannot be seen for the crawling, speckled beasts, and the air is filled with the sound of their honking and lowing, and the sea roars as it breaks against the cliffs.

Now Agni saw that the people of the village in Braj had built funeral pyres and were burning the bodies of their children, for the soldiers had made a raid on the fiends and snatched back many of the bodies. And Agni saw that the warriors were guarding the village intently, and he wondered what to do. But then he told the fiends to be ready to attack, when he should cause panic in the village, catching the soldiers off guard, and he went into the village and blew the flames of the pyres onto the houses, so that they all caught fire. The villagers ran here and there trying to put out the flames, but there was no water to throw on them because there was a drought and they were besieged. And some of the soldiers came to help.

But Agni got an ox-cart and rode to Nanda's house, before they knew of the fire, and he disguised himself as a holy man, and said 'Quickly Nanda, Jasuda, Balarama, leap into my chariot, and I will take you where Krishna is.' And because Agni seemed in such a hurry, and would not let them ask questions, they all three leapt in, hoping to save the village, and Agni made the ox gallop, and swept out of the village through the soldiers. And he cried out to the fiends to let him pass, and he drove the ox-cart full-pelt towards the desert, where there is no living thing.

And when the demons saw the village in flames, and the soldiers

130

leaving their posts to fight the fire, with a shout they poured into the village, and ran among the people. And with a touch of their claws or a bite of their tusks, or merely by their eyes and hideous faces, they made the cowfolk run mad. And soon the village was boiling with flame, and raging mad with devils and people, and the uproar echoed even from the walls of Mathura it was so loud, and the citizens there stopped what they were doing when they heard the noise, and shuddered and blanched with fear.

Then did all the demons in and outside the village fall on every living thing and suck out its life. The cows and pigs they bit and drained of life. The trees and crops with their breath they caused to shrivel. Beasts of the jungle and birds on the river all were sucked dry and turned to dust. And the mad cowfolk and the soldiers they would leap on and pull down to the ground with their numbers, and then, like piglets or calves clustering round the udder, they sucked out the life from the top of the cowfolk's heads, and the bodies of the cowfolk and the soldiers turned instantly to yellow and grey, and their flesh went wrinkly, and their eyes went pale, and their lips they shrivelled into blackened holes. Soon the very earth itself was drained of every colour, brittle and dry, like ashes of burnt logs on a winter's fire, that keep their shape a while in the whispering flame but crumble to dust when any draught should blow.

And while the demons did this, Agni flew on in the ox-cart with Nanda, and Jasuda and Balarama, and came at last to the stony desert where is no living thing, and he stopped the cart and said 'Here is the place Krishna was put down. Where he has gone since then you can now seek!' and he thrust them all suddenly out of the cart, and with a crack of his whip drove on over the sands and out of sight. And Krishna's father and mother looked at one another and saw they had been tricked, and they knew they were alone in the desert and far from any water, and they saw that their death was near.

And Agni rode on in the cart, but when he had gone some way off he jumped out of it and left it and flew on alone, for a god can travel faster than any human transport. And he flew until he came to the red hills of Bihar, where all is hot and dry, and he came to a mighty cave in the hillside, huge and dark and deep, and this was the cave in which Vritra had gone, the giant dragon which Indra had defeated. Agni went into the mouth of the cave and he roared down into its echoing chambers 'Vritra, awake, your day for revenge has come.

The earth is parched and dry like tinder. The people are all struck by fiends. The gods are gone. Arise, O greatest dragon of the world, arise and swallow earth in flame!'

And out of the cave came a deep booming voice and said 'Who is it wakes me from my endless sleep?'

And Agni cried 'It is I, Agni, the schemer of the gods, that licks up the sacrifice and loves the fire. Awake from your sloth. The days of old are come again, the far off days when all earth was but flame. Come, there is everything to glut your hunger.'

But the dragon's voice boomed out 'This is some trick. You seek to lure me out to throw me again into Indra's wrath, and pour down on me the hurtful rains, for the time of the year is come. Last time I was sore tried, and suffered agonies of thunderous water, and escaped only with my life, and the treasure that I keep in here. Away, you cannot tempt me. Leave me to sleep.'

But Agni said 'Indra has sworn never to harm you, nor any friend of Yama's. The days of peace among the gods have come, and none will fight the other. Then is it time for you to arise. Indra shall not oppose you: he is bound by his oath. No human can oppose you, they are all dead with thirst. There is no rain to oppose you, for the cloud-warriors are lost and gone, and Indra refuses to lead them. All is ready for the holocaust. Come, then, come. Vritra, arise!'

But Vritra's voice came again and said 'Very pretty it sounds. But how do I know you are not lying and tempting?'

And Agni said 'Can you see me at the cave's mouth?'

And the deep voice came 'I see a little man in holy clothes. Can that be Agni? Agni was once a mighty god, and never kept a peace between his fellows. You are a puny little man, and seek to trick.'

Then Agni rose up and flamed as his true self in the mouth of the cave, and the whole of the caverns of Vritra, and all the gold treasure and the iron mace were lit up by the glare, and far beyond, the flashing of the dragon's eyes could be seen down a massive tunnel. And as soon as he had done this, there came a roar, and the voice cried 'Agni you are. I come, I come. Let us go together and devour the world!'

And the dragon shot out from his mouth a vast sea of flame that roared out of the cave and bore Agni flying into the air outside, and Agni screamed with joy. And all the sand outside the cave began to melt with the heat and turn to glass, and Agni danced in the flames and sang a song of destruction.

And the dragon lumbered forward in the long stretches of his narrow caves, heaving his gross body through the rocks. The hill trembled as he brushed its sides, and smoke and dust poured out of crevices among the mountain, and a dark cloud began to form over the hill. And while he came, finding once more the movement in his long-dead limbs, and heaving himself out with strength and pain, Agni sang on as he pranced in the furnace of the swimming sands 'Doomsday is come, and all shall go back: back to the flames and the bubbling rocks. Doomsday, doomsday, fire and heat, and the dragon that is Vritra shall eat this world.'

But all this while Mother Earth, the goddess called Prithivi, who suckles every living thing, lay angrily enduring the outrage of the fiends. But when they attacked the village, and fell on the beasts and crops, she could suffer it no longer, and rose from her primeval caverns in the earth, where since ancient days she had reposed, when Dyaus the sky-god quickened life in her teeming womb. And Prithivi arose and went among the people in Braj, and with a balm anointed them, keeping just enough life in their bodies to stop them decaying into dust. The plants also she treated and the beasts and birds, and the houses in the village she caused to burn without decay, so that the flames licked on but no wood or stone crumbled at their touch. And when she had done this Prithivi went to the mountains and found Indra, her son, gloomily looking at the plain from his solitary crag. But neither he nor his mother had so far seen anything of Agni and Vritra, but believed that the trouble on earth was only that of the drought and the fiends.

And Prithivi spoke to Indra and said 'Indra, my son, how can you watch and bear these insults offered by the fiends on the body of your mother? Do you not see how they are ravaging the earth? Arise and rout them, my beloved warrior. Did you not rout Vritra in the days gone by? Then you were a powerful god, now it seems but an idler and prone to fits of sulking.'

And Indra turned to his mother and said 'Mother, you are right to upbraid me. But look, what can I do? The whole earth teems and is alive with devils. There are more demons than I can rout. Besides in far-off days, when the dragon Vritra fell to my blows, I made myself the target of much jealousy among the gods, and I swore then to my brother Yama, in the regions underground, that I should never more ride out against his demons. The gods are all at peace now: it cannot be that we should fight each other.'

But Prithivi said 'Must the forces of right give way to evil in the name of peace? O wretched coward, you will have the scorn of both good and evil for believing that! Look at the world. See how it seethes with strife. Demons are out draining the whole earth of life. Surya the sun sits in the sky and helps them with his burning. And you that should long ago have brought the clouds, and poured the life-giving rain on earth once more, you sit here gazing too, helping the fiends. Are all the gods gone mad that they should be so feeble-hearted? And Yama too, whom you have sworn never to cross, he sits in Hell pondering on sad things, and lets his fiends be swayed by others. Agni's the man. He is the trouble-maker. He from his birth has always been a-scheming. But Yama and Surya are to blame, and you, that have let him and his pranks prosper so far.

'Because you idled in a cave in Braj, because you neglected to bring in the monsoon rains, because you did not control your warriors of the clouds but let them scatter over the earth's face, because you were routed by a little cowherd Krishna, because you sulked because you were so, because you were too weak to rule the gods and keep Agni to his place among the sacrifices and the pyres, not burning and scheming in the whole land over, because of all this, and because you are too stubborn to admit where you were wrong, and leave this sulking, and stupidity, and weakness, and feeble-heartedness, and fly to untie all this knot of trouble and toil of desperation that is vexing and ravaging and bringing the world to ruin – O, that I should call you son of mine, and live to be a witness of your weakness!'

And Prithivi was silent and wept with indignation before her son. And Indra's head was bowed to the ground, and he was overwhelmed with shame. And at last he said 'O mother, mother, you are right indeed to scold! I see now where my pleasant ways among the caves of Braj have led me. The land was sweet there once, but I was a fool to be so taken with the place. I should have been here, ruling the gods of heaven. O mother, what can I do now? What is to be done? Where are my warriors to fight these fiends? How can I rally the mass in time for the wars? See, the earth is almost dead. I know not what to do.'

Prithivi was silent, sharing her son's anguish, yet for all that she

134

thought the case was not too bad to be saved, and waited a while for Indra's spirits to revive. And it so happened that Indra turned his eyes down towards earth, and the far-off land of Bihar, and then he saw the flames and the lumbering form of the dragon Vritra, burning up the world, and Indra's eyes blazed, and he leapt up and shouted 'Where are the gods? This is not to be borne!'

And Indra went storming down from the peak into the streets of heaven, roaring for his shield, his sword, his chariot and the other gods, and little gods dashed here and there, terrified of their master's rage. A small god that looked after the Northern Lights was seized by Indra and shaken so that his teeth rattled, and Indra roared 'Where are the other gods, you dwarf?'

And the little god said 'So please your divinity, they have all gone to the realm of Varuna to ask his advice.' And Indra threw him to the ground, leapt into his chariot and went immediately to the Western Ocean. And Prithivi saw all this from the lonely peak, and smiled to see her son himself again, and wrapping her earthy mantle about her she went back soberly to the dark caverns of her ancient home.

And Indra roared to the Western Ocean and splashed into its glassy surface and burst upon the gods sitting in Varuna's court, and he yelled 'Arise, O gods, you lazy, idling creatures. We have all been shamed. We have all led a life of idleness and weakness, and it is time to throw off our sloth and arm ourselves for the fight. Arise then, and follow me. The dragon Vritra is in the world, and we are to overthrow him.'

But Varuna smiled and said 'Brother, sit down. We have been long debating these things, and know of all the trouble upon earth with fiends and such like, although the news that Vritra has arisen is both new and grave. Remember, though, that you have sworn not to fight against your brother's kingdom, and there is little therefore that you can do yourself.'

But Indra burst in and interrupted him, and said 'Did I remember oaths the day I drove Vritra to his cave? To Hell with oaths! Now I am roused, I'll fight.'

But Varuna went on and said 'Brother, the time has gone for speeches such as this, nor are you the hero that will rout these fiends. We are the gods and never more must go to war on one another, for the new age that is to be ushered in cannot grow ripe in heavenly strife and discord. Peace must be universal on the earth, and fiends

135

and dragons must be slain by heroes. for men are men now, and must look after themselves. So, brother, sit down with us gods on the pleasant bed of old Ocean, and be patient but a little while, for soon he is to come who will deliver all.'

And Indra, though puzzled by these words, was nonetheless by Varuna's wisdom calmed, and Varuna said 'Come then, let us all feast together, for the lord of the gods is friends again with us all, and we are all united in a common aim.'

And Indra's wife came to him and offered him a shell of nectar to drink, and Indra looked at his wife and took it, and after he had drunk he smiled at her and thought 'Why do I wish to be playing among the caves of Braj, when my wife has so much beauty of her own?' And he gave her a kiss, and all the gods turned aside their faces to hide their smiles. And once more the gloomy ocean bed echoed in all its weedy caverns with the feasting of immortal gods.

But then Indra said to his wife 'My dear, who is this that Varuna speaks of: one that will soon come and deliver all?'

And the goddess hesitated a while and then whispered in his ear 'Krishna.'

And Indra looked horrified and shouted out aloud 'What, is that little pipsqueak that lifted my mountain to be the saviour of us all?'

But Indra's wife smiled and lifted a shell of nectar to her husband's lips, and said 'Come, my lord, you have punished him for his sins, and now you must forgive him, and show you are divine.'

And the gods laughed, and Indra frowned and looked glum, and he said 'And when is this Krishna due to arrive? And how is he to get here?'

And Varuna said 'Leave all alone, and he will come to us.'

And the gods continued feasting, and all in their minds began to wonder where Krishna could be, and whether Vayu had found him or not on his mighty search. But then they thought that Varuna had said Indra would come and he came, and then they thought that Varuna had said Krishna would come, so they bided their time, and waited for his arrival.

Book Twenty-six

Krishna Wounded

Krishna meanwhile had been feasting and dallying with the beautiful nymphs of Kubera, who were overjoyed at last to meet the one they had loved so long. And maidens in striped saris with threads of pearls in their hair waited on him and brought him amrita to drink, and other lovely girls danced for him, thumping the glossy floor with their bare feet, and jingling their anklets of gold. And all Kubera's court with its paintings and sculptures, its musicians and poets, its dancers and singers, was glad.

But Vayu, who had been sent to look for Krishna, had met with no success. He had searched the land of Braj and the deserts, and the far-off mountains and the seas, but had come across no sign of Krishna. And he was so weary and confused by all his travels that he was flying back to heaven to report to the gods, forgetting that they had all gone to the land of Varuna, the sea-god. As he passed Kubera's palace he heard the sounds of laughter and music, and felt so sad and weary that he thought he would call in, and drink with him. And when Vayu strode into the great hall of Kubera's palace, who should he see sitting on the terrace, surrounded by lovely girls, but Krishna himself, the man he had sought so far? And his mouth fell open with amazement, but then he sighed, and went towards them with an anxious face.

And Vayu said to Krishna 'Krishna the cowherd, you and I are to go at once to the Western Ocean, for all the gods of heaven are there waiting for you, and they have a mission which you are to go on, and accomplish great deeds. Arise then and come with me, for we must fly there this instant.'

And Krishna jumped up and said 'I will indeed. Am I to do great deeds? Then I shall be a hero, and famous among men.'

But all the girls cried out and protested and said 'Vayu, who are you that you should take him away from us? Krishna is our paramour, and he is to live with us for ever in heaven, and dance and feast with us in Kubera's court.'

They set up such a wailing that Kubera arrived to see what all the noise was, and Kubera said 'What is this howling of female jackals? Have you all begun to argue over who shall have Krishna to dance with her?' But then he saw Vayu, and Kubera said 'Vayu, my honoured god, you are here with us again? There is no need to ask me questions of Krishna now, for as you see he is here among us. The nymphs of my court have been thrown into ecstasies and I think will never be the same again.'

And Vayu said 'My Lord Kubera, forgive me for this haste, but I have been sent by the gods to find Krishna. They wait for him now among the caverns of Varuna's ocean. He and I must fly this minute to that land, for there is a great mission which he must accomplish.'

And Krishna said 'I am to do great deeds, and be a hero!' and he growled at the girls and chased them about, and they laughed and screamed.

Vayu seemed weary and anxious and looked to Kubera hoping for his support and said 'You will not mind if we go at once?' But when he said this all the girls flocked round him and cried 'You shall not!' and Vayu looked at his wit's end.

But Kubera laughed and said 'Go this minute, my dear friend. But one thing yet bothers me about your journey, for you are a god and may easily fly to the Western Ocean, but Krishna is a mere man, and how shall he fly with you?' And Vayu looked distressed, for in his haste, he had forgotten this also. Kubera laughed and said 'Look down in the courtyard yonder.'

Kubera and Vayu and Krishna and all the girls went to the edge of the terrace and looked down into the paved courtyard, and they saw a mighty chariot of gold, gleaming in the sun, with bright spoked wheels, and sculptured sides, fit for the King of gods himself. And Kubera said 'That is the chariot my dwarfs have made for Indra. He was to ride it in these coming rains, but as you well know Indra has forgotten all of rain and duty. Let Krishna ride in that, my friend, and soon he will be flying to the Western Ocean.'

And Kubera called for his servants to fetch the flying horses from the stables, and they were led forth, three steeds of blushing rosy hues, throwing their manes of gold back in the wind and neighing loud. Krishna's eyes gleamed like stars at the sight of the rich chariot, and he leapt in, and he and Vayu made to fly off into the sky. All the girls ran round to Kubera and begged him to stop them flying away,

138

and they crowded around the chariot and tried to hold back the horses, but Krishna with a flick of a golden whip set them in motion, and Vayu leapt also into the chariot to save his weariness, and off they flew together into the blue sky. And all the nymphs and fairies of Kubera's court could not bear to be so soon parted from Krishna, and they took to the air also. Like a flock of cranes or storks that in the autumn wing their way over the Bosphorus to Africa, when the winter's days are crowding in again, so did the nymphs fly around Krishna's car, and the sky was like a festival with their coloured robes.

And so Krishna and Vayu and the nymphs came to the great spaces of the Western Ocean, and left the land of India behind them, and they drew near the place where they must plunge into the sea and go down to the realm of Varuna. But the cloud-warriors of Indra, which he had told to scatter when Krishna the cowherd had routed him from his mountain in Braj, had all gone flying wide over the Western Ocean, seeking what storms or typhoons they could stir up, and all this time they had been winging aimlessly about, and had grown moody and dissatisfied with life. And it so happened that many of these warriors saw in the morning air these nymphs flying with Krishna, and they rejoiced at the sight and flew towards them. Some of them summoned on their horns the other warriors about the ocean, and soon they were all flocking round the flying car.

Now Krishna, ever eager for new amusement, greeted them all, and asked them who they were and what they did.

And the warriors said 'We are the Maruts, the warriors of Indra, that at the time of the rains bring in the clouds and battle with thunder, and fling down the rains upon earth. But this year we have brought no rain, and so we fly about the ocean and feast and sing songs of battles in the past.'

And Krishna said 'Then all's well met, for we also are a happy crew and prone to feasting. Let us feast here, warriors and nymphs together.'

And the Maruts were all delighted and they called up their clouds and spread them in the gloomy air, and Krishna and the girls sat about on the clouds and soon they were all feasting. The Maruts all sang jolly feasting songs and shouted their battle cries, and poured wine and soma over each other's heads, and Krishna laughed and joked with them. And all the nymphs who were at first a little afraid of the boisterous warriors soon began to join in the fun and feast and sing with the men. And the fishes looked up from their glassy home and saw a mass of black clouds sometimes flashing with light, and from the cloud came an uproar of laughter and drinking songs, and they could not understand what had happened.

But Vayu was horrified at all this, having brought Krishna so near the place where the gods waited, for they were all feasting directly over that part of the ocean where the gods were. And he smote his brow with his fist, and wiped the sweat from his neck, and tried here and there to shout over the noise of the feasting that Krishna was to come with him to the gods. But for all that he could not make himself heard, and at last he sank down on a cloud with his head on his fist, and nearly wept with weariness and frustration.

Now when Indra had ordered that Krishna should be sent out into the desert because he had insulted him by lifting up his mountain, he ordered three gods to punish Krishna with three things. One god he ordered to take away Krishna's memory, one god he ordered to push Krishna into the desert, and one god he ordered to shoot Krishna with a shaft of love. Now the two gods who had been ordered to take away Krishna's memory and to send him to the desert went immediately to their tasks, and they came to the man that calls up spirits and got him to do these things. But the god ordered to shoot Krishna with a shaft of love was Kama, the love god, and he had been more slow.

What happened was that he went to his wife, once Indra had told him to shoot Krishna, and told her that he would go down to earth on a mission. But Kama's wife was very loving, and could not bear to be parted with him, so she at once threw her arms round his neck and stopped him leaving. And when he had comforted her and quietened her laments, he fell asleep, for he was tired with all his efforts. And while he was asleep his wife got up and shut all the windows and nailed them close and when he woke up again she told him it was night, and that he could not go out while it was yet dark, and she began to say she would die if he left her. So he had to comfort her again, and satisfy her laments, and so he fell asleep again, and when he woke up it was still dark. And with this trick Kama's wife kept him from going down to earth to shoot Krishna, and so it was that he neglected his mission, and Krishna's heart never suffered the pangs of love as Indra had intended.

140

But after three days and nights, when all the gods had left heaven and gone to Varuna, and all the land of Braj had been overrun by fiends and Krishna had gone to the ends of the universe and back, Kama saw what had happened and ran out of the house fearfully to look for Krishna. He slung his quiver of arrows on his back, and dived over the walls of heaven, and he flew straight down to Kubera, and asked him if he knew where Krishna was.

And Kubera laughed and said 'Had you been here an hour or so ago, you would have seen Krishna feasting in my court. But now he is gone to the Western Ocean, and it is there you must haste if you wish to catch him.' And immediately Kama flew off towards the Western Ocean to find him.

Krishna meanwhile with the warriors and the nymphs was rejoicing in good fellowship and festivity. The warriors blew their horns and boasted about their deeds in the past, and talked over old campaigns which they had fought with Indra, and the nymphs all grew sleepy with the drink and kept blinking their eyes to keep awake. Cups were upset upon the cloudy tables, and the torches guttered on the misty walls.

Now Vayu who had been brooding unhappily at the end of a long dark thundercloud saw that it was time to put his plans in action. He leapt up, and, as it was now quieter, spoke out to all the warriors at the feast and said 'Cloud-warriors, and Krishna, prince of men, well have you feasted and talked long of action. But all the while you feast and talk there is action to be done which you neglect. Do you know how the earth is while you sing your songs? But none of you have been there for so long, how could you know? You have all been neglecting earth, and have failed to bring the rains which it is your duty to pour down now that the time of the monsoons is come. Look then on earth, and see the plight she is in.'

And with that Vayu blew at the clouds, so that a great channel appeared in them, and through the clouds he caused them to see far into India and the land of Braj. And Krishna and the warriors then saw what was happening on earth. The land of Braj was swarming still with demons, and all the villagers and cattle lay dead on the ground and dry of life. The houses of the village were still burning, throwing up flames and fumes into the blackened sky. And on the plain beyond the fiends swarmed still, fighting among themselves, and swearing oaths, frantic that further pleasures were no longer coming. And far beyond this, but advancing ever nearer, from the red hills of Bihar, there came the dragon Vritra. All before and behind was flaming and burning, and beyond Vritra they could see Agni dancing in the flames he had brought, so that the horizon was one sheet of flame. And all the warriors were struck with awe at the sight, and the feast became still, and all the hall was quiet.

But then Krishna sprang up and said 'What are those villains that are ravaging the earth? What is that devil with the fiery breath? Who shall endure this sight? Not I. Warriors, come round that will. I shall lead the fight against those scavengers!'

And Vayu rejoiced at Krishna's rage, and saw that the gods' behest might now be obeyed, and Krishna would lead the army of warriors against the fiends. The warriors all cheered Krishna's words, and they lifted up their hands to signal they would fight, and drew out their swords, and cried the battle-cry. And the whole cloudy hall was filled with the spirit of war and the courage of heroes, and the clouds began to ring with thunder at the charge.

But it so happened that at that minute Kama the love god arrived, and, perching on a cloud, he saw Krishna standing bravely in the midst of the warrior clan, so he took an arrow of love from his leather quiver and strung it on his horned bow and pulled the string back so that it touched his chin. Then he let fly, and the arrow flew to its mark and pierced Krishna's chest just in the region of the heart. The tip went into his heart, and its potion at once was at work.

Krishna staggered back, his hand clutched to the arrow in his heart, and he pulled out the shaft. The lids of his eyes dropped heavily closed, and he fell backward from his chair, as the warriors cried out and the nymphs screamed and wailed. And Krishna fell back quite through the clouds, and fell down through the sunny air beneath, and down into the glassy surface of the sea, and down through many fathoms past the fish and sharks, into the darkness of the ocean deep and the silence, and sank right to the middle of Varuna's court and rested on the coral floor, among the phosphor lights and ruby shells and weed.

The gods were astonished to see Krishna, and at first they were surprised and glad, and Ganesha cried 'Vayu has done his work.' But then they saw that Krishna did not move, and seemed as if dead on the ocean floor. But as they were wondering if he was dead or stunned, there was a splash and Vayu came down speedily, and then another splash and Kama followed.

And Vayu raced towards the gods and cried 'I have sought Krishna over the ends of the earth, and travelled ceaselessly, and found him at last, and through a thousand difficulties shepherded him to the ocean, and through more setbacks and puzzles roused him to thoughts of battle against the fiends, and all had been accomplished at one stroke when up comes Kama, later than late, three days late fulfilling Indra's task, and now overlate and quite contrary to Indra's present mind, and shoots Krishna through the heart, and ruins in one action whole days of my mission and striving and travelling. It's almost too much to be endured. I shall never again go on missions of the gods, for all I've got from them is trouble, weariness and strife!' And with that he flung himself on a coral chair and turned away from them all and wept, and the gods looked at each other not knowing what to say.

But Kama looked at them, as they turned to him, and made a wry face like a little boy caught stealing jam when his mother is away, and he said 'My wife played a trick on me. I could not start earlier. And what have I done but obeyed Lord Indra's wish?'

And Indra scowled at him and said 'Yesterday's wish is tomorrow's fear. Do my tasks speedily or not at all. Look, here lies Krishna as like not dead. If this is so, the destruction of the world is on your head, and all through your tardiness the dragon Vritra shall burn the earth and the seat of gods. How shall you ever bear a shame like this?'

But the wise Varuna said 'Lord Indra, do not be too hard upon little Kama, the love god, for if he had obeyed your wish and shot Krishna directly, Krishna might very well have not made his way here today. But let us end this talk, and attend to the patient. See, I think he begins to stir.'

And Krishna began to move, and opened his eyes, and his eyes even in the ocean were wet with tears, and he cried out in a weak voice 'Radha,' and sank again in the swoon.

And the gods looked at each other puzzled. And Kama said 'Radha is his love. I struck him with a love arrow, and so he thinks of her. O, he will suffer cruelly with love now till he sees her.'

And Varuna said 'If he has had his memory taken from him, how can he remember the girl he loved in Braj?' But when none of the gods could answer, Varuna said 'He stirs again, I will speak to him. Perhaps all his memory has come back with the arrow.'

143

And be bent down to Krishna and said 'Mortal, who are you, that you visit thus my regions of the sea?'

Krishna opened his eyes and said 'I am.' But then he began to writhe as though in pain and said 'Where is my Radha, my beloved Radha? O, there is such pain in my heart for her. Will no one bring me to her?'

And Varuna said 'What is your name? Where do you live?'

Krishna said 'I am. I do not know. I have no memory of things like that. Such thoughts are but cluttering in the mind, and I have none. But where is Radha? Is she in this land?'

And Varuna said 'No. She is not here. She is in a land that you must go to quickly. And you must fight the devils there, and battle with the dragon, and send them all away. And in that way you will achieve your love.'

Krishna said 'Are they the demons in the land of Braj? I saw them in a vision in the clouds, before I was struck down by an arrow of love. That I remember well. And the great dragon.'

And Varuna said 'That is your home, that land you saw invaded. That is where Radha lives. Come now, be strong. Get up now, and shake off this sickness, for you must go and win Radha from those fiends.'

And Krishna's eyes flashed and he said 'I must, I must,' and he started to struggle up.

But as soon as Krishna made the effort to get up off the ground he cried out in pain and clutched his heart, and swooned and fell back again. And whatever the gods did to try to help him was no avail, for as soon as Krishna stirred or tried to rise, he was overcome by pain and swooned. He could not even stand or try to walk.

And Krishna said 'I cannot move. This agony in my heart is more than I can bear. O bring me Radha, or I shall die for pain. O Radha, Radha, when will you come back to me? O my beloved. O my soul. My life.' And he fell back, groaning and sobbing on the ocean floor.

So the gods left him in the care of Indra's wife, who stroked his forehead, and gave him soothing nectar to drink, and cradled his head in her mother's lap. But the gods spoke of Krishna a little way off, so that he could not hear, and Varuna said 'His heart is paralysed with love. He could not fight in battle now, nor lead the warriors, unless his heart is healed by seeing Radha or hearing her, and I cannot think what can be done. The warriors wait their leader. The earth

144

waits her deliverance. But we are as far now from achieving it as we have even been. I cannot pierce this problem. My wisdom's done.'

The faces of the gods went white as they heard this, and none of them knew what to do. And they sat together in a gloomy part of Varuna's court, listening to the roaring of the tides in the deep ocean, sucking and rushing through the coral rocks, and it was like the roaring of a waterfall or the last torrent of the earth's long life, when all shall fall, and go again to darkness.

But then Ganesha the little elephant god said 'My Lord Varuna, it is not like you to look uncertain. When we wanted Lord Indra, you told us but to wait, and he came. When we wanted Lord Krishna you told us to wait, and he came. If we wait now, will not Radha come to us also?'

But Varuna looked at him and said 'That I had not foreseen. Krishna is a hero, and can cross the waves and dive into the water, but Radha is a mere girl, and how may she come to us here? Perhaps though, for she must be somewhere on earth, we might send Vayu again to seek and find her.'

Varuna turned to Vayu and said 'What would you think, my friend, to another journey, though from your face I see you would not think much of it.'

And Vayu said 'My lord, weary though I am, and reluctant to go on any more travelling, it was not that that drained the colour from my cheeks. Can you not know what has happened to Radha? Indeed you cannot, for you have not been on earth as I. My dear gods, she is dead, and gone down to Hell. There is no hope that she could come anywhere upon the earth.'

And the gods gasped, and looked round anxiously to make sure that Krishna had not heard what Vayu had said, but he lay there too weak in the goddess's arms, and had no time to eavesdrop on their talk. And the gods looked at each other with fear and anxiety.

Varuna said 'My dear friends, then there is nothing we can do. Krishna lies stricken with a wound of love, and cannot move unless Radha will call him. Radha is dead and gone down into Hell, and so can never call or have a mortal voice again. She alone it seems could save us, but she is dead. What is there to do now, but wait for the end?'

And the gods sat gloomily and thought of Radha, and it seemed that all their hopes had gone down with her to Hell.

145

Book Twenty-seven

Radha in Hell

Radha had indeed gone down into Hell, and the three dog-fiends hailed her to the gate of death, and left her before its gloomy jaws. And they ran off, and their barking echoed away in the darkness. And Radha was horrified at what had happened, and in her mind she struggled still, just as if she were in the prison courtyard, and Kamsa was hacking at her brother, and the fiends pulling her by the hair. It was a long time before her heart was quietened and she knew where she was.

And when she saw that she was at Hell's gate, she groaned aloud and said 'Alas, is this then death? O my poor life, had you to end in such a way? What hideous tumult brought me to my fate! O ghastly vision of that torturer's courtyard, how shall I ever rid you from my mind?' And she stood still, and at last sorrow came into her heart and brought her rest.

But then a dark spirit appeared, that was a guardian of the gate, and spoke to her and said 'Radha, come in. Here is your home henceforward.'

Radha looked up and said 'What are you?'

The warden said 'I am the warden of the gate of Hell. All souls that have done with life come to me here, and I lead them to Yama, the King of the Dead, who judges them and puts them to their place in Hell.'

And Radha said to the spirit 'It is strange that you know my name already. One minute I was in the courtyard with Kamsa and the fiends, and now, after a little fall into the darkness, I find myself in this country, and a warden waiting. How did you know that I would come?'

And the warden said 'The soul is a book. Whoever comes, it is but to read, and they are known. Come then, and let me take you through the regions of Hell.'

And Radha looked at the man and said 'And do all come with you willingly? What of those who have not yet done with life? What of those who have left on earth loves that they shall not part with, arms that wait still their embraces? What of those who did not come here by death's usual road, who have no wound, nor bodily hurt, who were hailed by fiends, and are alive here still?'

And the warden smiled and said 'Such cases are not for the warden of the gate. Souls cannot choose but come with me. If you are determined never to accept the state of Hell, then it is Yama you must greet with your strange conditions. Hence then, and come to him, and see the lands of Hell.' And the warden took Radha by the arm, and led her through the gate, and she found she could not resist him, but followed on that gloomy journey.

When they came through the gate, there was nothing but darkness before them, and the warden said 'To get to Yama, we must traverse three regions. One of them shall be your home when Yama has been your judge. They are three countries of the mind, and have no body, therefore it is but a kind of falling to pass from one to the other. In them will you see the souls of the dead, locked eternally in the state they attained on earth. They are all quite free to move about in Hell, but none of them can, for they believe only in their surroundings. Come then, let us see the landscape of the first region.'

And the warden became grim and snatched Radha at once to the highest plain of Hell. Here they suffer who have lived a life of love. And the warden looked here, and smirked with a scornful smile. He pushed Radha into the rolling hills of green that overlooked a grey ocean from chalky cliffs, and she felt on her face the gentle falling of small rain. And she heard sighs and saw many people sitting on the cliffs, gazing out to sea and weeping tears, and she felt pity for them all.

And the warden said 'See here an end of love in endless sadness. Take away what is loved from the loving heart, as the cycle of time comes by, and see: the ache of grief, the pain of separation. These souls suffer this eternally, and what of them has loved is vanished into thin air.'

And Radha saw her brother sitting weeping on the grass, sighing and looking out to sea. She went towards him, and the brother saw her coming a long way off, and sprang up and said 'Radha, did those dog-fiends then drag you to this place? Alas, my sister, yours was the fate meant for me. But that fiend Kamsa has our blood on his hands, and there is one that shall revenge us both.'

147

And Radha said 'O my poor brother, are you stranded in these gloomy fields? O saddest life, how are you littered with our broken selves! O let us sit and weep together, and gaze upon this sea, looking for hope.'

But the warden said 'Come, leave your whining. I have more to show.'

The tears burst forth from Radha's eyes to be so parted from her brother again, and she ran to embrace him on that rainy cliff, but as he came towards her the love in his heart caused him to melt away like mist on a stream, and she was left with nothing in her arms.

Then the warden snatched her down to another Hell. They came to a barren land of deserts and of ice, where the sky was dark and thick with snow, and there were people on the ice, some running here and there eagerly, some sitting shivering, groaning with despair, and those that ran were upon hot sand, and those that sat on the ice.

And the warden said 'See here the common throng of all mankind. These are the millions who fall continually from greed to boredom. See what they do. Look how they chase those shells.'

And Radha saw that littered over the ice and sand were little shells that glinted like silver and gold, and people would run towards the shells eagerly, and some would quarrel over them and fight each other, but once they had picked them up and looked at them they looked away again, and the shells dropped from their hands. And when they were tired of all this they sat down on the ice and howled with despair, and the snow and hail piled up against their backs.

And Radha saw there the wicked priest of King Kamsa. He was running picking up the shells and saying 'This will not please him. This will not please him.'

And the warden laughed and said of him 'See what an end mankind comes to. What fatuous beasts! What brainless fools!'

But he then turned to Radha and took her by the hair and hailed her round and round. 'Now,' said he, 'down to the other kind!' And whirling her so, he cast her and himself into a darker place, where there were screams of pain, and bellowings of rage. They came to a place of harsh rocks and of trees all iron with leaves that were of knives, and there were people running madly at each other, pushing their fellows into the slicing branches, making the trees clash and jangle, and there were blood and hewed limbs goring the place around.

148

'Here, Radha, here! See these!' cried the warden, and he pulled her round by the hair and held her towards the knives. 'And here, Radha, here! See these!' he cried, and ran again, and hailed her after him, and he shook her head into another place.

And here were people tossing and thrashing in lakes of boiling fire, and they screamed as the flames licked them and flickered in their hair. And they ran mad, and clambered on each other. There was a deafening noise, the air belched black smoke, there was a smell of burning flesh, and a rain of blood, and all was in turmoil.

The warden shrieked and danced as if possessed, and he suddenly screamed to Radha 'Do you find Krishna in your heart in the middle of all this?' And a thousand faces appeared in the air, red like glowing coals, with horns like devils, and they flew around Radha on bat-like wings, and buzzed like hornets, and they all screamed so that it tore their throats 'Krishna! Krishna! Krishna!'

And the warden dragged Radha to a black lake, where there was a figure fishing, and he cried 'Take her, Rakshasa.' And the figure turned and caught Radha in his slimy arms, and pressed against hers the face of a gibbering ape, and leapt backwards with her into the black lake.

And Radha found herself in Yama's court, and the King of the Dead sat before her in a granite throne, and she sank before him on her knees, and swooned.

But when she stirred from her swoon, Yama called his guards and said 'Make the woman stand to receive her sentence.' And the guards lifted her up, and Yama gazed into her eyes and read the book of her life.

And Yama said 'You are the girl Radha, that lived in the land of Braj. You are the lover of Krishna, the blue cowherd. Your place in Hell shall be as you lived on earth, for Hell is no more a thing than the past, and what has gone. Will you speak before you are judged?'

Radha looked wearily at the great King from half-closed eyes, and said 'Who are you, dark Raja, that sits on a throne in Hell?'

Yama frowned, and said 'I am your judge, Radha, the King of these regions, and I am to assign you your place in death's realm. Have you anything to say on the crimes of your life? Will you repent of this love for the blue cowherd, Krishna?'

But Radha did not answer him, but gazed a long time ahead of her and said 'Am I then truly dead? Am I no more to see my earthly joy, nor never more to take him in my arms? Is this my home now for eternity?'

And Yama said 'There is no home in Hell. All here are exiles, and you now come among them. Say then of your love for this strange herdsman. Do you repent it?'

'Must I repent?' said Radha. 'Is there no love in Hell?'

'Love has no place in Hell. Those that were lovers have a place for all their sorrow. They go to the grey cliffs and weep towards the sea. But when the impulse of their love overtakes them they fade from my region like small rain in the wind. You, if you are to come here, must repent you of this loving. I do not wish my subjects to have ways of freedom.'

And Radha said quickly 'Then forget me, dread King, for I am not yours at all. I was never killed on earth in the ordinary way. No common fate of adder's teeth or fever brought me here. But your dogs, King, that were conjured by a wizard, they dragged me bodily to Hell before ever I could die. I shall not stay here, whatever place you put me.'

And Yama smiled at her words, for he saw that she had courage, and would stand up even to the devil himself.

And Yama said 'Can you fall into the black pit of Hell and never die? You will be rare indeed if ever you could do that. No, there is no help. You cannot leave Hell now. Here you are fixed in what place I assign you, and so must dwell until eternity is gone.'

Then Radha sighed and said 'Alas, so this is death, this knowing and not being, this gloomy cave, this absence of a spring. O my love Krishna, was that the last I saw of you, when we two said a brief farewell, imprisoned by the soldiers? Will you not come again? O death, then am I now your bride, and must I live away from him for ever?'

Yama looked at her and said 'Aye, that you must, and Krishna must you put out of your mind. He and this place can never go together. Love and this place can never be together. Him and love you must forsake for ever.'

And Radha said 'How can you know of Krishna? He is but a poor cowherd in the land of Braj.'

Yama said 'What is this Krishna I can never tell, and surely he will never be before me to be judged. Krishna has a ring, a bracelet of discernment, and he that wears it is protected from Hell. The ring

150

gives wisdom, and wisdom reveals that all things are unreal and
vanishing. How can a man who knows such unreality ever be prey to
these delusions of my realm? Aye, we are all thick dreams and massy
shadows, and he that knows us is proof against all devils.'

And Radha said 'Then he will not come here? That gives me
courage then. I would not wish my love with me in Hell. Let no dog-
fiends drag him down, no warden seek to frighten him with pictures
of Hell's pains, no thronging shapes and turbulence assail him, no
tempest, and no hubbub, and no grief.'

And Radha sighed, and said 'O that in Hell there could be endless
sleep, for I am weary of this restlessness!'

Yama said 'Now, woman, now, let us about your sins. What of this
love for Krishna? Through your love for him are you come to this
place. Do you repent your love? Will you renounce him?'

And Radha said 'Should I renounce what it is that renounces?'

Yama replied 'But you will admit your love has led you straying?
How, if you had not loved, would you have come to me now?'

And Radha said 'It was not Krishna brought me to this place. It
was the devil Kamsa I must thank for that. He, the black King that
darkens all the land of Braj, he with his filthy plots sought to make
me marry him, and with his crowd of jugglers and magicians summoned the fiends that brought me to your den. O, if there were but
me and Krishna in this world, there would be no scope in it for Hell
and devils.'

Yama said 'So you alone are pure, and all the world is evil! That is
a human thought, if ever was. But come, you will not slip me with
these excuses. Time enough you had on earth to get your soul
absolved, to snuff your passions, to blend again your spirit with the
eternity it moulds, but you chose dallying in the woods of Braj. And
because of it you are in my kingdom, damned with the rest, lost with
the whole tribe of human fools. Come now, admit you have been led
a-wandering. Do you still cling to this love of Krishna when it
brings you here?'

And Radha said 'Krishna's love will keep me from this place.'

Yama said loudly 'But love of him brought you here. From love of
him you were caught. For love of him you were tried in Braj and
condemned. For love of him you were brought to that deathly King
who sent you to this place. How can you love what has been your
ruin?'

And Radha looked calm then, and sighed, and smiled slightly and said 'Who would not love Krishna?'

Yama slapped his hands upon his thigh and said 'O these human fools! How they cling to the snake that bites them.' And he looked at Radha, and said 'Let us argue no more then, but send you to your doom. In Hell there are many places. The spirit is free to go from each to each. One that is set among the belching fires can wing upward easily to the cooling showers above. But so great is the ingrained habit of the soul that few souls rarely stray from their natural lot. The state on earth you had, that is your state in Hell, for Hell is but the past and what has gone. And in your place your mind is satisfied, for whatever images it has of life it sees before it, as if made of matter. Your sad man sees sad things, your vile things vile, and like a dog trained to root out one scent, so out of a universe of changing things you see only the image of your mind. So to one place I'll send you. There you'll stay. And all the other realms of Hell will be but shadows. You are a lover: to the cliffs you'll go, and sigh and fade into the sea-borne mist.'

And Radha shrugged her shoulders and said 'Well, I shall love then for eternity.' And she smiled a little and said, lifting her eyebrows, 'Not even you, O King, can stop me there.'

Yama looked angrily at her and said 'Should I send you to the fire you could not love, nor could you love fighting among the leafy knives, nor could your heart grow warm among the ice, or hold steadily to its loving on the deserts and the shells. Were you among those places and in pain, you could not even think of love. Nor do my demons have it. We do not hold with it, nor have faith in it at all. Sometimes a creature strays into love's realm. He turns back, for he sees it is not real.'

And Radha said 'Hence you are all prisoners, for you cannot doubt your chains.'

Then Yama looked angrily at her and said 'Come, I shall make you doubt your love. Why should you lovers have such fortitude in Hell, and fade out of my kingdom as the wind blows cool or warm? Why should you, Radha, have such faith in all your loving? What is this Krishna then that you love so much? Let me tell you what he has given you that you repay him so. Nothing but scorn and neglect. What has he done but taunt you and play jokes on you, but shame you in your life with your good brother? What has he done but send

152

you to this place, for you were tried for loving him, and Kamsa tortured you because of Krishna. What has he done but desert you when you needed him? For when you were taken and tried he vanished away, and never has come to your assistance yet. Where is he now? Is he thinking of you? Does he care where you are, what has become of you? Or is he bent, as always, on pleasure and laughter, forgetting all that has past, to glory in the fleeting gilded minutes as they fly by? O, what a fool you are to love this fellow!'

And Radha said 'These are the pranks for which I love him. Nothing on earth holds Krishna in its chains. Would he were here, how he would joke with you!'

Yama looked fiercely at her, and said 'Joke in Hell? I shall show you something now that will stop that merriment. I shall show you where Krishna is. You will see how he misses you, and weeps his time away that he has not you with him. You shall see him now.'

And Radha put her hand to her heart, and tears came to her eyes, to think of seeing once more her dear love, now that all hope of seeing earth again was gone.

Yama saw that she was moved and said 'O now I see you care. Yes, yes often on earth you have scolded him for neglecting you. You have nagged him for running off with other women. Do you fear now that he might be up to his pranks again? You lovers can be jealous, it seems, and jealousy will lodge you a little lower in Hell for all that. Look out that way then, into the darkness, and see if you can love him now, being where he is, doing what he does, this Krishna.'

And out of the darkness, as if spying through the whole thickness of the earth, appeared a vision of Krishna, and what he was that minute about. And it so happened that this was the time that Krishna was in the court of Kubera, and Radha saw him there among all the lovely girls. Krishna sat among the glossy halls of the palace, and the jewels of the goddesses and their glinting gold anklets and necklaces were reflected in the marble floor. And on soft carpets of camel-hair and goat-hair sat musicians that played on flutes and drums, serenading the group of revellers. And Krishna sat on a terrace, overlooking the blue and misty mountains, and round him were goddesses clothed in saris of mauve and gold, shot like a peacock's throat and sewn with gold, and they gave Krishna drinks of nectar from small cups. Radha saw that the court was like a great sultan's palace, and that riches dripped from the walls like hanging

153

trophies, and works of art, intricate mouldings of gold wire and ivory, lavished among the rooms, and scattered on the chequered floors among the bellied cushions, and it was all like spring when the magnolia petals stream in the gardens and scents of musky pollen are born along the wind. And Radha saw a goddess, the chief there, take from her purple hair a yellow lotus and give it Krishna. With smooth arms she wound it in his glossy hair and kissed him. And Yama laughed and clapped the flat of his hands upon his throne, and with a crash like thunder the vision vanished and the thickness of the muddy earth closed once more in the way of seeing.

Yama cried 'Now do you love him? Now you see how sad he is that you have died and gone to Hell.' And he laughed on and on, and and when he had finished he turned to Radha for her answer and said 'Well?'

And Radha said 'Send me to my doom, great Yama, now you have had your sport.'

And Yama said 'Aye, so I will. The case is hopeless. His love is so hard fixed in your heart that not eternity will root it out. So be it. You have a place in Hell. Now you will hover on those upper regions, among the weird ones that we scorn in death.' But he turned to her again, and said 'Will you not say at least that he loves you not?'

And Radha said quietly 'I have only to call him once, and he will come to me from the ends of the earth.'

Yama said 'What? Call him? You have only to call and he will come? O foolish girl, how can you think you can do that? You are dead. You are past. So are we all in Hell. There is nothing we can do to change or move. All is gone by, all time, all future days. Once you are here, or you, or I, or any of these millions, all the earth's dead of man and bird and beast, there is no more. In Hell and death there is no further forward. All here is past and all are lost in it.'

And Radha knelt on the floor and wept.

Yama looked at her and sighed, and he said 'Such is your fate. Such is the pain of Hell. And now I think you know your punishment.'

And Radha said 'Endlessly sad is human life. O poor dark souls! O spirits of the fathers! How are you all like shattered urns that no more can be mended. Alas, great King, how sad is death and Hell!' And Radha wept as though her heart would burst for grief.

But Yama sat and wondered at her, and he knew not if she wept for

154

herself or for him. And he began to muse in himself and said 'What is this in my heart? How comes this stirring? The reason of all things is shifted, and I see a light behind the furthest barriers of time. How can she weep for Hell, that is in it?' And Yama looked at Radha and said to himself 'Strange is this thing she feels!'

Yama looked at her for a long time in silence, and Radha ceased weeping at last and looked up at him and saw that he was staring at her and yet lost in thought. So she said 'Shall I go now?'

Yama sighed and said 'When you first met this Krishna, did you love him then?'

And Radha smiled and said 'I loved him from the first.' *

Yama said 'How did you know you loved him?'

Radha replied 'How does one know? Love comes in many guises.' And she smiled after her tears a little and said 'Sometimes we suffer when we are apart. Sometimes our hearts leap when we go to him. Our thoughts are ever on him, and our times with him, times past and time we wait for. And all things else but him are but shallow things and shadows. Sometimes we weep. Sometimes we laugh.'

Yama interrupted her and said 'But all this is but symptoms of a love: these are preoccupations, not the thing itself. How do you feel when you are with this Krishna?'

And Radha sighed and said 'When I am with him all things have come home. There is but peace and comfort, nothing to stray further. We are contained in all, and all in us.'

'And how is that?' asked Yama.

And Radha replied 'Once we were in the forest on a night in spring. A shower had come and dampened the young grass. and smell of mangoes and magnolias was in the freshened wind. And in an arbour among trellises of rose and dusky roseleaves we sat and heard the drumming rain beat on the bamboo roof, and saw it smoke in the blue forest like a dragon's breath. Of love and lovers' pastimes we had gorged our fill, of love and lovers' oaths we had both spoken all we could. Now was there no more to do or say, but sit together in that little arbour. Then did I see that all fears were but foolery: we cannot be lost, we cannot fall out of ourselves. And I saw that everything was contained in me: the forest, the rain, the future, our love, Krishna himself: they all lay in my heart like a child at its mother's breast. And then I knew that love was all in all.'

Yama's eyes caught fire at this, and he spoke fervently, and said

155

'O tell me what is love. Tell me but this, and I shall grant you anything you ask.'

And Radha laughed and said 'What, a boon from the King of the Dead? This is like a story-book of an olden hero. Will you grant me anything if I tell you this?'

Yama said 'Anything, my girl, but satisfy my craving. For a long time and all time have I sat here, the King of these regions. Four brothers, we took upon ourselves the rule of the world. Indra, the sky and the North had in his power. Surya the East, where as sunlight he would rise. Varuna, the wise one, he went deep into old Ocean. And I, in my gloomy fashion, fed myself on these dusky realms. Long have I sat here, lost in sadness, brooding upon time and the gods of old, watching the years turning like wheels on Vishnu's cart. But always your kind have puzzled me most deeply. Humans, so frail, yet with such strange desires. They fall to me continually like leaves from the shaken branches, but their hopes and minds are always yearning upward, and they break upon the rocks that sharpen between all matter and one mind. Tell me then what is love, and I will grant you a boon, for love is the great secret that you strangers hold, and eagerly would I hear of it, and hope to pick those locks.'

And Radha said 'Then let me tell you love is all, and no more need I say. Love is completeness. Love is whole. You puzzle how we love, and yearn towards the sky, while falling ever earthwards. But love is the fabric that survives your fires. Love is the resolution of these knots of death, dissolver of all lines between this and this. The fresh spirit that quickens in the life of things, and brings them all to ripening like a sun, this, this is love.

'You are puzzled that we love in all these torments, and loving fade from them, a shade from shadows. Love in our hearts is a sad lullaby, and lies our cares and worries all asleep. Love is all comfort of release from clods of matter or the pangs of life. Love is outside the tangled knot of things, and in renouncing them we fall in love. With love the essence of all things is seen: the trees are friends, the moon a helpful guide, the snows and mountains are a lover's smile, and the grey clouds, like children playing in their mother's clothes, come blushing in the sun of love, our dear ones. O love is holy, love is fair. Love is all comfort, sweetness, purity. Love is the very substance of our soul, and leads us on, and round, and makes all one. Love is the conqueror of your region, King, and when I love, then am I safe from it. Seek in

156

your heart, O mighty Raja, seek, and see if what I say of love is true.'

So Yama sat in thought a great while, and then he sighed and said 'What is your boon now? Ask something of me.'

And Radha said 'O, let me see him but once more.'

Yama said 'A little I can give you in this way. And yet the jaws of fate cannot be slipped. Go back to earth this day, stay for the next, and on the third day come again to Hell. This can I allow you for my promise's sake. Give me your word though you will come again, for as yet I have not judged you, and for a little while I can keep sentence. Swear then to hold your bargain.'

And Radha said 'I swear, O King, bitter bargain though it is. To have a sight of earthly happiness, and have it snatched away, that too, King, is Hell. But I shall go, for something calls me back to seek among the troubles of the land of Braj. So I shall go, and in three days I will return. Farewell, then Yama. I thank you for this boon.'

'Farewell, rare girl,' said Yama.

But as Radha turned to go, Yama spoke to her again, and said 'By what way will you come back to me? By fire, by steel, by poison or by water?'

And Radha said 'At the noon of the third day, I shall come back by water. In the Ganges shall I drown myself, and so complete the bargain. Can you perform the rest?'

And Yama smiled and said 'Drown in the Ganges, and you'll come soon enough.'

And Radha left the hall, and began the journey up again towards earth.

Book Twenty-eight

The Great Battle

So from the depths of Hell Radha made forward on her journey back to earth, the land that was to be hers for but three days. Through the boiling lakes of Hell and the woods of knives she passed, through the great thronged deserts of sand and ice, through the green cliffs that overlooked the sea. And she passed again the blackness, the desert and the decaying bodies, and came once more to the gate of Hell, and so passed back into the living world.

Radha found herself climbing a winding stair that went round and upward with the pit on her right side, and she came out into the court-yard of the prison and shuddered to remember the fiends and her brother's murder there. And she climbed up the tower to see out over the city and the plain, for all was strangely silent, and no warders were to be seen. And Radha looked out over the country that had been her home, and lo! it was a mass of fiends, blackening the earth, choking on one another in vile heaps, writhing like worms.

And the city of Mathura was in their grip, for they lolled against the walls of the dark streets. The plain was thick with them, like the fields of Egypt when the locusts come, and they basked in the sun, bewildered by the continual light, and full with all the lives they had sucked dry. Radha saw far off the village in Braj, and it burnt glaringly and threw up a great plume of black smoke into the air, and the smoke hung like a brooding cloud over all the land. And behind the village the hill in Braj was dry of life, and all the trees were leaf-less and bleached white. It was a sight more foul than all the Hell she had been trapped in. Radha grew suddenly weary and near almost to despair, and stood silent on the tower gazing out over the spectacle of doom.

And Radha said 'Lo, here an end of human life, an end of peace, an end of love, for in time the fabric of this world catches its own flame and destroys itself. And gone are all those things we laboured for: the ascent of man, the birth of love, the toil and craft, the wisdom and the joy. All cities end, all homes, all the bright pinnacles and rearing walls and towers all tumble down, and shaken by the tide of time fall back into the dust. O wretched man, did you set out upon your mighty journey but to come to this? Is this the end of all? Can this be doom?

'O Krishna, come, come, revisit the world, rise from your sleep. Krishna, come back, come back. O love, O peace, O happy days. O come, too long has all this war and toil, too long the scorching of the sun, the creeping death, the circling fiends, been our repast, our waking and our death.

'O Krishna, come, come, I have been true, I have borne everything and never lost, I have stayed firm amongst the fiends and tyrant, Hell itself, because you live in me. But come now to us all. Wherever you be in this vast universe, come back to Braj and free your people from this darkening terror. My heart is all in grief. I cannot weep. Bring me the rains. Come, Krishna. Come, come, come!'

And when Krishna, on the ocean bed, heard in his heart that he had been called by Radha, he suddenly found his courage and sprang up, and Indra's wife was amazed and gasped, for the moment earlier he had been in pain on the sandy ground.

And Krishna shouted to the gods who were still brooding on their troubled thoughts a way off among the rocks 'Shall I go alone, or will you come with me? The warriors wait me in the clouds. The Maruts are eager to go. Let us waste no more time but speed to the rescue of Braj. Come!'

The gods were amazed to see Krishna on his feet and so full of life, and they came towards him, and Varuna said 'Do you feel no more pain? How can it be you are so quickly well?'

And Krishna said 'Let us not waste time, O mighty god, with idle questions. The people of the land of Braj are in great danger. I have seen the demons. I have seen the dragon. I have heard in my heart the call of Radha, my dear one, and I long to be hastening to smash those fiends of Hell.'

And Indra rushed forward and took Krishna's hand and said 'Krishna forgive me. It was through my spite that you were thrown into the desert, and through my spite smitten just now with an arrow of love. I was angry with you for the past when I was foolish. But these fiends now are a threat to the very gods, and a revolting sight to be sprawled so over the earth. Let us have at them. And in this fight, since I cannot take an active part and wield a weapon, let me be your charioteer and drive you speedily among the war in my golden car. Accept this offer, Krishna, and henceforth, let us be friends.'

And Krishna said 'Gladly will I, my lord. Let us fly then.'

But Indra's wife came forward and said 'But Krishna, can you really be well? Such agony you were in just now. Is your heart healed so soon?'

And Krishna said 'My heart is not healed. For ever will it bear this love's deep wound. But my love has called me, and that is why I go.'

And Indra's wife said 'But what of your memory? Do you remember now the land of Braj?'

And Krishna smiled and said 'A little I recall. The wound has opened some of what was passed. But Radha fills my mind, vivid in my memory, the far-off days, the moon in the green woodland. I long to see her again, my heart's darling. Be patient with me then, great goddess, for I am grateful to have been your patient. Ever shall I remember your help and my refuge here in the glass-green kingdom of the waves. But now it is time to go, and I must fly to my love and release her from the enemies that ring her round. Come then, you gods, let us advance, and be a-warring.'

And Varuna came forward and he held in his hand a twirling conch shell, such as sheltered a great sea-creature in the past, bored with a hole to be a horn to blow, and Varuna said 'Krishna, this conch has been in my kingdom for long years. Shelter it found with me, after the dragon Vritra stole other parts of Vishnu's treasure. This is the conch of skill, and whoever masters it shall have the power to summon up the great forces of Nature to be his aid. Take it then, Krishna, for it is yours. Use it in this good fight, and all the universe will help you to rid earth of demons. Go now, and power and skill be with you on your quest.'

Krishna took it, and thanked Varuna, and he put it to his mouth to test it, and blew a great call that echoed through the deep. And all the dark caverns of the ocean rang with the sound, and the Maruts in the clouds above heard it and knew it as their summons, and they roared with joy and drew out their swords ready to fight. The booming of the conch echoed over all the earth, like the trumpet of doom, and the hills and mountains shuddered at the sound, knowing a great battle was to come.

And Krishna rushed upwards in the gloomy water, thrashing a bubbling wake as he soared higher, and the gods, taken by surprise by his sudden recovery, hurriedly collected themselves and made after. They roared upwards out of the deep, like a mighty flock of cranes that have stood long in a fishy lake, but then in one great impulse all leap forward, and run along the water, and glide into the skies. So did the gods follow Krishna to the surface, and then in a mighty burst of spray and foam they all soared out of the Western Ocean and flew up into the skies. And Krishna had risen so fast from the ocean bed that he leapt out of the glassy sea and straight onto a cloud, and the Maruts all roared and welcomed him as their leader.

Krishna said 'O mighty Maruts, warriors of the clouds, we have all long dallied about this mighty ocean, but now is the time for action. The people of Braj are at the gates of death from drought and fiends and all manner of evil. It is time the thunder and the rain awakened them from their swoon. Then man your chariots and let us race the clouds. The time of the rains has come, and there shall be an end of fiends. Forward then, cloud warriors. Follow me. On to the land of Braj and India!'

And with this the whole rout of warriors and gods lunged forward, and in a thick mass of thunderclouds advanced on the parching land.

In the desert meanwhile where Agni had in his spite led Nanda and Jasuda with their son Balarama, the sun beat down and they were scorched with thirst. But Nanda and Jasuda were now alone, for Balarama, as soon as Agni had turned them loose and ridden off in the chariot, had chased after him, hoping to wound him with a stone. But it happened that Agni did not notice this pursuit, and when he quitted the chariot flew away without seeing Balarama in the distance. And so Balarama caught up at last with the ox-cart, and leapt in it and drove the tired ox back again to Nanda and Jasuda. And so the old parents saw their son again bringing them rescue and were overjoyed.

But Balarama said 'There is great mischief plotted by that man. Take the ox-cart for yourselves and go back at once to Braj and guide the people, for when we left the houses were on fire and all were in great danger. I will stay in the desert and await the man's return, for something he is planning, and I wish to thwart him if I can.'

But Nanda said 'My son, how can we leave you in this barren

161

place? We are near dead with thirst, and you so far from home will surely die.'

Balarama said 'Good father, go. I am a match for fiends, and will quench my thirst by drinking their fiend's blood. Delay no longer. Go.'

And so Nanda and Jasuda unwillingly left their son, and hurried in the ox-cart back to Braj, hoping that the whole village had not caught fire and that they would be able to save it.

And Balarama turned and journeyed the way the man had gone, all unknowing that he was the god Agni, and sought to see what mischief he was up to. Balarama had not gone far when in the distance he saw smoke and flames, and running nearer and straining his eyes to see in the heat haze he saw the horizon all on flame from North to South. The flames flickered, and in the mirages looked as they were burning upon water, and Balarama thought 'How can the whole horizon be aflame? What is there to burn in the desert? Sand cannot burn unless in a mighty furnace.'

And he ran nearer, even though now far off he began to feel the heat of the flames on his face, and he felt dizzy with the sun's heat and the flames. And the flames now he could see clearly, writhing and twisting on the sand, like a glaring army slowly advancing. But then he caught sight through the flames of the dragon that was throwing them from his mouth.

It was a huge black monster with a snake-like head, cracked open from ear to ear in a great fiery mouth. Its eyes were green among the flames with little pin-point pupils, and from its head thick fins of oily leather, studded with plates, rose up and bristled down the winding spine. It lumbered forward on thick legs all armoured over and wide as redwoods in the lonely forests, and jet-black claws leapt out and dug the sand, and as it walked its body lurched with each step, like a great anchor tugged from the sea-bed, or a huge rope that pulls a log along. Vaster than a fortress he towered up, gazing upon the ground with evil eyes, and belching flame and smoke that flapped the ground.

Balarama was astonished to see such massiveness, but he ran on to try his best. And yet the heat of flame soon overpowered him, and he found he could not get near to the monster to attack, but staggered back with singed hair and singed eyebrows, and felt his throat go parched as he drew in the hot air. And the dragon Vritra saw Balarama and bellowed at him like the sound of chains clanging against an iron door, or splintering ships that crash upon the rocks, and it lurched forward hurling forth its breath. And each time that the dragon lurched Balarama hopped back from the sheet of flame. So they advanced together over the scorching desert while behind the dragon on the melting sand Agni danced round and round in hectic ecstasy of the endless heat.

But when Nanda and Jasuda came back to Braj, weary after the journey through the desert, they were appalled by the scene before them. The village burnt still, the flames sustained by Prithivi, the villagers lay as if dead, with only the smallest spark of life retained in them by Prithivi. To Nanda and Jasuda it was like a vision of doom. They stood together too horrified to move or speak, and cast their wincing eyes over the bodies and the ash. And far off, in Mathura, Radha too looked down upon the scene.

And Radha on the tower said 'He has not come. Earth has gone back to Hell. Why should I then prolong my days of grief? What are three days of this but worse than Hell? Hell is itself, but earth has lost herself, and all here now is sickening and wrong. Come then Radha, you are a fool of hope. You thought he'd come. You hoped for holidays. Ah, why do I have a faithful heart? It only serves to bring me misery. I shall return to Hell and damn myself.'

So she turned and went to go down again from the tower, but as she went her ear caught a long-forgotten sound far off, that stole upon her memory with fragrance of happy days. It was the sound of thunder in the West. She turned and lo! faint on the West horizon was a smudge of white, a hovering line of hope, and Radha put her hand over her brows and gazed and saw that they were clouds. And then the thunder rang again, and it was like a bell within her heart remembered, and she leapt for joy and clasped her hands together.

And Radha said 'O Krishna is it you? O my love come. Come quick and circle me within your arms. How I have waited for such a sight as this!'

The thunder rang loud now, promising rain, and the fiends began to stir uneasily on their slimy beds, and wake from their besotted slumbers, and some of them got up and looked about, but sank again to sleep for they saw nothing. But some there were in Braj that sniffed the air, and the smell of dust and fire was gone in it and it had a fresher taste, and the fiends began to whimper and run about snuffling and peering. But the fiends had not a sight as keen as men, and they saw nothing, nor did they yet hear the thunder clearly, and other fiends awoke and struck at them for moving, and they became still once more.

And the thunder rang again louder than before, and a trace of lightning flickered in the West, and Nanda and Jasuda saw this and looked at one another, but they dare not speak for they saw the fiends beginning to move. But they took each other's hands and squeezed them, and all their mounting joy was in that squeeze, so that Jasuda wrinkled her brow with joyful pain. And they stood close together and watched the horizon.

And the thunder rang and the lightning flashed. But the light now was answered by another light, for in the East the flames of the dragon could now be seen, and a wide horizon of flame answered the darker one of cloud, and the two elements of fire and water glared at one another over the plain and threatened. The dragon lurched on, belching forth his fires, and Balarama still hopped back before the flame, waiting for a chance to strike, while behind them Agni still screamed and danced his joy among the melting sands.

And the thunder rang and the lightning flashed and the clouds now began to pile up on the horizon, bank on bank, like a great leafy wood or jungle in the steamy heats of Guinea, where tree towers over tree and all is green. The clouds stretched up almost to the summits of the sky, and they flickered and clashed with thunder and lighting. And Radha cried aloud 'O deep dark clouds, you are the body of my blue-limbed Krishna, and flashing lightning, you his golden chain. O now the peacocks cry and the swans look up from the lotus lake, and shake their heads to hear the coming rain. And clouds black as zebus, you are my Krishna's chariot, and he comes as a conquering King to the country, and from towers on black elephants rain down the flashing arrows. O now the cranes with their echoing call flying white against the dark-pelted clouds, they are the laughter of my Krishna as he comes. O pierce me with your arrows, my love, and come to me.'

And the thunder rang again and the fiends now leapt up alarmed, for it was loud now and deep and booming and they quaked for fear, and some of them more happy in the darkness winced with the lightning and covered up their eyes. But then turning away they saw the flames advancing and the dragon and they began to hope he was their rescue, and they streamed away from the village and towards the dragon's path.

And the thunder rang, and Nanda and Jasuda were delighted now the fiends were leaving the village. Nanda said 'Quick, let us try and wake our friends from their swoon,' and they went round tending to the cowfolk and seeking to restore them, but the cowfolk lay motionless and seemed to have no life in them. But Jasuda saw the flames and then thought of her son and said 'But what of Balarama amongst that fire? He must be near it, for we left him that way.' And they stood close together anxious again, and watched the other way where the flames advanced.

And the thunder rang and Radha cried 'Come then my lover in black clouds, for the clouds are my breast and my heart is within. Strike your thunder hammer, clash your shield, rout these fiends. Lightning is like a golden lamp carried in a storm through a ghostly palace. Hurl down your spears. The frogs are croaking in the marsh, the egrets cry, the peacocks spread their tails. Now is the time to rain your love on us. Drench my black hair and soak my breast with tears.'

And the thunder rang, and Balarama gave ground more and more as the dragon came on, and the monster with the cracking jaws and the raging throat loomed forward, filling the sky with his huge bulk, his leathery flanks like thunderclouds that mocked the other side. And now the fiends began to come towards him, rejoicing to see such a prince of demons, and Balarama found himself surrounded: the flame in a vast sheet before, the fiends in a black mass at his back. And he turned to fight the fiends, and dashed many a devil to the ground, opening up crevices to Hell. But the fiends thronged round him, and began to overpower him, and the burning fire of the dragon flashed onto his cheecks and singed the flesh. And Balarama was about to sink down before ever his brother could rescue him from his plight.

But high in the sky the clouds split open with a thunderclap, and revealed within were the hosts of the Maruts, and Krishna and Indra in the golden chariot, and a throng of gods above them laughing loud. And a blaze of golden light shot down and lit the countryside so that all the barren trees rejoiced in the cooling glow. But the fiends howled with amazement and fear, and looked up shielding their eyes. Then with a mighty roar that seemed to shake the whole earth and echo from the caves of the deep the Maruts, at a signal from the purple Krishna, flung down their spears, and rain poured on the earth.

Rain, the soft rain, the blessing of the gods, rolled in grey curtains from the sky, and shook its fragrant balm over all the parching ground. Like the grey-eyed nymph of dusk that sprinkles from her copper bowl the dew of slumber, and strokes with a sleepy branch the foreheads of the restless babe, so did the rain fall drumming on the soil. The air was cool, the breeze was perfumed, and earth gleamed now as in a winter frost.

And now the battle started, and Krishna and the Maruts poured down on the fiends with savage battle cries. There was a groaning and a howling and a grinding of broken limbs, and a thump of swords driven into spongy bodies. And there was blood and steam flying in the air, and demon arms and legs hacked off, and screaming heads shooting away in the wind. And with a thunder of the Maruts' horses' hooves, and a whistling of slicing scimitars, and a thump of clubs, the Maruts advanced, swinging their swords, piling the fiends in heaps, causing the blood to flow in channels in the ground.

Now did a Marut race his chariot up to a group of fiends that were like wolves howling together, and stuck them on his spear, one after another, so that they bayed together bleeding on the shaft. Now did a Marut fall on a goblin with a club and batter it to the pulpy sand. Now did a Marut charge with his scimitar a flying fiend, and as it launched cut it in two, so that its wings flew separate ways to the ground. And the Marut shouted 'Take not to the air, O flying fiend. Your place is under earth, boiling in the pits below.'

And Krishna and Indra were rattling in their chariot across the plain, slicing and tangling serpent-fiends in their chariot wheels. Krishna told Indra to spur the rosy horses to a crowd of fiends like hairy gorillas, threatening with tusks and stakes, and he fell on them with his flashing sword, and as he struck them blood shot like steam out of their heads, and Krishna and the chariot were splattered in gore.

And Krishna flew on, and there were vampires lunging towards him with their teeth foremost, and he jumped among them and smashed their teeth with his sword-hilt, and struck off their heads. He stood on their bodies and shouted 'Death to all devils that pollute the earth. Hellwards with hell-hounds. On then your Maruts, and drive the darkness before.' and the Maruts roared as Krishna raised his bloody sword, and shouted aloud their battle-cries. And the sound was like the angry sea that tosses up whales in one night on the beach, and crumbles the houses that stand on the cliffs.

But now running up in a group at Krishna's back came a body of fire-fiends, red as blood. They gleamed all over with oily heat, and had crusty horns sticking from their heads, and they whistled at Krishna like owls in the wood. And one ran up and clung on to Krishna's back, and shouted to his fellows to stab him in the belly, but Krishna leapt back against the chariot and crushed him. And he sprayed the others with sand and rocks, caught them by the horns and broke their necks.

But the dragon Vritra, suffering from the drenching rain, reared up on his hind legs and snapped at the clouds, and his body was like a sudden mountain that cast a gloom over all the land. And Krishna saw this and said 'Quickly Lord Indra, let us fly to the dragon and knock him down, or he will burn away the clouds with his fiery breath.' And Indra and Krishna rose up at once from the battle-ground, and rushed with their rosy stallions to the dragon in the sooty clouds, and they crashed the chariot against its face, and the dragon fell back. But as Vritra fell he tumbled onto the mountain in Braj, the very mountain from which he had stolen Vishnu's treasure so long ago, and falling on it he made it crack with a deafening thunder, and a split came in its sides so that all its caverns could be seen. And Vritra lurched away, and headed backwards towards the desert, where the rains had not yet come.

And the fiends were now being pushed back all over the plain. And they began to retreat to Mathura, and rushed howling towards the pit that led to Hell. And the fiends leapt down it in so great numbers that they choked it up, and others on top pushed their fellows down with poles to keep it clear.

And now Krishna fell on his enemies with redoubled force, and even Indra was amazed at his strength. Spattered with black blood and gobbets of flesh, Krishna was like the god of war, his hair all tangled and on end, his limbs stuck over with dust and sand, his sword flashing like the lightning that crashed above.

Rushing into a thick knot of fiends, Krishna leapt into the air and fell in their midst, and he was engulfed in the writhing mass of evil. Indra feared that he would suffocate, as other fiends leapt on to the heap to pummel him, but soon, as a great porpoise or feeding whale shoots up from the surf and shows his face in the foam, so Krishna reared out of the fiends and scattered them dead about him.

Then did Krishna run mad among the fleeing devils. He spun round on his heel like a top and sliced them with his scimitar, and as they ran upon him he sprayed the country round with their red entrails. And the storm above crashed on, and washed the ground of all the filth and gore, and the battle raged on on the ground and in the clouds.

But Agni who all this time had been dancing in the flames not knowing for very joy and madness what was happening in front, now saw the dragon coming towards him, and he shouted to it 'Back, Vritra, you come the wrong way. Back and burn Braj. This is the final stroke.' But the dragon loomed on and with his paw swept Agni away and made back into the desert. And Agni was enraged by what had happened, but just as he turned to follow Vritra he saw Indra and Krishna in the skies, and knew that he had powerful enemies now. And for a moment his heart quailed, and he stood apart, not wanting to be seen.

But Indra drove the chariot now in pursuit of Vritra, and overtook the lumbering beast, and landed on the sand. And Krishna hopped out onto the ground and stood in the dragon's way. They had come so far they were by the cave's mouth where the dragon lived, far in the red hills of Bihar. And they waited until the dragon came in sight.

And Indra said 'Now is the final test, Krishna, for your power over the demons, for this dragon Vritra even I did not slay in the days of old. He is a vaster fiend than any in earth's history; he is the final dragon that shall eat the world when time is done and we must all away. Strike him now, and drive him down to Hell, and the earth is sure of peace and happiness for ages longer than man's memory.'

And Krishna said 'I shall kill him, for it is time he is slain. When you Lord Indra battled with him, the earth was young, and man had not come so far. But now this final barrier is to be thrown down, and the world of spirit is to come at last.'

And Indra said 'Krishna, we have made up our quarrelling. Take then my mace to fight the dragon, for with this I summon the thunder-clouds.'

168

But Krishna said 'No, I have with me all that I shall need.'

And Indra gazed at him and frowned, for Krishna had no weapon at all about him.

And now Vritra came near, but stopped far off when he beheld the pair by the chariot, and Krishna saw that he was cowed. And Krishna felt pity for the dragon that lived by fire, for the time of fire was past, and so he screwed up his courage and ran swiftly towards the monster and the dragon ducked and winced as though he knew his end had come.

And Krishna shouted to the dragon 'Vritra, the time has come for you to die. Sleep shall you no more in your gloomy cave. The fires of Hell are yours. Under the ground then must you!'

When the dragon saw that it could do no more, it began to rear up, and it blew fire to burn up Krishna, with a hideous roaring. But as Vritra reared up he showed the soft skin underneath his neck, and Krishna swiftly took off from his wrist the bracelet of discernment and flung it like a discus at the dragon's neck. And the ring hit the dragon in the throat, and split it asunder so that flame shot out, and the channel to its belly was exposed. Then all the fire that was inside it exploded and shot up in a vast towering cloud to the sky, and pieces of the dragon after a long while began to rain with blood upon the desert, and soak into the sand. The silver ring lay upon the ground untouched, and the dragon was no more.

And Indra smiled when he had seen this, and said 'Had I known you had such power that day you lifted up the mountain in the land of Braj, I would not so angrily have flown back to heaven to set about your downfall. But wise enough are we all by hindsight. Give me your hand, my fellow great one.'

Krishna took the hand of the great god, and they went then to Vritra's abode and saw all the treasures that the dragon had been guarding. And when Krishna had found the mace he brought it out, and together they closed up the mouth of the cave so that the dragon's gold could sleep safe for all time. And they started back across the sandy desert.

But when they turned back they found their way opposed by the angry Agni, who flamed at them and said 'Vritra have you killed, O small blue cowherd. But you shall soon find a greater match.'

But Lord Indra spoke to him and said 'Hence, Agni, you have raised enough of Hell. No god shall fight a man, so go back. Or if you

will fight, then prepare to make with me your battle, for you and I
have been at secret enmity long enough.'

Agni replied 'And indeed I shall. You are an old god, Indra, and
swollen with pride. My fires shall soon lick your windy, puffed-up
strength.'

Then Indra seized his mace and held it aloft, and Agni made of
flame a fiery spear ready to throw, and the two gods faced each other
threateningly on the burning desert plain. And there had been done
sorry work that day, and heaven had been shaken by the combat of
its great ones, had not Yama looked up, even amid the confusion and
rout of Hell, and moved to forestall the battle. For he summoned to
him a messenger-devil, and dispatched it to earth with a stern word
to the gods, and the messenger flew upward and rushed between the
combatants.

And the messenger said 'Lord Indra, Lord Agni, my master Yama
bids you desist, and these are his words he bade me tell you. It is a
shame and a disgrace that gods should ever quarrel. He wills that you
cease at once, for he shall not abide by the outcome. Whichever of
you is killed, Yama and Hell will reject, for already are the regions
overflowing with the spurned, and devils choke every passage in the
gloomy caves and tunnels. It is fated that there shall be room left this
time for one mortal woman, a certain girl who has made a certain
pact, but for any other combatants, and especially those of the gods,
Yama will accept no more. He urges you both to return to the courts
of heaven and be reconciled, for enough mischief has been made on
earth by disorder among immortals. But this also he urges you, if you
are not willing to be satisfied: let each of you choose a champion, a
fighter from the men of this land, and let a tournament decide the
outcome of your quarrel.' So saying the messenger dived back into
the exploding earth, and left but a sulphury smell of his presence
behind.

Then did Indra nod his head and say 'What Yama proposes is just.
Let us indeed choose champions. I will have Krishna to fight for me.
Let you pick who you will.'

And Agni said 'Chanura the King's wrestler I choose, who has never
been defeated in the whole land of India. I am content to let these
two fight for us.'

And Krishna smiled at the two gods and said 'Strange is it how
we choose what is fated to happen. There is an old debt to be paid

170

between Kamsa, King of Mathura, and me, for long ago he urged me to a wrestling bout in a tournament with the very Chanura you have mentioned. In the webs and coils of time this tournament has been postponed, but now comes the season for the challenge to be renewed. For Kamsa lives still, who began all this evil, and still is this matter to be settled between us. Be content then gods, for your champions will fight, and good it is that heaven itself will anxiously watch the issue.'

And Lord Indra laughed, and said 'This will be a match well worth the viewing. I will rejoice the gods with news of the coming spectacle. Yet no doubt have I of the end.'

'Nor I either.' said Agni cunningly. 'Farewell till that day, for I'll return to heaven. I have a fancy there is a demon you have missed, somewhere in Mathura, stirring into life. I leave my affairs in the hands of a new man.' And Agni flew up in a column of fire to heaven.

Now Indra and Krishna looked at one another puzzled for a while, but then in the chariot they returned again to Braj, And they left the red hills of Bihar and returned again to the rains. The dark clouds and grey spears covered all the thirsty land, and the soil drank and drank, making a gurgling sound of pleasure. And Krishna met his parents and Balarama whom he had saved, and they embraced and wept to be reunited, and together they stood and gazed over the village and the land.

And where before all had been charred and burnt and choked with bodies, now it was all full of laughter and song, for the land was thronged with spirits that went about reviving the dead. And these were the fays of the forest which long ago Vritra had imprisoned in the mountain, and in this very battle on the day of his death, he had released them from their chambers by splitting the aged seams. In a pageant of green the nymphs went forth, tending to each creature and man, with cool palms soothing them and restoring their flown breath. And the trees had sap again and sprouted with joyful leaves.

And Lord Indra took Krishna aside to bid him farewell, and he said 'Krishna, henceforward we are ever friends. You are as mighty a warrior as any among the Aryans, since they came from the steppes where the wild grasses roll. See where my rainbow is shining above Braj. That shall be a sign of this new compact between us. All the gods shall attend on the heroes of mankind. And now farewell. Well have you fought, and the battles are done. Peace is yours to live in hence, and in this land now all things shall be well.'

And Krishna replied 'Thank you, O mighty King. With your troops this day have we made a great victory. I hope to maintain the record in the coming strife I go to. And Kamsa the tyrant, I feel, will also abide in the outcome. Though the country is sweetened and the devils are gone, yet the source of their advent remains in that tyrannical Raja. I shall not rest until he has also paid his due. The tournament shall settle all these things together. But farewell, my lord. We shall meet on earth no more. It is strange times when god and man campaign together. Now you return to your place in the heart of things.'

And Indra leapt into his chariot and cried 'Luck go with you Krishna. Farewell, indeed farewell.' And he flicked his whip over the glossy flanks of the rosy horses, and leaving a sparky trail he sped up into the clouds. Krishna watched him go, and the sun flashed on the gold sides of the car and it shone like a meteor against the darkness of the clouds. And all the war-torn landscape Indra blessed.

And Krishna now felt a great sadness in his heart, for he did not go at once to the cowfolk of the village, but strolled alone among the creepers of the jungle, and thought to himself of everything that had passed, saying 'Strife behind and struggle before. The lot of man is wearying and unsettled. What fights I have seen this day! What fierceness! From a seabed sickness to war with the hosts of Hell. A madness drove me forward into the heart of battle. And now must I go on to a further test, and take up a sterner strife, and grunt and tug against a wrestler of the King. Is there no peace extending in all time before me? These compacts and onslaughts, are they really to be mine? O Krishna, now I see again what I have always been. In these smoky hills, beside these idle waters, I have lazed a useless life away. I have pursued only pleasure, with mischief as my brand of strife. O happy days, but now farewell to them. The farce is now ended, and the laughter runs out. Now must I take up causes, and rest only in my soul. O where then is my Radha, my little one, my love? Where among these teeming hills is the bower she makes for me? Let me but taste her lips once more, before I go further forward. For men can only make what is already built in their heart.'

And searching for his love among the reedy beds and creeper-hidden groves, Krishna moved on through the rainy landscape, longing for the meeting in the enchanted wood.

PART VI

Rasmandala

Book Twenty-nine

Kamsa Plans Poison

And Kamsa sat still alone shut up in his room and the darkness, and would see no one, he was so overcome with fear. And there he listened to the howls and sounds of battle.

And the courtiers came and shouted at the door for him to hear 'Great King of Mathura, come out and rule your people, for the fiends you called up to punish the land of Braj have all been sent back to Hell by an army in the clouds.' But from the shut door of Kamsa's little dirty room there came not a sound, nor any reply.

And other courtiers came and shouted at the door 'King Kamsa, come out and tell us what to do, for the dragon Vritra has arisen and been killed, and two men there are in a flying chariot that have slaughtered every one of the devils.' But from the shut door of Kamsa's little dirty room there came not a sound, nor any reply.

And other courtiers came and shouted at the door 'King Kamsa, come out quickly and save us all, for Krishna is come back to the land of the cowherds.' And from the shut door of Kamsa's little dirty room there was a gasp of terror and a cry.

And the courtiers talked with one another, and wondered what they should do, but whatever they tried to arouse Kamsa from his fear failed to get from the shut door any kind of a reply.

But there was a demon called Drumalika, that all this while sat and watched the invasion of Braj from a forgotten part of the city, where he lived in a dried-up well. When he saw that all his fellow-demons were scourged from the land, Drumalika got up and went to the palace of King Kamsa. And he kicked in the door of Kamsa's little room and went in to him as he lay cowering from the light, blinking at the glare of the sudden day,

Drumalika said 'Kamsa, you coward, why do you shut yourself away from the light, and speak to no one? Is this the way to rule a kingdom you took such pains to gain? Rally your spirits, O miserable man. I am ashamed to see you so afraid.'

175

And Kamsa looked up at him and felt his courage beginning to return after this reproof, and he said 'Who are you?'

And Drumalika said 'That shall you know in but a little while. But first tell me why you cower in this way. What is it that has frightened you out of all shape of a man?'

And Kamsa trembled and said 'Krishna is come back. He has come in the blue sky. He will want to hurt me and kill me for the harm I have done.'

And Drumalika looked scornful and said 'Krishna? A puny little cowherd? And you are afraid of him, who are a King?'

And Kamsa said 'But Krishna is more than all this, I know it. He can kill fiends, and lift mountains, and fight with dragons of drought.'

And Drumalika said 'And cannot he be killed with a little prick of your dagger?'

And Kamsa said 'No. There is nothing that can harm him now.'

And Drumalika said 'Then you are a fool and know nothing about him. Listen while I tell you how he may be killed, for it is to give you this secret that I have come to your palace today, and it is with this secret that I shall show you who I truly am. O Kamsa, you are a fool to give way to fear. You do not even know what allies you have to help you, let alone the fatal weakness that is the death of your enemies. I would have come long ago, but all went well without me. Now though is the time to settle things for ever, so listen well Kamsa, and Krishna's secret will I tell.'

And Kamsa listened eagerly as Drumalika said 'It was your plan, was it not, to ask Krishna to a tournament, and have him killed by Chanura, your giant wrestler? Indeed you have already asked Krishna and he has accepted, and in two days' time is the day set aside for this contest. Well, have at it again. Continue with the tournament. Send out your messengers again to lure this Krishna, for he shall come to wrestle and to die.'

Then Kamsa began to look afraid again and said 'But how may Krishna be killed by Chanura the giant? Krishna can kill even dragons with his giant's strength.'

And Drumalika said 'Peace to your fears, and listen to words. In his youth was Krishna enchanted against all wounds on his flesh. Spells were said and magic done to make the whole of his body un-woundable by any steel or arrow, and part of the enchantment was to dip him in the Jumna, and everywhere the water went was proof

176

against all harm. Well, the magician that dipped him was a stupid fellow as all magicians are. When he plunged him under the water so that all that grew wet would be invulnerable, he held the baby by his little heel, the heel of his right foot. Now this heel therefore of his whole body was the part that never grew wet and took the spell, and so of all his body that is the place which will not turn a sword away. Stab his heel therefore with a poison dagger, and Krishna is a dead man, and you are rid of him.'

And Kamsa's eyes began to sparkle at this, but he was suspicious always of his well-wishers and said 'How may I know this to be true?'

And Drumalika said 'Because I say it is.'

And Kamsa sneered and said 'And who may you be that I should believe you?'

And Drumalika said 'Your father, Kamsa, though you never knew!' And he laughed at the expression of surprise on Kamsa's face, and said 'O mighty King, how long have you been duped! You thought you were the son of the Raj of Mathura, whom you captured and threw in prison so that you, his heir, could be our King, but all the time you were my son, and no heir at all to this wealthy land. I am a demon, Kamsa. I am a fiend of Hell, and you then have my blood, and carry out on earth Hell's wishes. I came upon your mother in the park, where she strolled unsuspecting among the beautiful flowers, and as I have the power to make myself in the likeness of any living thing, I took your father's shape and lay with your mother on the grassy lawns. And then I told her: "I am a demon, and your son born to me will rule the earth." Up then, you coward, and fulfil my prophecy. Sit here no longer mooning in the darkness. Send one to stab Krishna with poison on the heel, and be rid of your foe for ever, and rule earth in the name of the fiends.'

Kamsa dashed out of his room and into the court, and summoned the holy man to come to him that looked into the future. And the demon Drumalika followed him, wondering what he was about. And Kamsa turned to the demon, and said 'In one stroke I shall test your word. And if you lie, O dark man, you will be hanged alive until your tongue is as black as your heart.'

And when the holy man came, Kamsa turned to him and said 'A third time I have summoned you to look into the coming days. Tell me now at once, holy man, shall Krishna be killed by a man and by a wound? If so, what wound and in what place of his body?'

177

And the holy man said 'Krishna shall meet his end among the thronging men of Mathura, and by a little wound made in his heel.' And with that the holy man went away from the court.

And Kamsa cried out aloud with glee and said 'O dark man, you were right. Now I shall be a-scheming. Go then, and thank your fate I did not hang you this day. And for your story of my birth, be it true or false I care not a scrap. I muse not on what I am, for I alone am myself, and I shall make me emperor of the world. I have done all. I need no help. I need no father nor no mother either. I am but I. Get you gone then.' And he turned to his courtiers and said 'Stir yourselves, scum. Prepare the arena for a tournament, in two days time. Have all the guards ready to parade. Bring Chanura the wrestler to me. Fetch Akrura here. Be off! Be off!'

And Drumalika looked at him as he raged about and said 'You are indeed my son. There is no trace of gratitude at all in that black heart. I save your life and you spare me a hanging. On with your schemes then. But remember me.' And he turned and made his gloomy way down the long corridor and out once more to the city.

And now the palace was full of bustle. One moment it had been still and fearful, while Kamsa their ruler had been locked away. Now he was out again and all was busy and fearful, as the courtiers hurried here and there on his commands. And now after the fiends had quitted the streets and Kamsa had risen from his despair, the citizens of Mathura went again about their business, musing that everything could so quickly be the same again after all that had passed.

And Kamsa found in himself greater energy and vigour than ever, and felt that he could alone do everything, and need not even rely on his courtiers for advice, for they had only tricked him and disobeyed him in the past. He thought to himself 'I shall be me alone henceforth. I need no one, I have greater powers than other men, and can see things that they do not. Had not that fool that calls the spirits persuaded me to raise up the demons to overcome Braj, I would never have put myself to such trouble and shame. All this quandary is come through listening to others. Now I shall listen to no one.'

And so Kamsa sat again on his throne and scowled, and threatened the people around him whom he thought such treacherous fools, and he thought again busily to himself 'Krishna cannot be overcome by demons, that is true. I knew this all along, had not those stupid conjurers persuaded me otherwise. But Krishna can be overcome by other men. This must be a fact, because the holy man has said that I shall kill him with a poison knife in his heel. Should I do it myself perhaps, and get the glory? No, I do not wish to come near Krishna. In two days time I shall have the tournament, as I had planned at first. It was my idea, and the best plan yet. The cowfolk shall come to Mathura, and Krishna will fight my wrestler Chanura, and him shall I tell to stab him with a poison knife in his heel. O this is a masterly plan. Left to myself I can master all things.'

Then Kamsa looked down on his courtiers and roared 'Where is Chanura the wrestler? I told you to fetch him. You hounds, I'll hang you all.'

And Chanura was standing in front of Kamsa all the time and said 'Here I am, your majesty.'

And Kamsa said 'You come when I call, that is good. Now Chanura, come here and let me whisper in your ear.'

Chanura stepped up to the throne and Kamsa pressed into his hand a little knife in a sheath, and said 'In two days time, my friend, you are to wrestle in the arena with Krishna the cowherd. Take you this little knife of mine and wear it in your loincloth. Its point is dipped in the most deadly poison. When in the fight with Krishna you spy your chance, stab his right heel with this knife. His right heel alone is where he may be wounded. Stab him and leave the poison then to work. Do this, my friend, and I will have you chamberlain. Aye, and my harem too shall yield you a choice of girls.' And with that Kamsa slapped the wrestler on the back, and Chanura went off, roused with new dreams of power and lust.

And Akrura then came to the court, for he had left the cowfolk in Braj, and the soldiers with them, to come again to Kamsa to ask what should be done. But in his heart now he plotted against Kamsa and hoped with Krishna to overthrow him. And Akrura bowed low before his King.

And Kamsa said 'Akrura, in two days time the tournament shall come as I planned it. Krishna is there to wrestle with the great Chanura. See that all things are made ready. You also have a crafty mind: devise some scheme to get rid of this Krishna, and clear us of his mischief.' And Kamsa turned to his court and said 'You all know well what mischief Krishna causes. These demons, my friends, came but to fight with him.'

And Akrura said 'There is an elephant that no trainer has been able to tame. It is imprisoned in a vast cage in the barracks. Let us set that at Krishna when he comes.'

Kamsa smiled and said 'Well done, my friend. Arrange it.'

And Akrura said 'I shall, my King, and tomorrow shall I go again to Braj, and remind the cowfolk of the promise to come and wrestle before the King.' And Akrura left the court and went to his own house. He planned then to tell Krishna of the treachery he had devised, and warn him so that he would not be harmed. But for all that he did not know of the other plan where Chanura was to stab Krishna with a poison knife, for that was a secret between the King and Chanura alone. And Kamsa dreamed on in his palace of his wicked plots. His fear and despair had been forgotten, and the defeat of his fiends, and he longed again to bring Krishna to ruin by the tournament alone. And now night came and all the citizens went to rest, after a day of war and demons, and the moon came out and lit the city from a crystal sky.

Book Thirty

Radhakrishna

Radha meanwhile had not been able to come down from the tower, for at first there were fiends thronging in the courtyard, and then there were people again, as the citizens went once more about their tasks. But when the night was come, and the moon lit her way, she decided to go again to Braj and seek for her love, Krishna, so she climbed once more down the winding staircase of the tower, and came out on the courtyard below. And the courtyard was empty, and without being seen she was able to steal out of it into the streets of the town. The streets were silent and full of hovering moonlight and shadows, and although she went fearfully there was no one to call her to stop and ask her who she was. And soon she was journeying again over the plain towards Braj, which she had thought never more to see.

When Radha came again to the village she went to the little village shrine and paid respects to the village god and gave her thanks that she was allowed once more to come to Braj. And she stood in the village square and felt happy to be back home. But then she hurried on to Nanda's house, hoping that Krishna would be there.

And when Nanda and Jasuda and Balarama saw her they were overjoyed. They sprang up and gathered round her, and embraced her and wept. And Nanda said 'O my dear Radha, you are with us again after all your trials. When I saw you taken with your brother to Mathura I thought I should never set eyes on your face again, so cruel is the tyrant within those walls. But you are here, after all that has passed. How did you survive the fiends? How did you escape from your captors?'

And Radha said 'O father Nanda, the tale is too long to tell. My brother did not escape his captors, nor did he have my fortune. He is already gone to death and will not see us more. Him we must weep for, when there is better time. But tell me, Nanda, is Krishna with you? All I have suffered is forgotten if I can but meet my love once more.'

And Nanda said 'He is not here. Nor do any of us know what has

181

become of him. He came in thunder, riding on the clouds; he was our saviour and drove the fiends from our land. But since that time none of us have seen him more, and we do not know if he is safe or harmed.'

And Radha sighed and said 'O pray that he comes soon home. I have not long to wait. If I do not see him, then my fate will be bitter indeed.'

But Nanda said 'He will come back. Wait but a day or two. But now my child, come sit with us and eat, and let us talk of all the things that have happened to us since we last met.'

But Radha said 'O my dear Nanda, forgive me if I do not. There is such a load on my heart, I will go home and weep. For long days also I have not slept. My life has been all turmoil with little time for slumber. Let me go now, and in the morning will I visit you and tell you all.'

And Radha left them, and went back across the square to her own house. It looked ghostly in the moonlight, and she wept to think her brother was no more here to look after the home that she too must leave in but three days. She pushed open the door and went inside, and walked through all the echoing rooms, thinking of Krishna and wondering what had become of him.

And Radha came to her room and sat down on her bed and looked out on the trees outside, past the curtain that stirred in the fragrant breeze, and her favourite creeper, the lady of the night, dangled over the window and let its perfume come to her. And it was so still that Radha seemed to see in the blue moonlight pictures of Krishna in the trunk of a tree or the glittering of lilies or the musing lotuses on the pond. But then she heard thunder, as another storm came on, and sank back on her bed to watch the rain come down. But then amid the rumbling of the thunder she heard another sound, a fluting coming from the depths of the forest, and she knew it was Krishna's flute.

Out then into the rain she flew, and ran out of the village towards the jungle. And without fearing the snakes or the bangs of the thunder she ran by the palms of the Jumna in the grey rains of Himalaya towards her love. The anklets on her mud-spattered ankles jangled in the woodland, and she ran on, following the silvery fluting among the stormy trees and climbed up the hillside of the mountain. And she found she was being led by the sound to the

182

enchanted lake where Krishna and she had strolled on the night when she refused to swim out with him to the island and live with him there, forgetting all the cowfolk. And soon she came to the lake and saw the moonlight playing on its misty waters, and the rain had stopped, and dripped from honeyed flowers.

But although she looked all round the lake, and though she still could hear the fluting nearer than ever before, Radha could not see Krishna anywhere among the trees, and she sat down puzzled and perplexed. Yet the fluting sang on over the smoking waters, and the sound was full of melancholy and love-longing, as though the forest itself yearned for a lover's arms. And Radha gazed out to the island, remembering it well, and wished that she had gone with him to that place, that enchanted spot, and left the world to go on alone into whatever grim-faced fate awaited. At that moment she saw Krishna on the island, playing his flute among the branches of a tree, and Radha leapt up and called with all her heart 'Krishna!' And all the hills around the lake echoed with 'Krishna, Krishna' like the voices of a thousand nymphs.

Krishna looked up when he heard his name, and saw Radha on the bank and cried out 'Radha!' and leapt down from the tree. And he dived into the water, and throwing up the moonlit spray he struck out towards the bank. All the woods and hills that were echoing still with Radha's call of 'Krishna' now echoed with Krishna's call of 'Radha,' so that each tree and rock seemed to cry together 'Radha, Krishna, Radha, Krishna,' as though the very stars were singing the tune. And Krishna swam to the weedy shore, and Radha waded into the water, and in a splash of spray they met and embraced and clung together, soaked with lake and rain. And they fell back upon the flowery bank and kissed warm kisses from their watery lips.

And Krishna strained her in his arms and kissed her lips and kissed her eyes and kissed her cheeks and hair and ears and throat and breasts and cried 'Radha, my darling, deep-hearted Radha, my soul, my love. I heard you call me from the depths of the ocean. My heart was struck with love and I was helpless, yearning for you on the very bottom of the sea, and you called me forth, and all my wars I made for you, merely to win you back again. O my love, never leave me more, O my heart's joy, my life, my self.'

And Radha lay back in Krishna's arms, her eyes swimming with salty tears, and seemed to sink into all comforts to be again in his arms, and to be near to swooning with her bliss. She could hardly speak, but only said 'O Krishna, how I have missed you!' And she began to sob and weep, and clung to him as if she were a baby that someone had tried to prise from its mother's arms, and she wrapped her arms round and round his warm blue neck and would not let him go.

And Krishna kissed her and cried 'Radha, you are my world. Your arms are my own body. Your name is my very soul. All the yearning of the world that stretches up its hands to the stormclouds when summer has burnt the fields is mine for you. All men's fond hopes, all comfort, you are all. O my dear love, what bliss it is to kiss again these lips. My soul is on my lips when I kiss yours. Those dear, dear eyes. That silver brow. Those little snakes, your eyebrows. O your sweet fingers, that taste like sugarcane. Your deep black hair.' But as Krishna was singing this song he saw that Radha with her head on his smooth shoulder had fallen fast asleep. Krishna laughed and kissed her sleeping eyes and wound his arms tight about her and lay still. And he sighed and dreamed of all sweet things, as they lay together on the bank of the moonlit lake.

Krishna would not move or speak for fear of waking her, and the moon went round the sky, peering at them through the trees. And another storm came on and rattled its thunder and poured down on them its cooling rain, while Krishna shielded Radha's sweet face from the rain. Still he did not wake her from her sleep, but thought 'O to be this for ever. Set as a tree in one lovely place, our legs entwined and sunk like roots into the water, and branchy arms twisting around each other, and blossomy lips like red ashokas blowing, just touching with their fragrant petals and soft. O let the world spin round and seasons come and go, this is my paradise, my luscious heaven.'

But then Radha awoke and stirred, and she laughed at having been asleep and said 'Forgive me, Krishna. I am so at home. Your arms are like a bed to me of smooth blue sheets.' And she smiled and kissed him.

And he said 'You have been taxed and troubled. The fiends have plagued you. Was it a hard time in the village while I was away?'

Radha looked at him a while, and saw that he did not seem to remember her trial before the villagers, when Krishna disappeared from the hut, and he knew nothing of her time in Mathura. And so

184

she said 'It was a hard time, but now you are back, we can easily forget all our troubles.'

And Krishna smiled and kissed her and said 'My love.' And then he looked at her, and leant up on his elbow and said 'Radha, I think you love me.'

And Radha lifted her hands up to his face and cradled it, and said 'O my dear darling, you are my soul. I would die this instant if you wished. Kill me. I should not blench.' She tried to say more, but she could not, and the tears trickled down out of the side of her eyes.

And Krishna said 'Come then, let us waste no more time. Let us swim out now to the enchanted island, and there live in peace together always. For on that island is eternity, and once we set foot on it, we are there for ever. O come, my love. Eternity waits. Let's leave this fractured, fragile world, and gain true bliss. It is but a short way. Look, across that water.'

But Radha turned aside and felt her heart grow cold, for she remembered now her promise to Yama, King of the Dead, that in three days she would return to him and drown herself in the waves of Mother Ganges. It was a solemn oath, through which she was now here, without which Krishna would never have seen her again, Krishna who now loved her so much. She longed to go with him and yet she could not. So she turned back and shook her head.

And Krishna said 'What? Why not? Radha? What is it?'

Radha said 'I cannot come, my love. Don't ask me why. Again, all my heart longs to be with you in that enchanted place, all my soul wants nothing more than to be always with you in such a spot on earth, but it cannot be. It cannot ever be.' And she began to weep.

But Krishna was perplexed and sad and cried 'Why is it you cannot come? Do you not then love me? Have I been untrue to you?'

And Radha's eyes at once fell on the lotus in his hair. And this was the lotus which the goddess in Lord Kubera's court had given him, when Radha saw it all in a vision in Hell. And she said at once 'Where did you get this lotus?' For she did not want to speak of Yama, and wished to keep it a secret that she had to leave him in three days.

Krishna touched the lotus and said 'I found it in the lake, I think.' For he did not want to get into an argument.

And Radha jumped up and said 'No, Krishna, you were given it by a goddess in Kubera's court. I know it all. You have always been

185

unfaithful to me, and teased me in front of the other girls, and arranged to meet them to dance with them in the forest. Now you have been dallying with a goddess, and I see you do not care for me at all. Come then, what's the use in sitting here, for look, the dawn has already begun to break, and the villagers will be looking for us soon.'

And Radha began to walk off to the crest of the hill, ready to go again down to the village. But Krishna ran after her and said 'Radha, what do you mean? You love me. You know I love only you. No one in the whole world do I love but you. How can you suspect me? O Radha, do not leave me now. I cannot bear it. Come back. Come back.'

And like a child that runs behind its mother, whining to be picked up and carried, Krishna followed Radha all the way down again from the mountain, and as it became light they came at last once more to the village in Braj. And still with Krishna protesting they walked again into the village square and towards Radha's house. But when the girls of the village saw Krishna they flocked towards him, crying 'Krishna, you are back. Now it is time to dance with us in the forest as you promised. O dance with us tonight.' And Radha heard their cries and turned and looked scornfully at Krishna, and went into her house, silent. And Krishna for very sorrow sat down upon the ground, and all the girls thought he wanted to talk with them, and sat round in a big troop talking and asking him of his adventures, for they had all forgiven him now that they had seen him in the clouds, and wanted to be his paramour like Radha, and perhaps become a goddess. And Radha returned to her room and sat down and sighed, for she knew not what to do.

Book Thirty-one

Krishna Takes the Challenge

When dawn with her rosy fingers had lit the streets of Mathura, all was bustle in preparation for the tournament. King Kamsa had announced to the whole town that the tournament was to be held as planned, and that this day now come was to be devoted to decking the streets and the arena for a great festival. The damage done by the fiends was quickly cleared, and everyone set about making the city spruce. The soldiers practised their marches for the parade in the arena, and the mad elephant was starved so that he would be ready to eat Krishna. Meanwhile Chanura the wrestler practised his throws, and the great bow of Shiva was set up by the city gate as a sign the festival was come – for there was a legend that whoever might bend that bow would become ruler of Mathura.

Akrura too went to Kamsa and said 'My King, I shall go now to the people of Braj and remind Krishna of his promise to fight the wrestler before the King. And to make doubly sure we have them in our power I shall bring them to the city gates this very day, and they may camp outside the walls, so that when the morning comes they may be ready.'

And King Kamsa said 'Be off then, and bring them here.'

And so Akrura went his way to Braj in a great chariot, and he crossed the plain and came to the village square. And the cowfolk seeing him coming a long way off were waiting for him, and Krishna was still in the square, sitting on the ground, surrounded by all the girls of the village.

And Akrura said 'Hail, O people of Braj, I come from King Kamsa and I am to remind you of your promise that you would come to the tournament in Mathura and that Krishna will wrestle before the King. The tournament is to be held tomorrow, and I ask you now to come with me to the city, and camp outside its walls in preparation for that great day.'

The cowfolk cried 'We will, we will,' and they wanted to run off at once and put on their best clothes and go to Mathura.

187

And Akrura said 'Krishna, are you ready to come and fight?'

And Krishna looked up from among the girls and sighed and said 'I cannot fight with anyone. My heart is aching with such pain I cannot move.'

And then Nanda came forward and said to Akrura 'Noble sir, my son is tired after his great battle with the demons. Were it not for him our whole land would be gone and sunk in flame, and Mathura too and your tyrant King. But now in any case we must think before we answer King Kamsa's request, for he has not proved a friend in the past. He sent soldiers into our peaceful land, soldiers at first that ruled us, but now are with us. He called up demons in his city and sent them to us, which plagued us and killed our children and burned our homes and took our lives, and were it not for my son coming from the ends of earth to be our rescue, none of us had been living, nor anything here but ashes. How can you expect us then to trust this monster Kamsa?'

And Akrura's eyes flashed with joy and he said 'Great Nanda, you are right. Don't trust the tyrant. Treat him with suspicion. But noble sir, this man has ruled our land enough. His time is come and he must be flung down to Hell which is his proper home. Krishna, dear hero, listen to my words. I am a servant of King Kamsa and have been his highest councillor, but all his deeds have grown so gross, and challenge the very peace of earth and heaven, that I can no longer brook his evil ways, and am determined to turn traitor against him. When I saw the fiends he sent, mangling your children on this plain, then my heart turned against him, and I knew of better things than rule and will and conquest. Krishna, he plans some treachery against you tomorrow in the city. By the gate there is an elephant, mad and untameable, fenced in a mighty cage. When you enter the gates it is planned to loose it at you and bring about your death. Be armed then, Krishna, against that attack. I have told you of it that you may be prepared, and overcome the tusker with your mace. Kill it, and on then to the games, and after you have beaten the wrestler, as I am sure you will, then you may fight with Kamsa and kill him, and rid our land for ever from the tyrant.'

The cowherds, who had been listening eagerly to all this, cheered lustily and cried 'Down with Kamsa! Down with the tyrant!' And Akrura blushed with righteous joy in what he had done, and turned to Krishna and said 'Come then, and let us be about it.'

188

But Krishna sat still among the girls and sadly shook his head, and said 'My strength is gone. I cannot fight with anyone.'

And Nanda turned to him and said 'What is it, Krishna? What can it be that saps your strength?'

And Krishna turned his eyes to the house of Radha and sighed. And then he looked to the ground, as though ashamed, and blushed and said 'Radha is angry with me, because I took a flower from a goddess in Lord Kubera's court.' And then he pulled a face, as though he was about to cry.

And Nanda rolled up his eyes to heaven, as if to say 'What a son I have! He routs all the fiends of Hell and now sits sulking like a little girl.' And then he said aloud 'I will go in and see her.' And Nanda turned to Akrura and smiled as though it was nothing, and said 'My son is a little weary. It will be but a minute.' And he went into the house and stayed a while and then came out and beckoned Krishna to come. And Krishna leapt up and went into the house, while all the girls protested and murmured jealously among themselves.

Radha was sitting sighing on her bed, gazing out on the trees among the garden, and it began to rain again and the rain rustled among the leaves. And Nanda came in and said 'Here is a man to see you.' And he pulled in Krishna, who was hesitating in the corridor outside, afraid to go in, and went away and left them together. All the people had begun to scatter because of the rain, and Nanda took Akrura to his own house, and told him all would be well if he waited a while. But the girls were still jealous and went murmuring to their homes.

Krishna sat a little way off from Radha and looked out of the window also, and the rain fell down over the mango trees and dashed the jasmine, bruising from its yellow petals a fresh perfume, and the distant woods looked blue and cloudy in the rain. And Radha and Krishna both sighed and were silent. He was thinking of all the times he had dallied with other girls in the past, forgetting Radha in the moment's heat, and he was ashamed of neglecting her who now was his only love. And Radha was thinking of how she had promised Yama to go back to Hell, and greater than her own sorrow was the sorrow she would bring to Krishna by leaving him, for she saw now that he loved her more and more.

And Krishna said 'O Radha, will you never forgive me for all my naughtiness? These girls bewitch me all, so that I forget even myself.

189

But now all is changed, for you are in my heart always and can never be forgotten. I want only you to be my true love. There is no one but you. O Radha let me throw this lotus away that was given me by the goddess, for though it is a gift from heaven I would rather lose heaven's help than your love. O my sweet, let me tear it apart.'

And he took the lotus, which was the lotus of love, given by Vishnu to man so many years ago, and went to tear it. But Radha put out her hand and touched his wrist and stayed him and said 'That is the lotus of our love. I know it well. There is but one in the whole world, and yet all lovers have it, for all love is the same. O my dear Krishna, guard it well in the days to come, and with that lotus remember me. I am not angry for your dalliance with the goddess. A man is honoured by such favours. Let us forget our quarrel and be friends again.'

And Krishna was so overjoyed he took her in his arms and hugged and kissed her, but she stopped him after a while and said 'You must go now. There are many waiting for your answer. Go and fight the wrestler in the city of Mathura, for that is your destiny which called you even before the soldiers came and we were put apart. Go then, and be strong now, for my sake.'

And Krishna got up and said 'For your sake I killed the fiends. For your sake shall I mangle that Chanura.' And he laughed happily. And then he knelt down beside her and said 'But tonight, when the moon is shining, let me call you again into the forest with my flute. O my darling, come to me then, and let us play as in the old days in the echoing woods.'

Then Radha's eyes filled with tears and she said 'I will my sweetest Krishna, my heart's darling. But tonight let us not go into the hillside, but let us play by the water of Mother Jumna, on the sands and among the reeds. There we shall be happy by that winding stream.'

And Krishna smiled and said 'If you wish, my love. There is a whole world now for us to play in, and all the coming years to be together, and we shall grow old, you and I, playing among the bounties of these woods and hills. Wait on my flute then, and then fly to me.'

And with that he kissed her lovingly and went. And Radha turned aside, and the tears from her eyes dampened the patterned coverlet of her bed, for she had told him to meet her by the Jumna so that she would not be tempted to go again to the enchanted island and neglect her promise. She wept for her fate and said 'O my sweet Krishna, how shall I bear to leave you? This night shall be our last night together, and we shall never dance again in the moonlight until the end of the world. This night must I bid you an eternal farewell, and be parted for ever from your loving arms. O bitter smile of fate, to mix our sadness with such sweetness. O let me die then in his arms, and know no more of this harsh, turning world.' And she stayed alone in her room, forgotten now by everyone, and was overcome with sorrow for all things.

But Krishna went skipping along to Nanda's house in the rain, kicking up the puddles and whistling, and he was roaring to fight Chanura for Radha's sake. And he went into the house and said to Akrura 'Come on, idle sir, let us be off to Mathura. We must not sit here chatting.' And so they jumped up and prepared themselves.

And after a while the rain had stopped, and the whole village was ready to march to Mathura. They gathered together in the village square, with all the carts they could find, loaded up with tents and dishes and firewood and chapatis. And there was a great babble of voices and barking of dogs and squealing of excited children.

But the girls who had sat with Krishna were all sulking because he had refused to dance with them and neglected them all for Radha. They refused to go to Mathura, and all stayed in their houses moping.

But then Nanda and Jasuda came out and Nanda gave the word to start and all the procession of villagers and carts and dogs made off over the plain. Akrura was in the lead in his chariot and with him were Krishna and his brother Balarama, a little red from the dragon's breath, and swigging wine from a bottle and singing. And the procession moved off and it was like a parade in a carnival, when everyone wears gay clothes and throws flowers at each other and there is a blowing of bugles and a clatter of horses' hooves.

When they came to Mathura they pitched camp, and all outside the red sandstone walls in a little village the tents went up and fires were lit and important villagers went up and down shouting and giving orders. And the tents were striped with red and yellow and looked gay inside and out, and on the floors were laid carpets of deep blood-red and mattresses for beds, all coloured round with peacocks and wishing-trees, and the bronze and copper bowls glinted in the kitchens.

191

And after they had all pitched camp, Krishna and Balarama decided to go for a walk round the town and see the city and its markets. A great gang of cowfolk went with them, and children too, and a few dogs. And as they entered the city news spread quickly that the handsome hero Krishna was parading in the streets, and women from all over the town ran to see him, and threw flowers and palm-leaves at his feet. They came running to the balconies and leaned over the balustrades, and they waved their scarves and handkerchiefs. And all in their hearts were joyful and hoped that Krishna would do such deeds in their town that Kamsa might be killed and the city released at last from its oppression. And they cheered him lustily, for all their hopes and hearts were with him.

And a gardener came up to Krishna in the street and took him into his house and showed him all the flowers that he had arranged in bowls of water, and he gave Krishna and the cowherds garlands of flowers around their necks and in their hair. And Krishna had a great garland of pink and orange marigolds and hibiscus, and it glowed around his smooth-skinned neck and was reflected in his azure chest.

And as they went in the streets a clothes-seller gave the cowherds all her clothes, and they were all fresh back from the Jumna and drying on her banks. The cowherd children tried to put them on, but they had never seen such courtly garments, such rich tunics of green brocade and trousers of shot silk, and they put the tunics on their legs and the trousers over their arms, and ran about and fell over in the flowing raiment.

After walking in the town and smiling at all the people, and after seeing the great temples and the markets and the rich houses with glossy floors and honeycomb windows, and after walking in the busy streets among the beggars and the cows and the ladies in saris and the priests in orange robes, they all turned and went back towards the gate.

And as they neared the gate a little hunchback girl called Kubja came forward and bowed to Krishna, so that her hump was where her head was. And she said to him 'Krishna, beloved hero, you are so kind. Take this perfumed ointment and let me rub it on your limbs, for it is very precious, and I have made it for King Kamsa, whose servant I am. But you are a greater King than he, and out of love for you I wish to give it.'

192

And Krishna smiled and said 'Come then, rub a dub! Let me be perfumed like a bank of musk and lilies.'

And the little hunchback girl's face broke out in such a smile that she could not stop herself laughing at what he had said, and tears ran down her cheeks as she tried to keep herself serious. Krishna jumped down on his haunches as though he were going to wrestle with her, and she rubbed the perfumed oil all over his chest and blue shoulders. And Krishna stood up, and his heart went out in pity to the little hunchback girl who had felt such love for him. She looked up at him, smiling, and he put his hand under her chin to lift up her face to kiss it, and with his other hand gently he straightened her back, and she was whole. And the people all round fell silent and still, for they saw that he had performed a miracle.

And then they went on and came to the gate, and Krishna saw the great bow of Shiva, and asked what it was, and the townsfolk told him that it was Shiva's bow and no man could bend it, only he who was to be the greatest King of Mathura. And Krishna leapt towards it and tore it down, and pulled the bow back so that the string was by his ear, and the bow snapped with such a deafening sound that it seemed the whole town had been split in two. And when the people saw what he had done they cheered, and quickly as fire the rumour went round that Krishna had snapped the bow of Shiva, and was destined to become King. And all the citizens were on fire with eagerness for the morrow, and hoped above hope that Krishna would be their saviour.

And the cowfolk went back to their tents, and the dusky evening fell, and in the blue twilight they lit their fires and cooked their suppers of rice and dal. The camp was quiet as the cowherds ate, and the moon came out above them and shone like silver over the whole plain, and the mists began to gather and hug the ground. And so they went to their warm beds, and each one dreamed of what the morrow would bring.

Book Thirty-two

Radha's Dilemma

When all in the cowherd's camp by the tall walls of Mathura were asleep, Krishna crept out of his tent, where he slept with his brother Balarama, and made his way across the plain towards the village in Braj. And all the girls who had stayed behind in the village because Krishna would not dance with them were sulking still, and they did not sleep. They stayed in their houses looking out on the moonlit night and gazing at Radha's house, for they were jealous of her, and did not want her to leave her house and go into the woods to find Krishna.

And Krishna passed by the far end of the village, and he wore his gaudy clothes that he had put on for the trip round Mathura: orange trousers of muslin speckled with flowers, and a great scarf of silk wrapped round his shoulders, and a spangled crown with a peacock feather. He carried with him his flute to summon Radha, and went towards the green lawns by the riverside, for this was where she had told him to call her. But one of the girls saw him, and she stole silently out of her house to follow him. And another girl saw her steal away, and she too stole away to see what was afoot. One by one all the girls in the village left their houses in the moonlight and went in a silent troop towards the river, and the word went round that Krishna had gone that way.

Radha meanwhile waited in her room, lost in the sorrow of her thoughts, and she was in torment, and spoke to herself and said 'Shall I ever bear to leave him? How can I tear apart what we have become? O wretched promise! Shall I then neglect my oath to Yama, King of the Dead, and live on with Krishna here in Braj? It is in my power to go back or to stay here. O sweet here, where Krishna is! How can I go to Hell and death where Krishna is not – an eternity of absence from those arms, an endless time of grief as all the happy days I've spent become my torturers? Better never to have met my darling. O death, I cannot come to you. I live, I breathe, I love. Must this love end? I shall go to the island with Krishna and once we are on its flowery

194

shores all shall be well. O Krishna, let us fly there now. Why does your flute not call me? O Krishna, come.'

But as she sprang up and paced about the room, holding her hands against her aching heart, she suddenly despaired and sat down again on the floor and said 'I cannot avoid death. What is it to cringe away from his embrace? We run one way to find him in another place: like the man that met the god of death in the market place, and saw him amazed with surprise, and ran away all day to another city, and there was death awaiting him, surprised only in the morning that he was so far away from his appointed place of meeting, and his death-hour so near. O Yama, I will come. You kept your promise. When it is time, then it is time. Shut the door when the sun has set, and bring in the chairs before the night. O my soul, take the last sweetness of this night, for it is to last a long, long time. O Krishna, come call me now with your flute.'

But Krishna did not have a chance to begin playing his melodies on his pipe, for the village girls caught up with him as he strolled along the strand. He was just about to put the flute to his mouth and call Radha to him when he saw among the palmtrees and flowering bushes of the bankside the girls shyly gazing at him, the moonlight glinting in their hair.

And Krishna said 'What's this? Naughty girls walking in the woods at moonlight? What would your brothers or fathers say if they heard of this? Off you go back to the village and go to sleep. You never know what might happen if you walk about in moonlight.'

But the girls were all shy and moody with him for talking to them like that. They pouted their lips, and twisted their hair, and drew patterns on the sand with their toes.

And Krishna said 'Go on, run off home. Or the wild beasts of the jungle, coming to the river to drink, shall eat you up.'

And one of them said 'Why are you so unkind to us? We don't want to go home. We want to be with you. And you promised us you would dance with us in the autumn, when you stole our clothes that day on this very river bank. The autumn is come, and you should keep your promise.'

And the other girls cried out 'Yes. Please dance with us. You said you would.'

And Krishna sighed and said 'You are silly creatures. Do you not fear what I might do to you? Dancing in the moonlight with a pack

195

of lovely girls, why I should jump on you all and crush you in my arms like demons and ravish you, and you would be lost and thrown out of the village.'

And one of the girls said 'But we all love you. We don't mind what you do to us, so long as you love us as we love you.'

Krishna's heart was stirred with pity for them, and he said 'And do you all love me? And have you loved me long?'

And they all cried 'O yes. We have all loved you, ever since you stole our clothes and gave us kisses. Please dance with us, Krishna. We played together when we were little, why can we not play now?'

And Krishna smiled and said 'I will play my flute and you can dance.' And at once he started playing, and the melody of his flute floated out over the waters of the Jumna and pierced the gloomy trees of the forest and echoed from the rocks and hills.

At first the girls were shy and would not dance, but as the music warbled on it struck their souls with its plaintive swoops and trills, until they could keep still no longer and began to move to the rhythm in a dance round Krishna. And as they grew more impassioned by the music they became as if drunk, and came to Krishna and tried to pull him into the bushes with them. They kissed him, brushing his blue cheeks as they filled with air to blow the pipe, and they planted kisses beneath his ear where his gold ear-rings shone, and his hair bristled with pleasure at the touch. And soon they were all thronging him so much that he laughed and broke off playing. And they played with him and kissed him and all rolled in a heap on the Jumna bank, laughing and crying out with pleasure.

And one girl began to think that Krishna was her own, and she pushed off the others and asked him to braid her hair, and while he was behind her twisting her tresses she gazed at him in a mirror so that she would not miss the sight of him. But when she told Krishna to send the other girls away, another girl came and asked if she could massage his feet, and Krishna let her and lay back on the flowery bank. But then another girl came and kissed him and asked if she could wear his ear-rings made of gold, but as soon as she had done this the girl massaging Krishna's feet hit her, and they started to fight. And soon all the girls were squabbling amongst themselves about who should have Krishna, and Krishna laughed to see them all fighting. But then to stop them tearing out each other's hair he strolled to a grassy lawn and played his flute again, and soon all the

196

girls had stopped fighting and were dancing once more to the sounds of his pipe.

Radha meanwhile was overjoyed to hear Krishna's flute far away in the woodland, and at once she sprang up and rushed out of the house. She followed the sound to the river, and then ran with jingling anklets along the grey shores of the Jumna. And she thought as she ran 'This meeting will make up for all. This shall be our night of play. With cheerful hearts we shall love this night, and forget all about the ugly future days. Oh my heart is merry already with the thought. O Krishna, I come. Shall I play a trick on him to start us in a jolly mood? Shall I growl and pretend to be a tiger? Or jump on him like a panther? Oh let us laugh this night along, and keep the stars twangling like musicians at our happy banquet.'

And with these words she came to the place where Krishna was, and she burst through a covert and saw him before her, fluting for the cowherd girls, and winking at them, and shaking his head. They thronged all round him, tugging his clothes, and Radha saw them undressing him, and soon he had nothing on but his orange loincloth, and they all kissed his arms and chest and hung on to him.

And Radha's hands dropped to her side, and tears came into her bright eyes, and she turned away and walked into the forest. And Radha said 'Well, here's an end of all our loving. And now farewell to all our happy days. O Krishna, will you ever be the same? Not faithful even one short space of a day? This is the last night I shall see you on earth, and here it is gone, lost to your pranks.'

And sadly as she walked the clouds covered the peaceful face of the moon, and the forest grew dark around her. She walked on and came at last to the enchanted lake and sat down on the banks, and the rain dappled the grey lake with a million rings.

But Krishna had seen Radha come forward from the trees and watch his dancing, and at once his breath failed so that he could not play his flute. But the village girls were so drunken with dalliance that they did not notice, and danced on. And Krishna ran after Radha, calling for her in the forest.

And as he ran he cried out 'Radha, come back, come back. My love, come back. Forgive me, Radha. Which way did you go?' But in the darkness when the clouds came on, he could not see her tracks, and did not know his way. And as he ran he cursed himself and said 'O Krishna, why ever the fool? O, what I have lost! I have missed all through my silly pranks. O Radha, she will hate me surely, and surely I deserve it. Why am I such a fool?'

The storm came on and shot the woodland full of lightning, so that the tree-trunks seemed to jump at Krishna. The bears and tigers went back to their caves, and the snakes slid down from overhanging branches. And Krishna ran, bellowing 'Radha! Radha!' like a mad elephant that crashes through the palms, and the forest echoed his cries as if mocking him.

And at last Krishna came to the crest of the hill, and he saw the lake below him, where he had lain with Radha on the bank. The sight of it was like a shining scimitar passing through his heart, and he cried out aloud 'Lo! our lake! She's gone and never more will tread these shores with me, and lie and smile under the moon. I have betrayed her. I have cast her off. O shame! O fool! O Radha, my love, my love!' And Krishna sat down on the bank, his chin upon his fists, and the big tears dropped down and splashed the flowers beneath.

But Radha heard him, sitting not far away, and it was deep love to hear him weep for her, for lovers often feed on one another's tears. And she walked to him through the rushes at the lakeside and the tufty moss, and stealing behind him she put her hands over his eyes, as if he were to guess who was behind him, and her soft palms grew wet with his tears.

And Krishna knew at once whose touch it was, and his weeping was stilled. He took her hands forward from his face and kissed them. And he twisted around to her kneeling behind him, and they kissed. And the rain stopped as their lips touched, and all things became still, and it seemed that the stars themselves ceased wheeling in the sky, and hung in silence over the perfumed earth.

And Krishna said 'O my love, my love, O never leave me more! To part from you is to tear my heart away. I cannot say how deeply I love you. Words do not reach into such depths. But in that ocean there is endless bliss. O my soul, your lips are paradise. I am your slave, kill me or beat me, treat me how you will, but every atom of my dust shall love you, even my ashes: touch them with your foot and they shall flower. O, kiss me, sweet. O smother me with kisses.'

And they lay back on the wet leaves and the tangled petals of milky gardenias and rich flags, and round their forms, borne on the wind like the spiced sails of argosies ferrying their Eastern riches to

Byzantium, the fragrance of mock-orange-blossom stole.

And Radha's swelling lips he kissed, and she fell sighing, and their love warmed like amber and grew strong. But Krishna stood up and pulled her gently by the wrist, and with a shudder from his mounting love said 'Come, let us swim out into the lake, and take our pleasures on the enchanted island. For there are bowers and little palaces and beds. Come, let us go now.'

And leaning backwards he pulled Radha up, and led her to tread in the cool water, and they looked towards the island where there were rose-trees blowing, azaleas all golden, and creepers' russet-flames, and there was a little pavilion there of white marble.

But Radha stopped and said 'Krishna, I cannot,' and she could say no more.

And Krishna knew nothing of her reasons for saying this, but joked and said 'What, cannot swim? Come on. Jump in the water.'

And Radha stood still and silent, caught again in the trap she thought to avoid, for had she gone with Krishna to the Jumna's side she never should have been tempted again with crossing to the enchanted island. But fate had led her once more to the turning of the ways, and all happy things lay before her, and yet she could not go.

But Krishna darted about, ignorant of all this and merry, and gathered lotuses for her from the lake, blue and deep purple lotuses on snaky stems, and some with centres like a golden crown, rusting with pollen. And he came back and heaped them in her arms. And when he saw her still silent he thought to cheer her, and splashed her with water, which sprayed up in the moonlight like a sea-mist, or storms among the icebergs of green snow. And he said 'Come, play. So solemn! Come, let's play hide-and-seek.' And with that he at once ran off, and disappeared from sight.

And Radha shut her eyes and said 'In Hell itself have I been tempted and tried, and seen all the horrors and sadness of that place. And by a tyrant have I been coaxed and threatened, seen tortures set for me, a brother put to death, and hell-hounds snuffling round me. And I have been by all my friends betrayed, and tried with jealousy and damned to death. O feeble, shallow sufferings! What are you all but gnat-bites on our flesh and bodily hurts, and bogie-men to fright us? O, I could bear you all again a thousand times, for my love led me on. But now . . .'

Radha gazed out over the lake, and although Krishna was not to

199

be seen yet she seemed to see him in every tree that bloomed, and in the glittering lake, and in the nodding irises. And Radha said 'I am called on by time, and cannot go. All happiness lies waiting and I must turn back into the darkness. To death I am pledged, being no more than dead. O unhappy ghosts, is this what you see, haunting the places and faces of your friends, seeing their happiness and cannot touch them, hearing their songs and cannot make them hear? O wretched human kind! Our spirits yearn for freedom and the body's jail decays. Our world is tears, and all our hopes an endless sea.'

But then Radha came to herself, and the sorrow in her heart was like a river at the floodgates, pressing upon the lock. And the gates were opened and the river was released and flowed on exulting towards the golden sea. Radha felt resigned to whatever might happen, and a spark of joy kindled like a fresh perfume in her soul, and she was happy.

So she walked by the lake smelling the lotuses, for she was determined not to be tricked by Krishna into looking for him, and decided to tease him by appearing careless, little knowing as she did this that he had a trap already sprung for her. She leaned down towards the lake to smell the flowers, and there was one huge blue lotus that floated just on the dark surface of the water, and Radha bent down so that she nearly touched it with her lips.

And the lotus kissed her, for it was Krishna's face. He sprang up in a shower of spray, laughing at how she had mistaken his face for a lotus of the lake and he had snatched a kiss without her knowing. And Radha laughed and hit him with her flowers for being such a fool.

And as they walked they came across a boat with a long pole to punt it along, and Krishna pretended to look astonished and opened his mouth in a big O, and said 'Well, well! The fairies have heard you were frightened to swim, and look! Step in, my girl, and let's put out. Come, my lovely. All aboard.'

And so with no more thought of right or wrong, nor any struggle in her heart of what she should do, she got into the boat and lay back on its varnished boards. And so at last, after their journeys through the earth and heavens and all their suffering and separation, they were together on the gloomy lake, and Krishna heaved at the shore with the pole and they nosed forward. The peaceful moon danced on the waves, swimming with them like a playful fish, and Radha trailed her fingers in the deep dark water.

And Radha knew not what was before her, whether she would be with Krishna for ever on the island or suddenly snatched away for the breaking of her promise, or whether even she could keep her promise yet, but all she knew was these things ceased to matter. And she looked up at Krishna as he punted her along, and his strong, smooth limbs seemed to glow with loving light. The moonlight lay on his bare breast and thighs like silver dew on fields of wheat in autumn, and the water ran laughing down his muscled arms and sprinkled in the lake.

Book Thirty-three

The Enchanted Island

And they landed their boat under the festive leaves of tall banana trees and palms, and pushed through the squeaking irises to the turf. As they trod upon the ground damp hyacinths tangled their toes that lay over the ferny floor like mist and made the glade seem as though spread with sky. And they walked through the rustling bamboos, beneath the dark trees where red orchids swirled on stems, and came to a clearing in the trees, and at the end of this, nestling among azaleas and the moth-haunted mimosa, was a white marble pavilion, set with precious stones, with leaves of sea-green jade and flowers of topaz.

And Radha, ravished by the sultry scents of stock and magnolia, oily-petalled flowers that smelt of milky mangoes, squeezed Krishna's hand, her fingers intertwined, and smiled with joy. And Krishna took her to the marble house, and with a laugh showed her the riches spread there, for round about over the glossy floor were cups and samovars of gold, chess-boards, and hookahs with red pipes, and by the low white balustrade were set long couches and huge cushions of brocade, in frosty colours on whose sheeny sides were scenes of hunting crocodiles upon the muddy Nile, or snaring birds of paradise among the blue-veined crags of Guinea or the steamy Amazon.

And by the gateway under trellises was a couch of sleek-skinned palm-leaves, strewn with flowers, and marigolds and lotuses and little jasmine littered it all over. Krishna turned to Radha with a flashing smile, and they embraced and swirled around, and as their limbs grew weak with the languor they sank down. Radha lay back upon the petalled couch, and Krishna knelt before her.

And Krishna said 'Now, my heart's darling, let us take off all our clothes and lie naked together on this couch, and nothing come between us but our flesh.'

And Krishna undid at his back the golden chain that held his orange loincloth, and showed her his manhood, and he said 'Look, Radha, how I love you. Come to me.' And his lingam stood before

202

her like a cobra swaying ready to strike, and it was smooth and blue, with rosy head, and full to bursting.

And Radha leant forward and hugged Krishna's waist, and kissed his smooth chest and its little nipples, and Krishna stroked her black hair with his hands, and then undid the clasps that held her sari's bodice, and she leaned back and drew it off and freed her milky breasts. And her breasts swung free and were as full as mangoes and as soft as foxgloves, and she embraced Krishna again, and cradled his manhood between them. And as he sighed, she bent down and sucked at it, like a calf that follows on the udder, and squeezed its head between her lips and tongue.

And Krishna gently lifted her head back and smiled and said 'Careful my love, suck gently at this sugarcane, or it will shoot.' And she laughed and he lay her back on the couch, and unwrapped the wide skirts of her silken sari, and drew it away, and gazed with love upon her smooth round legs, her belly like rose-leaves and her deep navel, and the smoky forest of her mount of love. And Krishna kissed her belly, and with his playful tongue drew patterns on it, and he kissed her fleshly womb.

And Radha sighed and Krishna leant over her and lay upon her, cradling his full lingam on her navel, and he looked at her through heavy eyes, his eyelids drooping with excess of love, and said 'Give me a sweet kiss from your lips, and it will suck my seed from me.' And Radha pressed her trembling lips on his, and from his manhood a surge of sweetness came which could not be held in, and he shot his seed up to her breasts and neck.

And Radha laughed and kissed his swooning eyes and kissed his ears and said 'O Krishna, are you so eager you begin the race before the starter calls? Look how you've wetted me, you wretched man.'

But Krishna lay on her and shivered with the joy of it and said 'O my love, my love, so long I've been away. It is such sweetness in your arms, too much to bear. O kiss me again.'

'And have you come again?' she said.

And Krishna laughed and said 'Not yet, although there's plenty more. You'll not exhaust my treasure-house of love. You scold me now, but wait. I'll have you begging me for mercy.'

And he began kissing her again, and fell upon her breasts and sucked them each, and he drew long on the sweetness of her rosy nipples, that stood up like the buds of spring on breasts that swelled to burst, breasts big as drunkard's jars, shaming the slender girl. And he would browse and she look down on him, growing ever more languid, and he would stop and kiss her lips, full now as blushing roses, soft as cream. And with his hand then Krishna stroked her mount of love, that swam with oily sweetness and grew drunk, and Radha writhed and breathed hard, and grew feverish and restless for his love.

And Krishna lay her down upon her side, lifting her upper leg to knee the ground, and he lay over her, his one leg kneeling set at her slender back, and into the woody cave he sent his serpent, gently and tenderly, for it was big, and drew it out again and pushed it in, and so softly made on, and Radha threw her arms against the ground and moaned. And Krishna played then with her breasts together, sliding his hand between, and he stroked deeper and churned round and round, and Radha with a cry shuddered and came. And she twisted round and flung her arms about his neck and wept. And Krishna waited until she grew calm.

And then he slid his lingam out, still full and hard, and lay back on the couch himself, and said 'Come then, my love, repay me for my work, and let me lie and dream, and watch while you are tussling.' And Krishna's lingam lay up to his navel, now flushed and wet, and Radha took it in her hand with eagerness, and knelt over her Krishna, and slid it again into that tight warm spot, and Krishna closed his eyes with pleasure. Then was it Radha's turn to thrust up and down, and lustily she rode him, like an eager jockey that sees the winning post within his reach. And Krishna stroked and squeezed her bulging breasts that bounced in front of him, and Radha babbled with sighs and talk as she came nearer to her goal, and her black hair flew out around her shoulders, and shivering suddenly she came again. And she slid her hands forward and fell on Krishna's face and pressed her nerveless lips over his eyes. And long she lay there, with pleasure quite overwhelmed.

And when she sat back and smiled at last, Krishna frowned at her and said 'Still nothing for me? This game is loaded. Twice have you thrown a six, and I but once, and that off the board. Onto your back then, Radha, and I'll take a turn.'

And Radha, still drunk and weak, rolled over on the couch, and Krishna crouched between her legs and wrapped those smooth limbs round him, and Radha dug with her toes round Krishna's ankles for support. And as he set about her, she to help him lifted her hips a little off the ground, and swayed them round, so that as Krishna plunged she would churn round, and so together could they thrust and squeeze. And Krishna relished this, and in his passion sucked the air backward through his teeth and growled, and rearing up so that he squashed her back, he came and shot his hot seed in her womb.

And Radha stroked his sweating head and tangled in his hair and smiled and said 'Let's rest now, Krishna, or I shall faint away. I am so gorged with pleasure all my flesh is rich. I feel it full and glowing like a rose, and should you give more I shall die.'

And Krishna said 'O my sweetest love, O how I love you. Why, I could love you for a thousand years and not feel any weariness or age. Love rushes to my blood and makes me strong. Come then, we cannot rest, for still we have not come together in one race. One more time and then we'll rest a while.'

But Radha leant her head on the leaves of her couch as though too tired or weak, and Krishna leant over her and kissed her, and rubbed his tool, still bursting, on her hip. And bowing her head as if in shame, Radha raised up her buttocks with a sigh, and Krishna knelt full close, and slid him in, and worked on her with lusty strokes, slapping himself against her dampened lap. And though he delayed as long as he might, he came without her, and frowned as he did.

And now since she was weary he lay down and nestled close to her, and lay down by her side, and drew her to him. And Radha smiled as if about to fall asleep. And Krishna kissed her lips and said 'Sleep then, my Radha, be my baby girl.' And she laughed and closed her eyes. But then she opened them again, for Krishna was burrowing at her lap, and she moved her lower leg under his hip, and let him gently in, and then he lay contentedly beside her.

And Radha said 'You're like a baby with its mother's breasts. Unless it's sucking something it will cry.'

And Krishna laughed and said 'You are my mother. From you I came forth, and into you I come, all home again.'

And they lay quiet on the soft-leaved couch, and Krishna said 'O what a journey I have gone to meet you. Would you think, Radha, I met a great white bird, and flew upon its back over the mountains, and even left the earth and went to heaven?'

And Radha said 'No,' and laughed.

And Krishna laughed.

And Radha said 'You no more went to heaven than I went into Hell, and saw all the tortures and met Yama himself.'

And Krishna laughed, and said 'That would have been an adventure. And he let you out again because you bullied him, no doubt?'

And Radha said 'Do you think once in you can ever come out of such a place?'

And Krishna said 'No. It is not possible. Although I am in you and come out often enough.'

And Radha said 'O, you ... you ...' but then she drew in her breath and sighed and said 'O my dearest love.'

And Krishna began to move slowly inside her and they gently kissed, and then with hardly any movement but only a soft rocking such as might be a lullaby to sleep they neared the peak of pleasure and slipped in, and they said nothing but lay softly embraced and mouth to mouth, halfway it seemed between dreaming and sleep and love. And so they lay embraced for a long time. And Radha felt as if she had come home, and in herself she knew that she was here and always had been here upon this island in this lake with Krishna.

And Radha opened her eyes and said to Krishna 'Krishna, my love, Seek now inside yourself. What do you see?'

And Krishna laughed and said 'That I am that, that you are that, and that all this is that.' And he smiled at her.

And Radha said 'I am. Now do I see that this island is eternity indeed, and we once on it never shall go hence, because on it we know the eternal now. O Krishna, why did I not come with you before? All those sorrows, then I would have seen they were but nothing, for this always is. We are released here from all time and place. And even love is otherwise than us.'

But now floating across the lakeside air came the voices of weeping, and it was the cowherd girls calling for Krishna in the woods, for after a while they had noticed that he had gone, and strayed far searching him fearfully in the jungle.

And Radha said 'Those poor girls, Krishna, you have left them all. Call them around you and be nice to them.'

And Krishna got up and looked about and said 'No, let us love again, and leave them go.'

But Radha searched and found her sari and twisted it around her and stood up, and she threw Krishna his little orange loincloth and said 'Cage up the tiger for a while, my lover.' And Krishna laughed and put it on, and fastened it around him with the golden chain.

And he looked out and saw the cowherd girls searching about the lake, calling out over the echoing water mournfully for Krishna. And suddenly he shouted out to them 'What, are you girls not in bed yet? Aren't you afraid of the jungle? What are you looking for?'

And they all stretched out their hands with longing to him over the water and cried 'Krishna, cruel Krishna, come to us again. We burn to dance with you as we did before.'

And Krishna shouted 'Trip across the water then. Hurry.'

And they wept and wailed that he was always teasing them.

But Krishna insisted they could do it, and to prove it to them he himself stepped out and danced on the surface of the water. And so in a great flock the cowherd girls ran over to Krishna, each one through her love finding she could stand on the lake. And they massed round Krishna and gazed about the island and stared jealously at Radha, who sat in the pavilion turning over in her hands the golden cups and looking at the Persian samovar. And they begged Krishna once more to dance with him.

And Krishna said 'Come then, the night wears on and soon the dawn will come. One final dance let us take on the floating mists of this lake, and to live in your memory of this lovely night, look, I shall make a palace on the waves, and we shall dance the great parade of time, the ring dance, like the circling of the world. And I shall call it the Ras Mandala, and all things from it shall take up their life.'

And a great palace of white marble appeared as if built from the mists of the lake, and towered above them all with a brooding dome of purity. From this vision in the afteryears were architects to draw, and that great tomb for Shah Jahan's beloved was nearest to this palace of the mists. And the moon glinted on the precious stones set in the walls and dome and fizzled in ruby sparks and argent and pale sulphur.

But the girls all wanted to dance with Krishna themselves and hold his hand, and it seemed that soon they would be quarrelling again amongst themselves, so Krishna told them all he would hold all their hands and bid them shut their eyes. And when they opened them again, lo! Krishna was with them all, and each of them held him by the hand and danced with him, and in a great circle round the island, they now stepped out the vast Ras Mandala.

And round the pavilion were there twelve maidens, each with a hand in Krishna's, so that twenty-four swift dancers twined and paced the ground. And round the island all were twenty-six maidens, each with a hand in Krishna's, so that fifty-two lithe dancers bowed and stepped the waters of the lake. And round the lake on the banks were a hundred and seventy-eight maidens, each with a hand in Krishna's, so that three hundred and sixty-six dancers slowly stalked along the rushy banks. And in their hands they held bright torches that reflected in the water, and the white marble walls of the vast fairy palace could be spied through whenever dancers passed.

And as they danced the dawn began to break and pale the sky, but the eager stars longing to keep the sight gazed down on the turning rings, and were so rapt they turned at the same time their frosty fires, and the whole universe was caught in it, so that all time and space centred upon that lake. And the great coiling of the serpent Ananta, whose sides were the swirlings of the milky way, wound round about them an embrace of stars.

Then on the floor of the pavilion Radha and Krishna sat together, and Radha poured him from the bubbling samovar sweet Persian tea, scented with cinnamon, milky, with nuts and flowers floating in it. And they laughed to be sitting on a blood-red carpet drinking tea, while all around them a thousand Krishnas danced, and they were at the centre of the universe. And Radha lifted up her cup to him and said 'All's one now, Krishna, the worlds dance round and round. The stars sing on within their burning spheres, the serpent space and the white bird of time wind on, fly on, in silent saraband, we at the centre drinking fragrant tea. Now there is no more further. Search is done. Longing is done, yearning and sorrow's toil, Now we can go a thousand ways apart, but always will be here, always, for ever, you, love, and I, love, this eternal now.'

And the dawn rose and blushed in the fiery clouds of the East, and the stars all faded but the morning star, and the dance ended on the enchanted lake. And through the trees the girls then sauntered home, all as they thought with Krishna on their arm, and he seeing them safe through the dark forest. And when they had all gone, Radha and Krishna left their island, and moored their boat, and Krishna promised her that when he had beaten the wrestler of King Kamsa he would call her again to dance upon the lake. And she smiled and knew no tears, knowing it could not be.

But as they walked together up the hill, Krishna stopped her and turned to her and said 'At the tournament today, when you watch me wrestle, wear this as a favour in your hair.' He pulled from his dark locks the golden lotus they had quarrelled over, and twined it in her hair, and Radha smiled and kissed him. Then hand in hand with wandering steps and slow they took their way back to the village in the land of Braj.

And waiting for them were the cowherd girls, all now without their Krishnas but so gorged with the night's bliss they yearned for nothing and together in a gay procession they left the village, a bevy of girls all in saris scarlet and pink and orange, with the Blue Krishna in the midst, laughing and glancing at them merrily. And so ended their night of dalliance, and so was danced the great Ras Mandala, and the earth was purged by the exotic sweetness, and signs of freshness and of purity began to rustle in the waiting sky.

PART VII

The Great Tournament

Book Thirty-four

Fun and Games

And now Vishnu, lying on the serpent of the universe, Ananta, looked towards his wife and smiled. And he said 'O what a tale of love is this! The very stars hold their breath, and all things become entangled in its sweetness. My Lakshmi, queen of the universe, this is your prince of stories. But come, I mean to stop you a little here, for I am concerned for Radha, the deep-hearted, ever-faithful girl. Surely she cannot now go back to death, and visit again the court of Yama, as she promised. You cannot mean to let her drown herself.'

But Lakshmi smiled at him, and she slid down on her golden thread another lotus onto the garland she was weaving, and she had now thirty-three flowers on the band, and Lakshmi said 'Out of the story grows its end. I cannot alter what must be. Radha must go where she had promised, and I cannot seek to change the ways of the world.' And she turned to Vishnu and said 'Have I not done well so far? I have wound on this thread of the tale yourself, your serpent, and your white bird Garuda, and I have also found a place for your bracelet, your lotus, your conch and your mace. And, as you asked me, Krishna has found himself.'

And Vishnu nodded, and thought for a while, looking out over the sea of milk, and he said 'Now make him see that he is me, and there an end. And now give me the kiss that you have promised, for your story has stirred me with deep love, and I long to touch your lips, so sweet and full.'

And Lakshmi laughed and said 'When the last lotus is in place, and the garland around your shoulders, then will I kiss you, Vishnu, and not before. Will you have the whole world stilled before our tale has had an ending? Patience a little while and I have done.'

And Vishnu sank back again on the twisting couch of the divine serpent, and gazed from heavy lids at his fair wife Lakshmi, and she was about to continue with the tale when Vishnu sat up and said 'My darling, there is one thing yet that has not found a place in your story, and that is my most dear and precious thing, the very substance

213

of this universe, the very life and action and its power.' And he looked at her lovingly and said 'Yourself.'

But Lakshmi smiled and glanced at him out the corner of her eye and said 'We'll see what can be done.' And she continued with the tale, as you shall hear.

And now as the glorious morning broke over the hills of Braj, and blazed with fiery splendour on the walls of Mathura and its towers, all things were joyful for the day's festival. The citizens decked out their houses with flowers and garlands, and hung across the narrow streets great lines of orange marigolds, and on the floor were palm-leaves, and paintings done with chalk. And the citizens all put on their best clothes, and wore rich saris of shot silk, scarlet shot with purple, purple shot with gold, and round their hems were woven silver threads in patterns of flowers and peacocks. And the streets were ringing with pipes and drums, and even the cows were hung with gaudy coverlets, and lotuses were tangled in their horns.

But King Kamsa, never having slept that night for fears and hopes, raged in his palace and bullied his guards. The wrestler Chanura he had brought to him, and questioned him about how he was to kill Krishna, and Chanura said 'Fret not, my King, with this little knife I shall soon fall on him, and I shall catch him in a grip that will bring his heel near my hand, and I will stab it with this knife and he shall die from the poison.' And when he said that King Kamsa held up his hands, as if pleading to heaven that this would be so.

And next Kamsa had Akrura brought to him, and asked him if all was well with the mad elephant, and Akrura said 'All is well, King Kamsa. The beast is mad with hunger and will fall on Krishna and spear him on its tusks. The cage is ready by the gate. Krishna will not even get into the city.' And Kamsa gripped his fingers together and clenched his teeth, hoping this would be so.

And then Kamsa went raging to the prison and he shouted to the jailers to bring out Vasudeva and Devaki, and these were Krishna's parents, as Vayu found out when he went on his second mission, and yet few people knew of this, and certainly not Krishna. And when Kamsa saw them he said 'Vasudeva and Devaki, whether Krishna be your son or not, whether you tricked me on that day so long ago, when it was told your son would slay me, and whether that daughter of yours that I tried to kill was yours or no, your lives will depend on Krishna this day. I shall take you to the arena for the great tournament, and you will watch Krishna wrestle with Chanura the King's wrestler, and should Krishna try to escape his fight with Chanura, you two will I kill before his eyes. And with this weapon shall I do it too.' And Kamsa snarled with rage and drew from his sash a glinting scimitar, as sharp as razors, and he threatened them with it, and then went his way.

And Kamsa came then to the great arena and he looked at it to see that everything was well, and the arena was a feast of colours, as banners and hangings were laid all around. Soldiers in glittering coats with shining armour marched here and there, rehearsing their displays, and there were horses and acrobats and dancers and elephants and panthers and all things ready for a great carnival. And Kamsa went to the huge pavilion, where his throne was, high overlooking all the games, and he arranged for Vasudeva and Devaki to be put there in chains. And he gazed out over the vast circus and thought 'This day shall be my day of triumph. This shall be Kamsa's glorious day. For I shall kill my deadly enemy that has stopped all my conquests and been my trouble, and there shall be a great festival to show I am truly King, King of Mathura, King of India, King of the world, King of the Universe, God!' And he laughed and cried out and stretched out his hands to heaven, and all the soldiers looked up and thought he had gone mad.

In heaven meanwhile, the gods themselves had all been reconciled, and they feasted to celebrate the coming of the rains. Indra was ruler again, and all the gods knew it, and Agni who had been defeated yet bided for the fight. But Indra's wife talked with Agni and gave him drinks of nectar, and made him happy to be with his friends again. And now, feasting together once more, the gods thought eagerly of the great festival to be held in Mathura, for they were all fond of Krishna now, and thought him a great hero, and as they talked of it Indra said 'Let us all go to the walls of heaven, and place seats along it, just as they have in an arena, and we may go and sit and watch this great contest taking part in Mathura today.'

The gods all rejoiced at this idea, and Indra summoned his servants and made them bring seats, and all the gods in a great troop left the feasting chamber and went in the clear air to the walls of heaven. And there they sat in rows along the golden wall, all among the shining dusky clouds, and the glint of their crowns and jewels flashed down on the earth. And Indra was there and Indra's wife, and Agni was there and Vayu, and Ganesha was there, the little elephant god, and all were laughing and eager to see the contest, and their great figures loomed into the sky, so that the stars might seem to be their diadems.

And so Krishna and all the cowherds came into Mathura. And as soon as Krishna came in the gate the servants of Kamsa lifted up the door of the cage which held the mad elephant, and the great tusker roared out of his cage and ran straight at the servants of Kamsa. And they all howled and shouted that he was to kill Krishna, but the elephant trumpeted and thrashed to seize them with his trunk, and they were dangling from the walls, and all the ladies screamed, and the servants cried to Krishna for help. And Krishna booted the elephant in its hind quarters so that it shot forward and broke its neck against the city wall, and its tusks broke off, and it fell in a heap, dead.

And then all the cowherds roared with laughter, and Krishna and Balarama picked up the tusks and went parading round with them, carrying them on their shoulders like spears, and the townsfolk all cheered and waved their handkerchiefs. And Akrura came up, who had seen all this, and said 'Well done, Krishna. It was a most untrusty elephant, for it was supposed to kill you but turned on its keepers instead. And yet it knew who had been starving it. Come now to the arena and let the contest begin.' And Akrura led Krishna through the streets of Mathura. And as Krishna went along all the townsfolk cheered him, and the word went round how he had killed the elephant that had turned on its keepers by kicking it in the rump and smashing its head against a wall, and the poor people of Mathura thought this was the funniest thing they had ever known, for they had never met Krishna before and did not know of his pranks, and they howled with laughter and fell on the ground.

And now Krishna and the cowherds all came to the arena. And the arena had become full of people, and all the townsfolk had crammed themselves in to see the contest. They were all cheering so loudly that Krishna waved to them and went out into the arena himself and brandished the elephant's tusks. And they all laughed at this and whispered amongst themselves 'Those are the tusks of the elephant that he booted up the backside and bashed its head against the wall.' And all those who had not heard the story said 'What?' and all those who had, told them the story all over again, and soon the arena was full of voices all telling the story of the elephant and its tusks, and

216

roars of laughter went up again. Krishna walked round the arena carrying the tusks like two lances, and the cowherds all followed him, and thought they were all heroes, and waved and blew kisses to the people, so that it all quite turned their heads. But just as Krishna was starting to do a little dance with the tusks as an extra pair of feet, King Kamsa entered the pavilion with Vasudeva and Devaki, and all his courtiers were with him, and Akrura too.

The people in the arena then fell deathly silent, and bowed low to their King, and all the cowherds, left in the middle of the arena, looked annoyed and frowned at the people and went to their seats. But as Kamsa sat down, and the people of Mathura buzzed with talk again, the cowherds began to quarrel over their seats, as they all wanted to sit in the front row. And at last they settled the matter by having half sitting on the front row of seats and the rest sitting before them on the ground.

Then did the games begin. A vast army of soldiers walked through the mighty gates at the far end of the arena and paraded around, and saluted King Kamsa. Then a rank of chariots clattered onto the sand, with a pair of horses each, great plumes on their heads, and they raced around and hailed King Kamsa. Then acrobats leapt on and performed feats of tumbling and jumping, and formed a great pyramid of people, such as Krishna used, to get the butter when he was a boy, and then they jumped down and ran off. And the cowherds were amazed at all this, and sat looking with open mouths. Then a troop of performing dwarfs entered, and began to run about on the sand, but the cowherds did not like these, and threw orange peel at them. And the dwarfs were so annoyed they refused to continue with their display, and complained to King Kamsa to send the cowherds away. The cowherds all booed and shouted, and Nanda stood up and shouted at the cowherds to behave themselves, and all was quiet again.

Then did the fighting begin, and in silence the cowherds watched the warriors of King Kamsa fight to the death with spears and swords. And they ran at each other in chariots and hacked as they passed with their scimitars. Then did other warriors fight with clubs, and crunched each other's limbs and heads. Then did slaves have to fight with tigers and leopards that were brought in in cages, roaring and hungry, and the slaves were torn to pieces and blood and gore littered the sand. Then was a mighty elephant brought in, and one

217

man alone had to fight it with a spear, and he threw the spear and it stuck in the elephant's side, and the elephant raged and picked up the man in its trunk and threw him to the ground and squashed him with its foot and skewered him on a tusk. And the elephant walked off with the man hanging bleeding from its tusk.

Then was an enormous cart drawn onto the sand, and it was covered over with a huge cloth, and the cart creaked and shook. And there was a great hush among the people as a soldier went up, and with a flourish pulled off the cloth and revealed the huge Chanura underneath, the King's wrestler, towering into the sky. And Chanura leapt forward and roared and bellowed. And all the cowherds who had pressed to the front of the seats panicked and scrambled over each other to get away.

But then Krishna leapt into the arena, and he imitated the roar of the wrestler, and stood as he did, and kicked him on the shins. And all the cowherds, looking back, cheered at this, and the people of Mathura fell about laughing again.

Chanura stood back, red in the face with anger, and he twirled his moustache. And Krishna pretended to twirl his moustache, and the people of Mathura howled and laughed, and tears rolled down their cheeks, and Krishna looked at them, thinking how easy it was to make some people laugh. And while he looked Chanura ran at him, and collided into him, and Krishna pretended to be dazed and went walking around the sand in a funny walk as though his head were ringing, rolling his eyes. Chanura chased after him, and Krishna pretended to be afraid and ran away. And they ran round and round the ring, with Krishna rubbing his fists up and down before his chest, as though running in a very eager way, leaning backward. And all the people fell off their seats with mirth, and rolled in the aisles. And every time Krishna ran past King Kamsa's great pavilion, he would suddenly stop and salute, and then run on again. Finally he ran around so fast that he caught up with Chanura's back, running after him, and kept kicking him and pushing him on, as though trying to make him run faster. And eventually Chanura sank wearily to the ground, for although he was a great wrestler, he could not run as fast as he might.

And now Krishna strolled seriously up before him, and as though taking great pains he crouched down and jumped up with his legs apart, and flexed his muscles and stood on his head, and jumped up to Chanura and jumped away again, all as though preparing for a great throw or clinch. And Chanura watched him until he was dizzy. But finally he got back his breath from the running, and became angry, and he darted out his hand and caught Krishna by the ankle of his right foot, and the heel of this foot was where he was to stab him with the poison knife. And Krishna cried out as Chanura took his foot, as though he was ticklish, and as Chanura turned his foot over to get at the heel, Krishna beat the ground with his hands, and pretended to plead as though he could not stand the tickling, and Chanura took out his knife, and held it behind his back.

Now all the cowherds who were at this minute behind Chanura saw that he had a knife and cried out, and Krishna stopped pretending to be tickled and put his hand to his ear as though trying to hear what they had to say. And as he did this, Chanura held down Krishna's heel on his own knee to steady it, and lashed down at it with his knife. At that minute Krishna stood up to hear what the cowherds were shouting and pulled his foot away, and Chanura stabbed his own knee with the poison knife. And staring down with horror at the wound he had made on himself, his eyes glazed over and he fell backwards onto the sand, dead. And because the cowherds fell silent when they saw this, Krishna gave up trying to hear what they were saying, and turned back to the wrestler, and he saw him dead on the ground and threw up his hands as if astonished.

But before the people could cheer Krishna for defeating the wrestler, King Kamsa sprang up and ordered his guards to seize Krishna, and a troop of soldiers rushed towards him to take him. But Krishna took the first and pushed him into the second, who fell onto the third, and soon he had piled them all up helpless before him.

And Kamsa then shouted 'Then, Krishna, watch these people die.' And he drew out a sword and seized Vasudeva by the hair, and Vasudeva was in chains and could do nothing. But as he went to kill him Krishna jumped up into the King's pavilion and seized Kamsa himself by his hair, and he jumped back with him into the arena.

And now the people of Mathura and the soldiers and the priests all leapt to their feet astonished at what Krishna had done. Even the gods themselves, watching from the high far off walls of heaven, gasped as he did this. And Krishna swung Kamsa round by his hair, faster and faster, and he stamped on the earth, and a great rift appeared in it, and flames shot out of the cavern. And into this burning pit Krishna threw Kamsa, and the flames shot up with a roar, so that even the gods flinched backwards, and the pit closed up again, and all was still. And there was a terrible silence throughout all the earth, and no one knew what to do.

But then high above in the clear air there was a rustling sound, and floating by came a pageant of peaceful signs, and the signs were as clouds that could be seen through, and there was a mace held by a laughing man, whose hair flew out behind like silver curtains stirring in the wind, and there was a conch born by a water-girl, and she had a fish's tail that glittered over with frosty scales, and her smiling teeth were like strings of pearls. Next in the pageant was a heavenly face and round its head a halo of white mist and the eyes of the face were like suns lighting the earth, and as the face shone there a neck formed for it and a breast and shoulders, and it was like a man formed out of sky, and at its heart shining with silvery light there was a lotus with a thousand petals, and the whole man appeared, and filled the bowl of the sky, and growing larger and larger he mingled himself among the earth, and his body seemed to fade into clouds and mist.

And immediately this pageant had passed by, the people in the arena and all the cowfolk cheered and clapped Krishna for what he had done, for he had killed the tyrant that had kept them all enchained and the signs of peace had shown, which meant that a new era had come. And the town of Mathura was filled with the sounds of rejoicing. In the streets the soldiers who were on guard heard the news and threw up their helmets with joy; the children of the city danced round and round waving streamers of silk; the women wept and waved their scarves and handkerchiefs; the men hollaed and bellowed with shouts of freedom, and all over the roofs of the city too the towers and spires of temples sprouted with spontaneous flags. And then above the earthly sounds of cheering, the applause of the gods could be heard, like a roaring waterfall high in a far off mountain. And the gods leaning forward from their golden walls threw flowers down, so that it rained with petals, and jasmine and hibiscus, lotus and rose, marigold and azalea, in all colours of the rainbow floated down, flooding the earth with perfume, dyeing the ground with richest hues. Petals twirled and settled everywhere, as in winter does the gentle snow. And in the middle of the arena Krishna stood, and he was silent thinking of coming days.

Book Thirty-five

Krishna the Prince

But now cheering crowds took Krishna to the palace of their King, and he was shown the riches and splendour of the court, and the rooms full of Persian carpets and the marble screens, the channels of cooling water and the rosy verandahs. And Krishna was amazed and joyful to see it all. And the people began to ask him what they should do.

And Krishna said 'Go, and tell everyone that has suffered from the cruelty of King Kamsa to come to the palace courtyard, and let us have a big feast to celebrate his death, and tell all the cooks to make a big banquet for thousands of people, and bring all the rice and curds and dal and chapatis to the courtyard and set them round for everyone to eat. And let every one be happy and rejoice.'

And the people said eagerly 'And let us kill all the guards that were the guards of King Kamsa, for they used to beat us and put us in prison.'

And Krishna said 'Go to the prisons, and all those that were put in there because they tried to oppose King Kamsa, let them free and bring them to the banquet. But all those who are in there because they have stolen things, let them stay or we will have no food left. And as for the guards, let them be waiters at the banquet, and those who won't bring them here to me, and I shall chide them.'

And the people flew off, eager for a great feast, and they all wanted to be the ones who set the prisoners free. And the word went round that a great banquet was to be held, and everybody came to the palace courtyard, for they all thought they had been wronged by King Kamsa, and all the cowherds came too.

But then a group of old councillors came forward, and they spoke to Krishna and said 'For many years we have served King Kamsa and given him our advice on governing the realm, and sometimes we were beaten for it, and sometimes our plans were accepted and we were ignored. But now we see that our King is dead, and there is no one governing Mathura at all. But from everything we have seen and done in the world, we know that a kingdom must have a King if it is to be strong, and now that Kamsa is dead there will be many people want to be that King, and Kamsa's brothers and cousins will be looking this way, and these people will soon find an excuse to come upon us, and revenge what has happened this day. Therefore Krishna, we would ask you to be our King, for you have shown yourself a great hero in your fight with the fiends, and if you would only govern us our kingdom would be safe. Let us therefore plead with you to take the crown, and live with us, King, in this glorious palace, and rule us, so that we shall live in peace all the days of our lives.'

But Krishna stood in thought when he heard this, for already he had been acting like a King and ordering people what to do. And then he said 'How may I be a King, when I am only a cowherd?'

And some of the cowherds, who had got into the court, shouted 'He cannot be a King, He is only a herdsman. Krishna, you must come back with us and look after the cows.'

And some of the people of Mathura scorned the cowfolk for saying this and said 'Silence, you fools. How can such a man be a cowherd, who can rout the fiends and kill the King himself?' And they all began arguing with each other, and the cowherds were pushed out to join their fellows in the courtyard below.

But Nanda and Jasuda remained of the cowfolk, and Nanda came forward and said 'Great honour would it be for my son to become a King, O wise councillors, but he is not of the kingly nor the priestly class. Were he a kshatriya or a brahmin, then it perhaps could be, but being as he is, a cowherd, I cannot see how Krishna may rule you. It were better that he returns with us to his simple home, and lived among us villagers as he used. Let us stay with you now for the great banquet, and then we must be going homewards to Braj again, and caring for our flocks.'

But now Vasudeva came forward, whom Krishna had saved, and he went to Krishna and said 'O mighty hero, you saved my life and my wife's in the arena when you snatched King Kamsa down, but for all your might in slaying him you did not know who it was you saved from his sword. Krishna, the signs are here, the time has come, you must learn now the secret of your birth.' And Vasudeva turned round to the throng of people and looked up and said 'Heaven strike me now, if I do not tell the truth.' And he turned to Krishna and said 'Krishna, you are my son, born to me by Devaki, whom you also saved. In killing Kamsa you saved the lives of your own parents. Now you are rewarded with the kingdom which is yours.'

And all the people were amazed and gasped when he said this, and they thought they saw now how Krishna was so mighty and so noble, and Vasudeva turned to Nanda and said 'Dear friend, you were a friend to me in trouble indeed, although you never knew. Do you not remember a snowy night when Krishna was born? Do you not remember how the Jumna raged and gnawed at its banks? Do you not remember the terrible storm around? That was the night I took my son away from the prison in Mathura, and on to Braj I went, for a voice had told me to go there, and my son I swapped with a little baby girl, born to Jasuda on that stormy night. Is it not true, my friends, is it not as I say? It was a prophecy that my eighth son should kill King Kamsa, and Kamsa knew of this, and it was to escape his anger that I put my little son among the cowherds. Now he is home again, and heir to a great kingdom, for Krishna is no herdsman as you thought, but as I, a brahmin, and fittest to rule. Now let heaven be my witness that I say true. Show us a sign, Lord Indra, with your bow.'

And suddenly in the air, far off over the hills of Braj, where the clouds gathered for more dusky rain, there appeared a rainbow, shining over the land of Krishna's youth, and then thunder roared as if confirming this fresh sign. And the people gasped, and they believed in Vasudeva's words.

And Vasudeva went to Nanda and took the old man's hand, and he took the hand of Jasuda standing near, and he said 'Dearest of cowherds, Nanda and kindly Jasuda, do not lament at this truth which is spoken. He is your son in nurture, far more than mine, and his most shining laughter is of you. Let us be both his fathers, both his mothers, making him twice blessed. And let us rejoice in this kingdom which must now be his, for though I shall press no rights on him as a father, yet must Krishna for the sake of us all become our King, and leave your land of Braj. Come then, let us smile, and think it all well done.'

But Nanda did not speak, but went to Krishna, and looked at him, and said 'Krishna, you are my son. Come home. The city is no home to you. Your home is Braj, your village and your friend.'

But Krishna took his hand and the hand of Jasuda and silently led them away. And they came into the courtyard, which was now thronging with people, and there were dishes and cups and bowls and trays everywhere, and fruit and rice and dal and curries. And the cowherds were already eating, and sitting on the ground helping themselves to the plates around, and supping up curds and junket, and peeling mangoes, and eating water-melons, and when they saw Krishna they shouted out 'Krishna, when we get home, we shall have tournaments every week and big feasts like this, and you can wrestle with elephants and tigers, and we can all watch and cheer you on. This is how we shall live in Braj now, not looking after the cows.'

And Krishna took Nanda and Jasuda apart, and said 'Dear father, dearest mother, to you I owe my life and my cherishing. I am your son indeed, and always will be the little cowherd from the land of Braj. But since the soldiers came, and I left the land of my friends, I have seen and learnt much about this turning world. It has come about that I am not your son truly, and that I have done certain things which have been prophesied. We must see then that however we act or think, fate is fulfilled and what was foretold has been. There is some other thing then in my life than being Krishna and looking after the cows, and I have discovered certain things which now I know I must make known. It is not my will that I should come to Mathura and be King. I should be most happy living on in the woods of Braj. But I came here just for fun and to wrestle, and look, with such a little action is all this come about. I must stay then, and I shall be their King, for they will be in danger and have no one to govern them. But you, my dear ones, come to this place with me. Live in the palace as my other parents. We shall laugh here as we have done in Braj.'

But Nanda was shaking his head at this, and Krishna stopped. And Nanda said 'No, my son. That cannot be. For we are cowherds, be you what you may. Let us say farewell then, and go back to our cows.'

But Krishna said 'O come, dear father Nanda, do not be cold with me. If we must say farewell, what, it shall not be long and we shall meet. If we must say farewell, let us say it with our hearts, my father.'

And Nanda looked at him, and tears came to his old eyes, and he said 'Farewell indeed, my Krishna, O my son. You were the jewel of our lives, and in your pranks our constant love and laughter. Still

224

and forlorn will be the forests now of Braj, sad shall be the banks of the Jumna. Farewell, farewell, I cannot speak any more.'

And Nanda fell on Krishna's neck and hugged him, and Jasuda next weeping pitifully, and they hugged and kissed, and would not be parted. And Nanda said 'Alas that this day ever began that we came to this city, which has always been a city of misfortune! Once already had we lost Krishna among the fiends, and now again, when he comes our saviour, so soon, so soon he is snatched away again.'

And Nanda went to the cowherds and said 'Come, cowherds, let us go home. Krishna will not be with us now. Krishna is to be King of this dark city, and to leave us villagers for ever, for he is not, as we all thought, a son of mine, but the son of Vasudeva, a great councillor and rich man of this city. Come than, poor herds, we must not stay long here. Here is the kingdom. Let us to our kine.'

And the cowherds were all amazed at this, and protested, both at Krishna and at the thought of leaving the feast so soon. They shouted that they would not, for they had all become rash and excited from the day's events, and some started throwing things at Krishna and the courtiers, and very soon it looked like a riot in the city. And the guards came, that were now the guards of Krishna, and seized the cowherds and took them all to the gates, Nanda and Jasuda with them, and flung them out to the plain.

And the cowherds howled and cried and threatened, and they burned with anger and cursed Krishna for what had happened. And all the girls wept to be so parted from Krishna, so soon after he had danced with them all in the forest by the light of the moon. But soon their anger cooled and they grew weary, and they took down their camp and made their way at last back to the village. And so once more the cowherds made across the plain, but how different was this procession, sad and weary and full of bitterness, from the jolly throng that came!

And Krishna meanwhile went back to Vasudeva and the others and said 'I have spoken with my friends, and considered all that you have said. If indeed I am not the son of Nanda, but am the son prophesied to be the end of Kamsa, as has fallen out, then I shall be your King, and guard you from your foes.'

The councillors rejoiced, and took Krishna into the courtyard at last. All was well there now, and the people of Mathura feasted peaceably, and Vasudeva said 'People of Mathura, today you have lost a King. But he that rid you of your King shall be your King. Krishna shall now be Raj of Mathura.'

And as he said this, the people cheered that were sitting at the banquet, and Krishna went down with his courtiers and joined them, and soon they were all feasting happily, and rejoicing at the new fate of the city. And the gods in heaven turned back from their seats, and all agreed it had been a splendid tournament, for only that morning was Krishna but champion of the cowherds, but now he was King of Mathura, and begun on a great reign that was to bring peace to the warring land of India, and usher in another age of wisdom and of light.

Book Thirty-six

Radha

And now came the time for Radha to return to Yama's kingdom, and to go to the Ganges and take the watery way to death, for such was her promise to the great King of the Dead, from whose mercy she had come once more to see Krishna. And now was she settled in her mind what she should do, for on the enchanted island she had found that all time was but now, and Krishna should be always with her. And she saw Krishna borne in triumph into the royal palace, and she turned away, and walked through the rejoicing streets of the town.

And when she came to the gate of the city, she turned back and looked towards the palace where Krishna was, and saw an old man sitting on the steps of a small temple, and he watched her closely, and this was the holy man that King Kamsa had often asked about the coming days, and he wore orange robes, and carried a trident. And Radha went to the man and said 'Which is the way to the Ganges' side, if I leave through the gate of this city?'

And the holy man looked at her and smiled and said 'Further than Ganges are you to go. Are you prepared for such a long journey? Is there nothing of the future which you wish to know?'

And Radha was surprised at his words, for he seemed to know all that was in her mind, and she stayed a little and said 'Can you then tell of the coming days, holy sir?'

And he answered 'A little of the future can I read,' and he gazed at her, and said 'Come then, ask me that question which is stored in your heart, and you may rest then well in whatever place you go to.'

And Radha felt her heart grow heavy with sadness, and she said 'Will Krishna then be King, and rule this land for many years in peace?'

And the holy man said 'Krishna shall be our King, and rule for many years.'

And Radha said 'Shall he be married, sir? Shall be be happy?'

And the man smiled and nodded, as though this was the question he knew she wished to ask, and he said 'There will be one who shall love Krishna as much as you, but she shall be promised to another prince. Krishna will rescue her and make her his wife. He will be happy with his love, as he has been with you.'

And Radha looked at the man a long time, and sighed. And then she said quietly to herself 'O Krishna, O my love,' and stood overwhelmed by the love in her heart.

And the man said sharply 'Come, you must off. The sun is already high. Take the right-hand path. It is long to the Ganges. Farewell.'

And Radha turned and left the city gates, and she made on then towards the East, taking a little winding path across the plain and walking under the trees to keep the shade. And as she went her heart lightened and she grew more cheerful, and she remembered all the things that Krishna had done that day: how he had paraded round the arena with the tusks, and how he had jumped in and kicked the wrestler on the shins, and how he had run away from the wrestler and saluted King Kamsa as he passed him, and Radha laughed through her tears at him for being such a fool.

But in the city meanwhile the courtiers had been talking with Krishna as he sat at the banquet, and they talked of a thousand things, of prisoners to be released, of laws to be revoked, or courts to be set up, of embassies to send to gain the friendship of foreign Kings. And they spoke also of Krishna's coronation, which they all planned must be an occasion of riches and splendour with guests from all over India.

And Krishna said 'While yet we sit here talking, I am still but a cowherd, and the laws of our country do not permit me to be so planning and ordering. Let me be quickly made a brahmin by my father Vasudeva, and all our talk will be more seemly and just.'

And Vasudeva said 'Well said, Krishna. This is indeed so. Let one be sent immediately to the Ganges to fetch the holy water, and when he returns I shall make Krishna a brahmin with the ceremony of the sacred thread.'

And Krishna said 'Send someone quickly in a chariot to fetch the Ganges water, and let them bring a big urn full to wash me over all. And I shall wash all the cowherd out of me, and be a proper King.'

And the courtiers all laughed, because their King had made a joke. And Krishna was very merry, and started talking of other things, and his mind was completely taken up with the tasks before him, so that he had no thought any more of the cowherds, whom he had had sent away from the city, but spoke eagerly of courts and kingdoms and wars and justice. And a charioteer was sent for the Ganges water, and raced out of the city gates and took the winding path.

But Radha by now, asking upon the way how far it was to the Ganges, found that she had a great many miles to go, and that the sun was already at the height of noon, and by this time she had sworn to Yama she would drown herself and come to him. When she saw the chariot rushing towards her from the direction of the city she waved to it, and brought it to stop.

And Radha said 'Sir, forgive me for stopping you upon your way, but I am on business for Krishna the cowherd, now a prince, and I see you come from the city of Mathura. I must reach the Ganges as soon as I can. Could you take me any part of the way?'

And the charioteer said 'Jump in, young girl, I go that way myself. I also am on business for the prince Krishna, for holy water is to be fetched for him that he may be a brahmin, for he is not the son of Nanda, but of Vasudeva, our courtier and a great man of our city.'

And Radha climbed into the chariot, and wondered at these things, and they galloped off, as the charioteer was bent on speed, and soon were sweeping past the roadside trees, and passing the bullock-carts and buffaloes that lumbered with their keepers from dusty village to village. And as they went they spoke of the exciting things that had happened in the city, and they rejoiced that the time of tyranny for Mathura was at an end, and that Krishna would be a kindly King, and rule the people well.

And Krishna meanwhile feasted on, and joked with the courtiers, and the courtiers clustered around and asked him to tell them of his life and adventures, and Krishna told them how he had been afflicted with a drink that took away his memory, and that he could still not remember everything of his youth and his days as a cowherd.

And Krishna said 'But since I took that drink, the events that followed I can well remember, but they are too long to tell you here. Why, I went on a journey through the deserts and through jungles, and I went across mountains too, and saw many a wealthy city, and I questioned holy men about their lives, and even among the stars I put my head, and saw the secrets of the universe.'

But then he looked at the courtiers and laughed and said 'I cannot expect you to believe me there. Let's talk of other things.'

But the courtiers were eager to hear, and Vasudeva said 'Tell us, dear son, of your fight with the fiends, For that is a dark time with all of us, and difficult is it to say what happened, so full of riot and confusion was that time. We can remember a day when Kamsa summoned up all the evil in the world, and the fiends paraded, in the arena where you triumphed, and they were sent out over all the world. But then our King went mad, or so it seemed, and locked himself up, and more fiends came, and seemed to steal our lives, although we have them now.'

And Krishna laughed and said 'That is another long tale, suitable for a rainy day. As for my part in that, I was a tool of the gods. They cared for me, and roused my fighting spirit, and though I was many thousands of miles hence I rallied the forces of the Maruts and led them in the clouds and we roared in together over the Indian plains. I was in a chariot swept along by the storm, and the power of the rains I felt bearing me to the fight. O they were mighty days, to be drawn in with that warlike throng, to be riding the clouds with such a pack of warriors! O my friends, great was it to be part of that charge and battle. The blood of the fathers of old, the great Aryans, sweeping across the windblown plains, then did it thunder in my veins and bear me to victory. The mace of power I found in the dragon's cave. Great is the mace, mighty such power. With this we have come forward in man's quest, with this we shall ride on to our goal.'

And the courtiers were all stirred by Krishna's words, and their fighting spirit was kindled, and they cheered his speech, and pledged him with their cups, and their faces flushed with the heroic spirit.

But when the cheering had died down, a courtier on Krishna's left said 'And what was it, Lord Krishna, that called you to our help, though you were many thousands of miles away?'

And Krishna looked amazed and clutched his heart and called out 'Radha!' and he leapt up from where he was sitting, and cried 'My Queen. Sitting with you here, talking of mighty deeds, I have forgot my love, my life. She was it called me to your aid. She is it shall be your Queen, my friends, crowned with me in our coronation. I must find her. Quickly a chariot. I must fly to her.'

And Krishna ran out of the courtyard where they all feasted, and rushed to the stables, and he saw horses and a chariot already hitched, and the horses were enchanted horses although he knew it not, and Krishna at once leapt in to the chariot and swept out of the city gates and rode over the plain towards Braj.

The cowherds were half-way back to the village in Braj, and when they heard the chariot they looked back, wondering what it was. Some thought it was a guard to drive them further away, and some thought it was a summons to call them all back again. But when they saw it was Krishna their hearts bounded with joy, and they thought that he was coming back to them after all.

And the cowherds cried 'Look, he has repented. He was hasty and flushed with his victory. Now he knows his true friends, and he is coming back to us again.'

And Krishna swept up to them calling out 'Radha! Radha!' and when he neared them they were all smiling and looking at him eagerly, but Krishna did not smile. He looked quickly at them and said 'Where is Radha? Why is she not here?'

And the cowherds said 'O Krishna, do you beg our pardons? You were very rude to us to throw us out. We are your old friends, and the friends of your home. You should not have treated us in such a way.'

But before they could speak any more, Krishna said again 'Where is Radha?'

And they cried 'We do not know, and we care not.'

But before they could begin to talk again, as they purposed, on how Krishna was to ask their forgiveness, and what he was to do, Krishna pulled on the reins of his horses and turned the chariot around and rode back to the city. And the cowherds were left open-mouthed, and they cursed him and lamented more than ever, and with set lips and white faces went on towards the village, vowing never to speak to Krishna again, for they thought he had had a change of heart but now saw that he was only concerned with his favourite, as he had always been.

And Krishna drove back to the city, cursing himself also, and lamenting that he was so forgetful, and he came to the city gates, and rode in under the echoing gateway, and stopped. And then sadly he sat down on the edge of the chariot, and brooded bitterly, for he did not want to return to all the feasting now that his heart was so heavy, and he wondered and tried to think wherever Radha might have gone.

And as he sat thinking he saw the holy man before him whom

Radha has spoken to, and the man smiled at him and said 'The loss is hard to bear, but fate is sure, and cannot be prevented.' And Krishna looked up at him.

And Krishna saw that the man was a holy man, and could read his heart, and he stared at him for a time and said 'What fate? What do you speak of?'

And the man said 'You are a King now, and the time is gone for playing. No more to the woods will Krishna go, nor play his flute among the moonlit trees. Comfort yourself, and brighten memory. There was no way but this. I speak of Radha.'

And Krishna jumped down and ran to him and flung himself on his knees before him and said 'Where is she? What has happened?'

And the man looked at Krishna sadly and said 'She told you nothing. You with adventures flew across the world, visited stars, and saw all happy things, and these you speak of, for they are delightful and worthy to be told. She for you Krishna suffered a thousand wrongs, and told you none of them, but kept her silence.'

And Krishna cried 'O Radha, is this true? What could she have suffered? Tell me. What is it you know?'

And the man said 'Your story, Krishna, is a book for me. I am the servant of the goddess Lakshmi, and these things have been told me. You have small memory of your time in Braj, and all was from a cup of potion that you drunk. But when you drunk that potion your Radha was already accused of unfaithfulness with you, Krishna, and brought to trial. All men were against her but your father Nanda, and they tried her and damned her to death in Mathura.'

The man looked at Krishna, but Krishna was stricken dumb, and he searched in his brain and found the memories reviving of that time, and felt it was true what the holy man had said.

And the holy man went on and said 'And in Mathura, Krishna, she met with King Kamsa, and Kamsa tried to force her to become his wife, and live with him, and flung her in prison when she would not. And he came again and threatened her with tortures and with demons, and he killed her brother before her face, and Radha was taken bodily to Hell.'

And Krishna stared at the man unable to believe this, and his eyes stood out like stars with horror at the tale, and the man said 'Hell, aye Hell, for she was taken by the fiends. And bodily she went to Hell and saw its horrors.'

And Krishna's head sank down, and he covered up his face with his robe, and sat still.

And the man went on and said 'And in Hell was she tormented by the warden, and Yama spoke with her to judge her and condemn her. But even in Hell, Krishna, even in Hell, Radha's deep heart was full of love for you, and though a thousand times in Hell and on earth she had been threatened and tormented to recant from her love, yet this she never did, for her love had become her heart, and filled its every motion. And this is how she came again to earth to be with you, for the god Yama, when he saw her love, was baffled and enthralled, and it struck him that she pitied even him and the fiends of Hell, and he let her return to the blessed earth before he judged her. Three short days were to be hers on earth with you, and then she gave her promise to return.'

Krishna looked up at the man, and the man said 'If you would seek her now, she has gone back to Yama. By the swift current of the Ganges is she gone, and so by water keeps her promise to death.'

But Krishna's eye caught fire and he said 'What, is she gone to the Ganges? And on foot too? Then I can save her. She cannot have gone long. O priest, all is not lost. I can cheat death. I must go to her now.'

And Krishna leapt into the chariot again, and cracked the whip over the enchanted horses and he sped out of the gate, crying 'Radha, stay. Stay.' And with a flurry of dust he clattered onto the winding road and made off across the plain, under the shady trees, the way Radha had gone, and he expected every minute to see her dear form walking by the way, and stretched his eyes always to the horizon, longing to glimpse her and her fluttering skirts.

But Radha meanwhile had reached the banks of the Ganges and the charioteer had stopped and filled the great urn from the swirling waters. He bade her farewell, and rode back again towards Mathura, and Radha stood and looked at the water, and said 'Dear Mother Ganges, be kind to me. Do not let me suffer much, for they say drowning is a painless death.'

And Radha turned round and looked back towards the land of Braj, and she cast her eyes that way the Western sun would sink, and scanned the horizon. And she said 'That way lies Krishna, He is a King now, and has another life. There is no place for me, and it is not so hard to leave him now. O my dear Krishna, farewell, remember me. Think sometimes of Braj, and the moonlit forest, think of our

233

dances on the enchanted lake, such happy days. O my good love, take care, be brave. Though we shall meet again on earth no more, and feel no more the sweetness of each other's arms, yet that we have loved will save us. In the still woods at midnight, at the shut of eve, by the grey Jumna, we shall be together, So now, farewell, my dearest love, my soul. Farewell, my heart. Farewell, my sweetest Krishna.' And Radha saw then that another chariot was coming, and she waded quickly into the swirling water.

And Krishna riding hard met with the charioteer, and saw he was carrying water back from the Ganges, and he called to him and said 'Did you see Radha on the way? A girl going to the Ganges?'

And the charioteer said 'Such a girl I brought to this place. She is by the water now. She had an errand for yourself, she said.'

But Krishna did not stay, but was already spurring his horses to the riverside, and he saw now, stretching out before him, the wide gleaming spaces of the Ganges, and he saw a girl's form in the river, wading in. And he cried out to stop her, and he saw as he neared that it was Radha, and he shouted 'Radha! Radha!' and saw her plunge into the water, and she was swept away by the currents and borne down to the depths.

And Krishna splashed with his chariot into the water, and leapt into the river, and swam out to her, falling downstream with the swirl of the current, but her body was gone. He thrashed about in the water, and swam under the surface, but he could not find her. And a little further down on a sand-bank he saw her body drenched and dead, and swam that way and picked her up in his arms, and swam again to the shore and dragged her out. But her body was drenched and her clothes clung to her coldly and she had no life in her limbs, and he came out of the water, carrying her close to him, calling her name, and looking in her face. And he lay her down on the dusty bank and knelt before her.

And Krishna cried 'Radha, Radha, answer me, my love. Come back to me. Don't leave me in this cruel world alone. Radha, O life, come back, come back.' And he chafed her cheeks, and tried to kiss life into her eyes, and hugged her to him to warm her. And he knelt like this, weeping and calling her a long time. And the sun began to sink in the West, and still she had not stirred with any life.

And at length a man came up to Krishna, and the man was nearly naked and smeared with ashes, and his hair was clotted with mud in long ringlets, and he crouched down by Krishna and said 'Prince, why do you hug that body so? There is no life in it.'

And Krishna looked at him and said 'She was my love, my friend.'

And the man said 'You have in your arms the body of your love. But she is no longer here. Return the body to the river, where it must go, and let Ganges bear her to the sea.'

But Krishna looked at him, and said 'Is there no hope to kindle in these limbs a little life?'

And the man shook his head, and said 'Her spirit is already gone. I that have sat long on these shores can see into men's souls, and many have I seen drown among these waters. Their souls fly down to Hell. She I saw go, and reach the gates of death.'

And Krishna said 'Alas then, all is done. O Radha, why did you not tell me of your promise? Could I not have fought with Hell, as I have done its fiends? She did all this for me. For me she was tried and damned; for me tormented and tempted by the tyrant; for me she went to Hell and stayed its tortures; for me and for my love she came again to earth. Then should I not with this dagger go into death to meet her? My soul will never rest until I have seen her but once more.' And Krishna drew out a dagger from his sash.

But the man said 'Stay. She is not in Hell.' And Krishna sheathed his knife and looked at him.

And the man said 'It was a strange vision, such as I have never seen, for the gods themselves attended at this maiden's death. But first, before I tell you what I saw, cast this poor body back into the river. For to the Ganges was it given, and to the sea it must now go.'

And Krishna looked down at Radha's face, and for all the love in his heart he could not stir.

And the man said 'Can you not do this? Then cannot I tell you more.' And he rose up as if to go, and tossed his long hair behind him.

But Krishna said 'Stay,' and the man turned back again.

And Krishna said 'Must she go from me? Must I never see this face of hers again?'

And the man said 'Why do you grieve for what will soon decay to silt and mud? Why do you stay to worship such brief things?'

And Krishna stood up and bore Radha in his arms back to the river, and he waded into the water and held her out above the muddy waves. And Krishna said 'For ever and for ever farewell, my little Radha. Farewell sweet face that I have loved above all earthly things. These arms were my heart's home. This form all heaven to me.' And Krishna drew away his hands, and the swirling current carried her away.

And Krishna came again to the bank, and said 'And now, say on. Where is her spirit flown?'

And the man said 'As I stood upon this bank, I saw her drown, and her soul slid from her body, and coiled in the confused waves. But such must have been her love while she lived, she did not sink as spirits do into Hell, but hovered still in the sunshine, as if content. And I wondered at this, and watched with amazement. And the guides of Hell came then, and went to take her soul into the gates, but for all their trying they could not bring it away. For each time they carried her a little way into Hell, her soul grew light and fluttered out of their hands, like a leaf in the wind that teases the cat jumping with outstretched hands. And long they continued in this way.

'Then from her depths did Mother Ganges come, the green-haired goddess of the sacred river, and she gathered your love into her arms, and wrapt her in a rainbow mantle. And Ganges said 'Leave her, fiends, she is not for you. Will you try to bring into Hell one that wears a jewel of Vishnu's treasure? See, in her hair the golden lotus. This is the flower of love, and in these regions Hell can have no power.' And the fiends turned back, and went again to Hell.

'There was a great white bird, an egret, standing near. To him now went Ganges with your love in her mantle, and she put her onto the bird's back, nestling her softly between his wings. And the bird flew then Northwards and winged in the high air towards the mountains.'

And Krishna was glad at what he heard, and smiled and said 'Radha, will you too be a traveller through heaven? Are you to be my old friend's voyager? Princely Garuda, guard her well. O that we three could fly together through the coils of time, and never part!'

And he turned to the man and said 'Friend, you have eased my heart with your kindly vision. May the gods bless your striving. I shall go now. I have another journey. Quick must I be, if I am to catch her soul.' And Krishna went back to the chariot and leapt in.

But the man cried after him 'It is too late. They are already flown. How can you catch them who have gone to heaven?'

And Krishna laughed and dashed the horses into the water, and they cantered on the river, splashing up the foam, and he turned them upriver and made towards the North.

And so again was Krishna heading for the mountains, and again far off he caught sight of their shining snows, and now they held for him the promise of Radha, and called him onward like a lover's arms. And at last he came to the vale of sages, which is called Rishikesh, and here the green Ganges rushes rejoicing from the hills, and babbles over breakwaters beside grey rocks, and all around tasting the bliss of gods the naked hermits burn fires in the jungle. And Krishna felt happy, as if he went on a country ride.

And so he drove upriver still, into the gorges and the cataracts, and on the banks bushes of gold azaleas bloomed, and pinewoods grew and cedars. And all was washed and pure of the dusty plain, and the hills flashed with veins of gold, that glittered in the spray of waterfalls, and mixed with rainbows. And Krishna came to the high ranges, where the clouds lead up like stairways into heaven, and he stopped his chariot in the purple air, and looked out once again at the golden snows.

But all around was silence, and no sign of the white bird among the mountains. And the stillness of the dusk grew ever deeper, and blue slopes melted into darkness, and quietness came and wrapped him all around.

And Krishna looked out over the roof of the world, and spoke softly to the ranges as if they were near, and said 'Will you not give me a glimpse, a shadow? Can I not meet her but for one more time? Now I know all her love, can I not see her?' And Krishna sighed, and sank back against the painted wheels of the chariot.

And now high above the mountain summits, gathering slowly in the dying air, as if made of the rustling curtains of the Northern Lights, Radha's spirit appeared before Krishna, larger than in life, and she was swathed in the scarlet sari she had on when they floated in moonlight to the enchanted island. And she smiled at him and said 'Krishna, my love, seek me no longer here, for I have gone to my eternal home, and am among the stars. Grieve then no more, my dear one, for your beloved Radha was not suffered to go again to Hell, but on the wings of Garuda, your friend, was brought to heaven here in the deeps of space. Come then, arise, and go back to the plain. Be brave, my loved one, and care for Mathura. And when the days have gone, and all the pain of loss has been resolved, then shall you meet another love, another dark-eyed girl, another Radha, and live with her in Mathura, your queen. Yet alas, all life must pass, and when years have come upon you, you too will come to this other life, by an arrow wound in your heel.

'But my dear love, why did you sorrow now to think you had lost me? Was it not you that took me to the moonlit bower; the island of everywhere in the lake of Braj? Did we not find there an eternal comfort? How could you think you and I could be parted? As long as on the earth love's lotus blooms, there in lovers' hearts we two shall meet again. Be happy then, sweet Krishna, for all the coming days are full of hope. Put off your grief and wipe away these tears. The world is turning into happier times. No more shall tyrants reign or devils plague us. No more shall parting or exile be with us. Nothing but well and fair shall ever greet us. And so I leave you. Farewell, my dear love.

With that she laughed, and took the lotus in her hair, and it shone gold in the evening sun among the silver mountains, and the mountains round them like a disc of milk. And, as a girl with a tame peacock on a marble terrace looks at it, and urges it to lift its crown and take the fruit she holds to it with outstretched hand, so did she gaze into his eyes, smiling, and urge him, as if saying 'Now do you see? Now do you understand?' And she took the lotus, and threaded it, and threw around his smooth blue neck the completed garland, thirty-six blooms upon a golden thread. And the ring of flowers at last was made, and all things had come home.